Are you having trouble making a needed transformation?

Are you stuck in your career?

Is your organization stalled in its progress?

Are you lagging behind competitors in innovation?

Are you having trouble making your diet
and exercise program work?

Are you overwhelmed by information?

It could be that you need to change your mental models.

Transforming your mental models can help you think impossible
thoughts and overcome the barriers to change in your life,
work and society. This book will show you how.

## It's almost midnight.

You are walking down a dark city street toward your car parked several blocks away, when you hear footsteps behind you. You don't turn around, but you quicken your pace. You remember a news story from a few weeks ago about a robbery at knifepoint in the neighborhood. Your pace quickens. But the footsteps behind you are also moving very quickly.

The person is catching up to you.

At the end of the block, under the street lamp, the steps are immediately behind you. You turn suddenly. You recognize the familiar face of one of your colleagues, heading to the same parking lot. With a sigh of relief, you say hello, and you and he continue on your way together. ■

## What just happened?

The reality of the situation didn't change at all, but the instant you recognized the face of your colleague, the world in your mind was transformed. The image of the pursuing attacker was transformed into that of a friend. How could so little have changed in the situation, yet so much have changed in the way you viewed it?

First of all, you had created a complete picture of what was happening based on a tiny bit of information—the sound of footsteps behind you at night. From this mere suggestion, you drew upon memories of news stories of crimes, together with your personal fears and experiences, to conjure up an image of a potential attacker. You changed your actions based on this assessment of the situation, walking faster to escape an assailant. This could be a great survival instinct, but in this case, you were fleeing an assailant who did not exist.

Then, just as quickly, in the flash of the street lamp, you gained a little more information—and the entire picture shifted. In a split second, you recognized the face of a colleague—again based on the vaguest hints. You didn't take time to stare or think deeply about it. There might have been other possibilities in the situation. Could the person have been an assailant wearing a mask to look like your colleague? Could your colleague be an assailant? These possibilities were so remote that you didn't consider them, and by the time you thought through them, you might be dead. You saw the face, and the footsteps quickly switched categories from "foe" to "friend."

Only a small part of this drama happened on the sidewalk. Most of it was created within your own mind.

Working on transformation initiatives with leaders of major global corporations, we have recognized a simple lesson with profound implications: To change your world, you first have to change your own thinking. Neuroscience research shows that your mind discards the majority of the sensory stimuli you receive. What you see is what you think. The ability to see the world differently can create significant opportunities, as companies such as Southwest Airlines, FedEx, Charles Schwab and others have demonstrated. But even successful models can ultimately become a prison if they limit your ability to make sense of a changing world, in the way that major airlines failed to fully recognize the threat of upstarts such as Ryanair or that music companies, locked into a mindset of selling CDs, failed to see the opportunities and threats of music file sharing.

From driving organizational growth to improving personal health and fitness to fighting international terrorism, your mental models shape your responses in every area of your life. How do you become better at recognizing and using mental models more effectively? This book provides specific insights and strategies to help you understand the role of mental models, and know when to change them—so you can transform your organization and your world. ■

Surely the human mind is not so malleable.
Are you saying we all have lost touch with reality?

We know what we see, right?

## Why don't we ask the folks who saw Bugs Bunny in Disneyland?

The "wascally wabbit" from Warner Brothers would be turned into stew if he actually showed up to cavort with Mickey Mouse and Donald Duck in the theme park of rival entertainment company Disney. Yet when test subjects were shown mocked-up images of Bugs Bunny shaking hands with tourists in Disneyland, some 40 percent subsequently recalled a personal experience of meeting Bugs Bunny in Disneyland.[1] They "remembered" a meeting that was, in fact, impossible. It turns out that many of us are not much more astute at avoiding the rabbit's tricks than his befuddled archrival Elmer Fudd.

How often in your daily life do you find yourself shaking hands with Bugs Bunny in Disneyland?

**OK, so we might be fooled by some sleight of hand in a theme park, but we certainly won't miss the signals that are truly important in our environment.**

## How about overlooking a gorilla?

Researchers asked subjects to count the number of times ball players with white shirts pitched a ball back and forth in a video. Most subjects were so thoroughly engaged in watching white shirts that they failed to notice a black gorilla that wandered across the scene and paused in the middle to beat his chest. They had their noses so buried in their work that they didn't even see the gorilla.[2]

What gorillas are moving through your field of vision while you are so hard at work that you fail to see them? Will some of these 800-pound gorillas ultimately disrupt your game? ■

## What you see is what you think.

Just as we can believe we see the "impossible"—such as Bugs Bunny in Disneyland—or fail to see a gorilla striding across our field of vision, our mental models shape the opportunities and threats that we can see in our lives.

To change, you must first see the possibilities. By understanding the power of mental models and the process of changing them, you can think impossible thoughts. These thoughts can transform the way you approach the life of your business and the business of your life. On the following pages, we'll explore a process for unlocking the power of impossible thinking. ■

## Rabbits and gorillas may be interesting, but why should I care about mental models?

Mental models shape every aspect of our lives. If you are stuck in your career, if your organization is stalled in its growth, an underlying mental model may be holding you back, or a new model might open opportunities for progress.

If you are lagging behind your competitors in innovation, it may be your models that are constraining your creativity. If you are overwhelmed by information, perhaps the models you are using are not up to the challenge of making sense in our information-rich world. If you are trying unsuccessfully to lose weight, increase exercise or improve your health, the mental models you use to understand these activities will have a dramatic impact on the outcomes you achieve and the quality of your life. If your personal relationships are strained, your mental models, and those of others, could be at the root. And if you want to change society or the broader world, you need to begin by looking at the mental models that shape your world and challenging them.

In any area of your life where you need to change and transform yourself, your organization or others, mental models play a central role. Yet we often have little awareness of what our models are and how they shape what we can see and do. Mental models can appear simple, and are often invisible, yet they are always there and have a significant impact on our lives. Changing the world begins with changing our own thinking.

**The world we live in is not out there on the street. It is in our own minds.**

Until we recognize this, we will always be running away from ghosts and moving toward mirages. In our business and personal lives, we often fail to see the true threats and true opportunities because of the limits of the way we make sense of the world.

This book is designed to creep up on your view of the world and shake up the way you see the world. It will help you understand how your mind uses only a small part of the outside world it perceives, filling in the rest of the picture to make sense. Your mental models shape your vision and actions. Knowing how this process works will help you challenge the way you view the world and the way you act.

This idea may seem quite simple and self-evident, and it is. But if you truly consider the implications, as we will on the following pages, it is a powerful idea. This transformation of thinking is where all the transformations of our personal lives, our organizations and our society begin. That's the power of impossible thinking. ■

**Do you hear footsteps behind you?**

# (AN ASIDE)
# IS THIS ANY WAY
# TO START A BOOK?

Some of the early reviewers of the manuscript liked the way this book opens, because they thought it drew the reader into the core issues. Others, operating from a different "mental model" (the way we make sense of the world), wanted instead a concise summary of where the book was headed and a diagram showing all the key points we'll be making. Others wanted more of an academic description, relating the discussion to what has been written in this area.

This is probably a good time to point out that your own reaction and experience is probably due as much to the mindset you bring to these pages as to what is written on them. The concept of a "book" is quite different when it refers to an extensively footnoted academic work versus a popular novel. Peter Drucker and Stephen King both write "books," but beyond the fact that they both use words, what they mean by "book" is completely different.

What did you expect when you picked up this book? Because it is coauthored by a university professor, were you expecting something more academic? Because it is coauthored by a former chief technology officer at a major corporation, were you expecting to see some opening tales from the trenches of business? Both these elements appear later on, but the opening is designed specifically to challenge your current thinking and perhaps make you more receptive to the ideas you will encounter here.

A fundamental message of this book is that what you see in any situation depends in very large part upon what you bring to the table. What you see in this book is no exception. You are involved as much as we are in the process of making sense of the ideas presented. More than what we have written here, your own experiences and mindsets will shape what you get out of this process.

If you think this *isn't* the way to start a book, we ask that you set aside your existing model and give us a little time to win you over. We also invite you to let us know your reactions so we can challenge ourselves and our own mental models (contact the authors at contact@impossiblethinking.com).

By the way, if you were looking for a roadmap of where we are headed, here is a diagram:

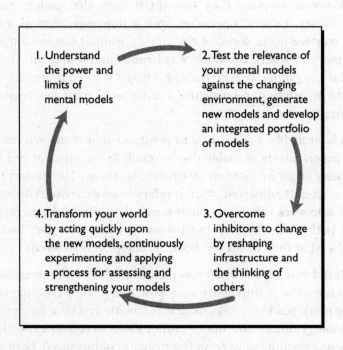

1. Understand the power and limits of mental models

2. Test the relevance of your mental models against the changing environment, generate new models and develop an integrated portfolio of models

3. Overcome inhibitors to change by reshaping infrastructure and the thinking of others

4. Transform your world by acting quickly upon the new models, continuously experimenting and applying a process for assessing and strengthening your models

# ENDNOTES

1. Braun, Kathryn A., Rhiannon Ellis, and Elizabeth F. Loftus. "Making My Memory: How Advertising Can Change Our Memories of the Past." *UW Faculty Server*. January 2002. <http:// faculty.washington.edu/eloftus/Articles/BraunPsychMarket02.pdf>; Gould, Ann Blair. "Bugs Bunny in Disneyland?" *Radio Nederland*. 7 May 2002. <http://www.rnw.nl/science/html/ memories020507.html>.

2. Taylor, John G. "From Matter to Mind." *Journal of Consciousness Studies*. 9:4 (2002). pp. 3–22. This experiment has also been mentioned in various other papers.

# PRAISE FOR
# THE POWER OF IMPOSSIBLE THINKING

"This is an important book that 'makes sense of how we make sense.' The authors provide a thorough, fresh, and compelling exploration into the dimensions of mental models. All leaders who want to be more effective in their actions would be served well to leverage the principles in this book to learn about how they think and make sense of the world around them."

*Nick Pudar*
*Director of Strategic Initiatives, General Motors*

"This is a really great piece of work. It is 'immersion into the process of insight.' Truly a valuable addition to any forward-thinking person's library in light of the rapid change we face in today's world—business and personal."

*J.Allen Kosowksy, CPA*
*Forensic Accountant and Director, ON2 Technologies*

"A masterfully written book that is sure to capture the attention of every thinking person who's willing to look at the world of business through new lenses. *The Power of Impossible Thinking* is both timely and intriguing."

*Kathy Levinson, Ph.D. Author of* The 60-Second Commute

"Tough-minded managers like to think they see the world as it is. Wind and Crook, drawing on recent neuroscience research, demonstrate that none of us, tough-minded or not, do anything of the sort. What we perceive as 'the world' is as much inside our heads as outside. By realizing that and making choices about how we see things, we can become much more effective managers."

*Rob Austin, Ph.D.*
*Harvard Business School and co-author of* Artful Making

"While most of us may recognize that the world we respond to is more in our mind than in any physical reality, often we don't have a clue why this is so. This very important book clearly explains how our mental models work to construct these distinct inner worlds. And more importantly it offers empowering advice on how we can use this knowledge to work for us rather than against us in creating a better outer world for ourselves, our organizations, and our societies."

*Charles C. Manz*
*Best-selling author of* SuperLeadership, Fit to Lead, *and* Temporary Sanity

"Today, life moves at hyperspeed. Hence, the age-old human skill of pattern recognition is more essential to our health and happiness than ever before in history. *The Power of Impossible Thinking* is a wonderful guide to help you understand the patterns you recognize and—critically—when those patterns serve you well, when they don't, and what you can do about it."

*Douglas K. Smith*
*Co-author of* The Wisdom of Teams *and author of* On Value and Values

"I have been trying to explain why Japan has fallen into a pitfall and cannot come out of even the simplest problems. One can call it an innovators dilemma, but that does not solve the problem. This book suggests we have to go back to the basics of reviewing our underlying 'mental models' now and then, and only then, have to construct a new model, perhaps plural, and move onto exploring the new terrain."

*Kenichi Ohmae*
*Author of the international bestseller,* The Borderless World

"Jerry Wind and Colin Crook have one of the most powerful messages there is about dealing with the present changing world. Perspectives are prisons, they say. The only way to thrive in the coming environment is to cultivate the ability to sense the new patterns and relationships as (and before) they emerge—otherwise you'll be locked in the past. This book can get you out of that jail."

*John L. Petersen*
*President and founder of The Arlington Institute and author of* Out of the Blue: How to Anticipate Wild Cards and Other Big Surprises

"*The Power of Impossible Thinking* is a health spa for the executive brain. Poor mental models can do more than ruin your reputation, your organization, or your team. How many times do we ignore market changes because of personal bias? Thanks to Wind and Crook we have a new vast insight into 'making sense' to help global leaders master the models needed for successful leadership behavior."

*Cathy L. Greenberg, Ph.D*
*Executive Director, Institute for Strategic Leadership,*
*LeBow College of Business, Drexel University*

"Everyone is familiar with exhortations for mindset change, attitudinal change and paradigm shift. But slogans are not solutions and words are not deeds. What is missing is a 'how to' book. Wind and Cook have brilliantly filled this chasm of need with an extraordinary book that revolutionizes businesses, individual lives and society."

*Dr. Y Y Wong*
*Chairman and Founder, The Wywy Group of Companies*

"Wind and Crook have written a marvelous book that can teach you how to think more effectively in personal and business settings. Read it and learn!"

*Drea Zigarmi*
*Author of* The Leader Inside: Learning Enough About Yourself To Lead Others *and co-author of* Leadership and the One Minute Manager

"We like to say, 'See it with your mind's eye.' Wind and Crook show us that our mind is our eye. What we think is what we see, and what we see directs how we act. Not only do the authors make this paradigm clear, but they offer concrete and practical ways to change our mind's eye and as a consequence change our actions and the results we get. The value of that is hard to top."

*J. Stewart Black, Ph.D.*
*co-author of* Leading Strategic Change *and Professor, University of Michigan Business School*

"This is a very important book. It deals with truly fundamental issues—both for practitioners as well as academicians—relating to making sense out of a variety of complex events in the real world, and how to keep an open mind regarding all of this. We often become 'prisoners' of set routines and behaviors, and thus gradually grow less and less effective. This book points the way out of this dilemma—in a most convincing sense. Models, properly focused around the best in human minds, are key here. These can help us understand paradigm shifts, maintain relevance, and keep momentum. To see things differently becomes central. The book makes seminal contributions here. It provides a strong, rigorous—and practical—conceptual base for this! I am equally impressed with the book's focus on implementation, both in terms of setting out an agenda for transforming one's world, as well as in terms of pointing out how action can be achieved—quickly and naturally—following the prescriptions of the book. All in all, I find the book to be a true seminal contribution, with a strong conceptual underpinning, convincing empirical verification, and realistic implementational focus. This book will become a must for practitioners and academicians alike."

*Dr. Peter Lorange*
*President IMD, The Nestlé Professor*

"The authors have done a masterful job examining the power and limits of our mental models and how to better accomplish change in the complex world ahead.... This book offers a road map with a real set of attributes that can help us make the tough choices in a time of transition.... I would put this book at the top of my 'keeper' list for those on the front lines of change management and mission accomplishment."

*Ken Minihan*
*Lt. General, U.S. Air Force, Retired*

"This book addresses some of the central challenges of management: How do you make sense of your situation? How do you probe alternative realities? What is your mental model? Understanding these issues is critical to each of us and central to key decisions that shape our professional and personal lives. Jerry Wind and Colin Crook offer a much-needed process for probing these issues in a structured way."

*John S. Reed*
*Chairman, New York Stock Exchange,*
*and former Chairman and CEO, Citigroup*

# THE POWER
# OF
# IMPOSSIBLE THINKING

Ideas. Action. Impact.
**Wharton School
Publishing**

In the face of accelerating turbulence and change, business leaders and policy makers need new ways of thinking to sustain performance and growth.

Wharton School Publishing offers a trusted source for stimulating ideas from thought leaders who provide new mental models to address changes in strategy, management, and finance. We seek out authors from diverse disciplines with a profound understanding of change and its implications. We offer books and tools that help executives respond to the challenge of change.

Every book and management tool we publish meets quality standards set by The Wharton School of the University of Pennsylvania. Each title is reviewed by the Wharton School Publishing Editorial Board before being given Wharton's seal of approval. This ensures that Wharton publications are timely, relevant, important, conceptually sound or empirically based, and implementable.

To fit our readers' learning preferences, Wharton publications are available in multiple formats, including books, audio, and electronic.

To find out more about our books and management tools, visit us at whartonsp.com and Wharton's executive education site, exceed.wharton.upenn.edu.

# THE POWER
# OF
# IMPOSSIBLE THINKING

## Transform the Business of Your Life
## and the Life of Your Business

Yoram (Jerry) Wind • Colin Crook
with Robert Gunther

Ideas. Action. Impact.
**Wharton School
Publishing**

Library of Congress Number: 2005931774

**Hardcover Edition**
Editorial/Production Supervision: Patti Guerrieri
Cover Design Director: Jerry Votta
Cover Design: Anthony Gemmellaro
Interior Design: Gail Cocker-Bogusz
Manufacturing Buyer: Maura Zaldivar
Executive Editor: Tim Moore
Editorial Assistant: Richard Winkler
Development Editor: Russ Hall
Marketing Manager: John Pierce

**Paperback Edition**
Vice President, Editor-in-Chief: Tim Moore
Wharton Editor: Yoram (Jerry) Wind
Acquisitions Editor: Tim Moore
Editorial Assistant: Susie Abraham
Associate Editor-in-Chief and Director of Marketing: Amy Neidlinger
International Marketing Manager: Tim Galligan
Cover Designer: Chuti Prasertsith
Managing Editor: Gina Kanouse
Project Editor: Rebecca Storbeck
Senior Compositor: Gloria Schurick
Manufacturing Buyer: Dan Uhrig

Ideas. Action. Impact.
**Wharton School Publishing**

© 2006 by Pearson Education, Inc.
Publishing as Wharton School Publishing
Upper Saddle River, New Jersey 07458

Wharton School Publishing offers excellent discounts on this book when ordered in quantity for bulk purchases or special sales. For more information, please contact U.S. Corporate and Government Sales, 1-800-382-3419, corpsales@pearsontechgroup.com. For sales outside the U.S., please contact International Sales at international@pearsoned.com.

Company and product names mentioned herein are the trademarks or registered trademarks of their respective owners.

Printed in the United States of America
First Printing
ISBN 0-13-187728-3
Pearson Education LTD.
Pearson Education Australia PTY, Limited.
Pearson Education Singapore, Pte. Ltd.
Pearson Education North Asia, Ltd.
Pearson Education Canada, Ltd.
Pearson Educación de Mexico, S.A. de C.V.
Pearson Education—Japan
Pearson Education Malaysia, Pte. Ltd.

**Receive Special Benefits by Registering this Book**
Register this book today and receive exclusive benefits that you can't obtain anywhere else, including

- Access to an audio summary of the book and an interview with the authors

- A coupon to be used on your next purchase

To register this book, use the following special code when you visit your My Account page on Whartonsp.com.

Special Code: olinking7283

Note that the benefits for registering may vary from book to book. To see the benefits associated with a particular book, you must be a member and submit the book's ISBN (the ISBN is the number on the back of this book that starts with 0-13-) on the registration page.

Ideas. Action. Impact.
**Wharton School**
**Publishing**

Bernard Baumohl
*THE SECRETS OF ECONOMIC INDICATORS*
*Hidden Clues to Future Economic Trends and Investment Opportunities*

Sayan Chatterjee
*FAILSAFE STRATEGIES*
*Profit and Grow from Risks That Others Avoid*

Sunil Gupta, Donald R. Lehmann
*MANAGING CUSTOMERS AS INVESTMENTS*
*The Strategic Value of Customers in the Long Run*

Stuart L. Hart
*CAPITALISM AT THE CROSSROADS*
*The Unlimited Business Opportunities in Solving the World's Most Difficult Problems*

Lawrence G. Hrebiniak
*MAKING STRATEGY WORK*
*Leading Effective Execution and Change*

Robert Mittelstaedt
*WILL YOUR NEXT MISTAKE BE FATAL?*
*Avoiding the Chain of Mistakes That Can Destroy Your Organization*

Mukul Pandya, Robbie Shell, Susan Warner, Sandeep Junnarkar, Jeffrey Brown
*NIGHTLY BUSINESS REPORT PRESENTS LASTING LEADERSHIP*
*What You Can Learn from the Top 25 Business People of Our Times*

C. K. Prahalad
*THE FORTUNE AT THE BOTTOM OF THE PYRAMID*
*Eradicating Poverty Through Profits*

Arthur Rubinfeld
*BUILT FOR GROWTH*
*Expanding Your Business Around the Corner or Across the Globe*

Scott A. Shane
*FINDING FERTILE GROUND*
*Identifying Extraordinary Opportunities for New Ventures*

Oded Shenkar
*THE CHINESE CENTURY*
*The Rising Chinese Economy and Its Impact on the Global Economy, the Balance of Power, and Your Job*

David Sirota, Louis A. Mischkind, and Michael Irwin Meltzer
*THE ENTHUSIASTIC EMPLOYEE*
*How Companies Profit by Giving Workers What They Want*

Thomas T. Stallkamp
*SCORE!*
*A Better Way to Do Busine$$: Moving from Conflict to Collaboration*

Yoram (Jerry)Wind, Colin Crook, with Robert Gunther
*THE POWER OF IMPOSSIBLE THINKING*
*Transform the Business of Your Life and the Life of Your Business*

# CONTENTS

## THE AUDIO YOU WILL FIND ON WHARTONSP.COM

Go to whartonsp.com, and register to be a member. There you will find downloadable audio, a unique feature of Wharton School Publishing books, included to give you a richer experience of the information in this book. You will find a short, 20-minute summary of the contents of the book, developed by Concentrated Knowledge Corporation, and an interview between the Editor-in-Chief of Concentrated Knowledge, the authors, and Al West, Chairman and CEO, SEI Investments. Listen to the authors discuss the book, and further implications of the book, during this audio supplement.

# PREFACE

---

## HIJACKING OUR MINDS

At first glance, mental models may seem abstract and inconsequential. But they cannot be dismissed as optical illusions, parlor games or academic curiosities—all in our head. Our models affect the quality and direction of our lives. They have profit-and-loss and even life-and-death implications.

The debate about U.S. intelligence following the September 11 terrorist attacks illustrates the difficulty of making sense in today's complex environment. Congressional post-mortems focused on who knew what when—on the information—but not on the more critical mental models that shaped how that information was processed. As is almost always the case in our information age, what led to the tragedy was not primarily a shortage of data. Plenty of data points indicated that an attack using an aircraft as a missile was possible, and there was even information pointing to potential members of the conspiracy. While more specific information could have been gathered and shared among different agencies, the failure was only partially one of data gathering. This was not a failure of intelligence per se. It was, at least in part, much more a failure *to make sense*.

Information was filtered through existing mental models related to terrorism and hijackings. For example, middle-class, clean-cut young working men with everything to live for did not fit the profile of the stereotypical wild-eyed young fanatics who became suicide bombers. So when these apparently more stable men began studying in flight school or asking about crop dusters, the possibility of terrorism was filtered out. Hijackings also followed a certain well-established pattern. The plane and its crew typically were taken hostage and flown to some remote location, where the hijackers made demands. Pilots were instructed that the best course of action for passengers and crew was not to resist. During the September 11 attacks, the information was filtered through a set of mental models that made it hard to see what was really happening until it was too late.

The events of September 11 also dramatically illustrate the power of shifting mental models. When passengers on the fourth plane, United Flight 93, received reports by cell phone from friends and family about the attack on the World Trade Center, several quickly realized that this was not a typical hijacking. They could see that their own aircraft would be used as a missile against another target. In a matter of minutes, they were able to transform their mental models and take heroic actions to stop the hijackers. As a result, the last plane failed to reach its target, crashing in a field in western Pennsylvania, a tragedy that could have been much worse if some of its passengers hadn't been able to make sense of what was going on and move to stop it. The passengers and crew of Flight 93 were presented with a picture that was similar to the hijackings earlier that day. What they suddenly developed, however, was a different mental model. They were able to quickly make sense of what was happening and to act on this new understanding. And that made all the difference.

## Mental Models

One of our most enduring—and perhaps limiting—illusions is our belief that the world we see is the real world. We rarely question

Romancing the Internet: The picture didn't change dramatically, but first we saw an attractive young woman, then an old crone. W. E. Hill, "My Wife and My Mother-in-Law."

our own models of the world until we are forced to. One day, the Internet was infinitely attractive. It could do no wrong. It was magnificent and beautiful. The next day, it was overhyped and ugly. It could do nothing right. Nothing had changed about the picture, yet in one instant we saw it as a seductive young woman and the next minute we rejected it. What happened?

This is called a "gestalt flip." The lines and data points are the same, but the picture is dramatically different. What has changed? Not the picture, but our making sense. What is in front of our eyes is the same. What is behind our eyes has changed. The same sight produces a very different *perception*.

We use the phrase "mental models" (or "mindsets") to describe the brain processes we use to make sense of our world. In recent decades, science and technology have progressed to the point where we can undertake direct observation of the brain. This is starting to transform philosophy and neuroscience. Instead of just thinking about thinking, we can now directly monitor brain processes as we think and observe. This research is generating a vast amount of experimental data. Confronting the incredible complexity of the brain, a range of neuroscience theories have emerged to explain what is going on inside our heads. In business and other organizations, these interactions become even more complex, as individuals with their own mental models interact through group decision making or negotiation, and they are susceptible to biases such as "group think" that can limit flexibility and constrict options.

As we were leading transformation initiatives at the Wharton School and Citicorp, and helping other executives transform their organizations, we began to realize how important these mental models are to the process of change. We have written this book to explore the implications of mental models for transforming our businesses, personal lives and society. This book does not support a specific interpretation of the neuroscience evidence, but it does recognize that the brain has a complex internal structure that is determined genetically and shaped by experience.

The ways we make sense of our world are determined to a large extent by our internal mind and to a lesser extent by the external world. It is this internal world of neurons, synapses, neurochemicals and electrical activity, with its incredibly complex structure—functioning in ways we have only a vague sense of—that we call the "mental model." This model inside our individual brains is our representation of our world and ourselves. (The appendix provides a more detailed explanation of developments in neuroscience that have influenced the thinking behind this book.)

Mental models are broader than technological innovations or business models. Mental models represent the way we look at the world. These models, or mindsets, can sometimes be reflected in technology or business innovations, but not every minor innovation represents a truly new mental model. For example, the shift to diet soft drinks was a tremendous innovation in the marketplace, but it represents only a minor change in mental models. Our mental models are much deeper, often so deep that they are invisible.

As a core component of our perception and thinking, mental models come up often in discussions of decision making, organizational learning and creative thinking. In particular, Ian Mitroff has explored their impact in creative business thinking in several books, including *The Unbounded Mind* with Harold Linstone.[1] These authors examine the need to challenge key assumptions, particularly in moving from "old thinking" to new "unbounded systems thinking." Peter Senge discusses how mental models limit or contribute to organizational learning in *The Fifth Discipline* and other works, and John Seely Brown examines the need to "unlearn" as the world changes.[2] J. Edward Russo and Paul J.H. Schoemaker emphasize the role of framing and overconfidence in decision making in *Decision Traps* and, more recently, in *Winning Decisions*.[3] Russell Ackoff, in *Creating the Corporate Future*[4] and other works, stresses the importance of approaching planning by challenging fundamental models through a process of "idealized design," starting with the desired end and working backward to the goals and objectives in reaching it. There have also been more rigorous academic considerations of these topics, such as *Decision Sciences* by Paul Kleindorfer, Howard Kunreuther and Paul Schoemaker,[5] and research on organizational learning by Chris Argyris.[6] Many other books and articles have touched in some way on mental models.

With so much having already been written on the topic, why another book? First, research in neuroscience is now supporting what we may have recognized intuitively in the past. This research makes mental models more substantial and, for us, more convincing, especially considering their inherent invisibility. Second, this book examines the impact of mental models more broadly, not just how they affect organizational decision making or learning, but the way they work and their implications for transformation—personal, organizational and societal. Finally, despite all that has been written about our mental models, the failure to see how they shape how we think and act is still leading to serious errors and missed opportunities. This is a lesson we can keep learning. This book represents an original take on the subject and an exploration of how these insights apply to personal and business life.

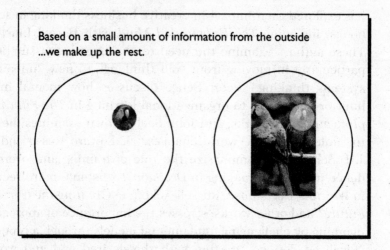

Based on a small amount of information from the outside
...we make up the rest.

## What We See Is What We Think

Whether considering a business move or a personal decision, what we "see" is not what we *see* (see sidebar, "The Difference Between Sight and Sense"). What we "see" is what we *think*. We usually trust what we see with our own eyes or perceive with our other senses. But research shows that we often use very little of the sensory information we take in from the outside world; most of it is discarded. Though we experience the process as seeing the external world, what the incoming stream of images actually does is to evoke other experiences from our internal world. This does not mean that the external world does not exist (although philosophers have argued this point), but only that we ignore much of it.

Most of what we see is in our minds.

The power of the mind in creating reality is demonstrated in the experiencing of a "phantom limb" by people who have lost a real limb through accident or surgery. The physical limb is no longer there, but the person continues to feel it. In a famous experiment, neurologist Dr. Ramachandran of the Salk Institute used Q-Tips® to touch a patient's face, evoking the reaction that he had just touched the patient's nonexistent hand. It turns out that the body map inside our brain has the hand and the face located in adjacent areas. When the hand was lost in an accident, the associated hand-mapping neurons moved into the adjacent face area for sensory input. The brain could now experience having its nonexistent hand touched. The person's experience of this touch was completely real. As Dr. Ramachandran observed in a series of lectures on the BBC, our brains are "model-making machines," and we construct "virtual reality simulations" of the world and then act upon them.[7]

While most of us have never experienced a "phantom limb," we have all had the experience of believing something and finding out suddenly that we were mistaken. This is the pivot upon which a magician's tricks often turn, as we are led to see a particular thing when, in fact, something quite different is actually taking place. Many of the great dramas and mysteries of fiction and of our own experience involve such twists. We are surprised and amazed by the shifts in how we make sense of the world.

## THE DIFFERENCE BETWEEN SIGHT AND SENSE

The ability to make sense is different from the ability to see. Mike May, an accomplished downhill skier who had been blind since the age of three recovered some sight through an operation at the age of 46. In his diary, he describes the experience of seeing the world for the first time.[8]

On his first airplane flight with his newfound vision, he looked out the window but couldn't figure out what he was seeing. He thought the white lines he saw against the brown and green of the ground were mountains. He turned to the passenger in the seat beside him and explained his situation and asked: "Could you help me figure out what I am seeing?"

The woman sitting next to him explained that the white lines were haze, and then proceeded to point out the valleys, fields and roads in the scene below. When he later looked at the night sky with his new sight, he experienced the stars as "all these white dots, so many white dots" before truly recognizing them as stars.

The process of recovering his physical sight was just the beginning of the process of learning how to make sense of this new visual information.

## The Importance of Mental Models

Mental models affect every aspect of our personal and professional lives and our broader society. Consider a few examples:

- **Personal—Wellness.** Every day, we are bombarded with new medical studies and other information. Some studies find that certain foods or activities have harmful or beneficial consequences. Some of these reports are contradictory. Even studies in respected medical journals are sometimes later overturned or found to be less conclusive than first touted to be in the media. We also receive other information about potential threats from diseases such as AIDS, mad cow disease, West Nile virus and SARS. How do we assess the danger and take appropriate action? We also face some more fundamental questions about our approach to health. For example, we can adopt the traditional Western focus on treatment of disease after it occurs, or we can focus on prevention of disease through diet, supplements and exercise. Or we can combine the two approaches. We can put our faith in allopaths, homeopaths, osteopaths or naturopaths. Our decisions in this area have a lot to do with how we make sense of the world. If we choose to adopt a diet to lose weight, we confront a cacophony of conflicting diets to choose from. The way we make sense of this picture has significant implications for our length and quality of life. How can we make sense of all these options? How can we become better at assessing the options and making decisions about our personal wellness?

- **Corporate—Growth.** Many companies have built their strategies around a traditional model of growth. Companies such as McDonald's, Coca-Cola and Starbucks have achieved growth in domestic markets and then sustained it by looking at overseas opportunities or new distribution channels. Other companies have grown through rollups and acquisitions. But the drive for growth has the potential to dilute the value of the brand—Starbucks coffee has a completely different meaning when served in gas stations and supermarkets. Yet the commitment to investors often keeps these companies addicted to growth. How can companies create healthy growth strategies, which either enhance the brand (reduce churn, maximize lifetime value of customers, capture market share, enter new markets, add new distribution options, etc.), extend the brand to new product/markets, or create new brands (new growth engines)? What other models have companies used to build and sustain successful businesses? Could you apply them to your business?

- **Society—Diversity and Affirmative Action.** Mental models also play a key role in debates on challenges for our society. For example, what is the best way to address historical inequities in the treatment of ethnic minorities or other populations (such as women) that have faced discrimination? One model, embodied in U.S. Affirmative Action programs, creates a formal structure designed to compensate for historical discrimination. As President Lyndon Johnson explained in a speech at Howard University: "You do not take a person who for years has been hobbled by chains and liberate him...and then say 'You're free to compete with all the others' and still justly believe that you have been completely fair." But opponents of these strategies hold a different model—that programs such as Affirmative Action are in themselves discriminatory and tend to emphasize and thus perpetuate the very racism they are designed to counter. President George W. Bush called an Affirmative Action program at the University of Michigan, "divisive, unfair, and impossible to square with the U.S. Constitution."[9] The choice of these models has serious implications for legislation and society—and individuals. The competing views have played out in a series of high-profile court cases.

In each of these examples, mental models play a crucial role in our thinking and actions. Our models shape what we see, and this opens or limits our possibilities for action. We will explore some specific dilemmas of personal life, business and society in Chapter 11.

## Thinking the Impossible

How do we engage in impossible thinking? The parts of the book that follow provide an overview of a process (see the sidebar, "Choices for Change").

First, we need to recognize the importance of models and the way they create limits and opportunities, as discussed in Part I. Then we have to find ways to keep our mental models relevant, deciding when to change to a new model (while adding the old to our portfolio of models), where to find ways of seeing, how to zoom in and out to make sense of a complex environment, and how to conduct continuous experimentation, as considered in Part II. Even if we are willing to change our thinking, we also need to recognize the walls that keep us in the old models, the confining influence both of the infrastructure and processes of our lives and of the slowly adapting models of those around us. In Part III we consider these obstacles to change and strategies for addressing them. Finally, we recognize that models are used in order to act quickly, and in the last part of the book we explore ways to access models quickly through intuition to transform our world.

## CHOICES FOR CHANGE

### RECOGNIZE THE POWER AND LIMITS OF MENTAL MODELS

- Understand how models shape your world
- Recognize how models limit or expand your scope of actions

### KEEP YOUR MENTAL MODELS RELEVANT

- Know when to shift horses
- Recognize that paradigm shifts are a two-way street
- See a new way of seeing
- Zoom in and out to make sense from complexity
- Engage in experiments

### OVERCOME INHIBITORS TO CHANGE

- Dismantle the old order
- Find common ground to bridge adaptive disconnects

### TRANSFORM YOUR WORLD

- Develop and refine your intuition
- Transform your actions

# ENDNOTES

1. Mitroff, Ian I., and Harold A. Linstone. *The Unbounded Mind: Breaking the Chains of Traditional Business Thinking.* New York: Oxford University Press, 1993.

2. Brown, John Seely. "Storytelling: Scientist's Perspective." *Storytelling: Passport to the 21st Century.* <http://www.creatingthe21stcentury.org/JSB3-learning-to-unlearn.html>.

3. Russo, J. Edward, and Paul J. H. Schoemaker. *Decision Traps: Ten Barriers to Brilliant Decision-Making and How to Overcome Them.* New York: Doubleday, 1989; Russo, J. Edward, and Paul Schoemaker, *Winning Decisions: Getting It Right the First Time.* New York: Doubleday, 2001.

4. Ackoff, Russell L. *Creating the Corporate Future: Plan or Be Planned For.* New York: Wiley, 1981.

5. Kleindorfer, Paul R., Howard C. Kunreuther, and Paul J. H. Schoemaker. *Decision Sciences: An Integrative Perspective.* Cambridge and New York: Cambridge University Press, 1993.

6. Argyris, Chris. *On Organizational Learning,* 2d ed. Blackwell Publishers, 1999.

7. Ramachandran, Vilayanur S. "Neuroscience: The New Philosophy." *Reith Lecture Series 2003: The Emerging Mind.* BBC Radio 4. 30 April 2003.

8. Sendero Group, "Mike's Journal," March 20, 2000, <http://www.senderogroup.com/mikejournal.htm>.

9. Greene, Richard Allen. "Affirmative Action: History of Controversy." *BBC News World Edition.* 16 January 2003. <http://news.bbc.co.uk/2/hi/americas/2664505.stm>.

# INTRODUCTION TO THE PAPERBACK EDITION

Since the original publication of *The Power of Impossible Thinking*, the world has continued to demonstrate the extraordinary malleability of our mental models—and their importance. We have seen this in diverse domains, from the paradigm-breaking shifts that create new market space in business described by Kim and Mauborgne in *Blue Ocean Strategy* (Harvard Business School Press, 2005), to the global technological and political transformations explored by Thomas Friedman in *The World is Flat: A Brief History of the Twenty-first Century* (Farrar, Straus, and Giroux, 2005). Mental models are at the core of understanding these and other changes—from work to personal life to addressing broader societal issues. Those who have been able to see the opportunities in these changes have been able to take advantage of them—from blogger-journalists to open-source programmers to Indian outsourcers. The world is changing in fundamental ways. It has many more degrees of freedom than it had in the past. But we need more flexible minds to see and act upon the freedom.

# THE END OF THE 30-SECOND COMMERCIAL

The changes in our world can have significant implications for individuals and entire industries. For example, the entire advertising industry was built around the 30-second commercial. Where would Budweiser be without its Clydesdale horses and slapstick frogs? Where would Pepsi be without its gyrating rock stars? But the importance of these short ad spots is now dissolving. The TV remote has already taken its toll on advertising. A study of the 15 largest U.S. television markets by CNW Marketing Research, Inc., found that more than 43 percent of viewers were actively ignoring advertising. Additionally, more than 71 percent of viewers with TiVo and other personal video recorders skipped advertisements altogether. In some ad categories, such as credit cards and mortgage financing, more than 90 percent of commercials were being skipped over by viewers with TiVo. How can advertisers continue to spend millions on 30-second spots that will be ignored by all but 10 percent of the entire audience?

While this is a disturbing picture, there is a silver lining. Companies that have adopted new ways of thinking about the world have been able to find tremendous opportunities. For example, two web sites, Google and Yahoo!, now account for more advertising revenues than the prime time schedules of the three traditional television networks (ABC, CBS, and NBC) combined. Google is now the largest media company, overtaking Time Warner in market capitalization. This would have been unbelievable just a few years ago. This is truly impossible thinking.

The decline of the 30-second commercial has been met by other innovations from managers who are not limited by the blinders of the old model. Companies are turning to other approaches, such as hosting events, creating buzz, and using product placement. For example, in launching its new Scion brand, which targeted youth markets, Toyota shunned traditional advertising, spending 70 percent of its promotion on street events. The remaining ad spending was mostly directed toward the Internet. In another example of innovative advertising, players of *Tony Hawk's Underground* video game cannot move up to the third level until they drink a Pepsi. As Robert Kotick, Chairman and CEO of video game maker Activision, Inc., commented during the Milken Institute's Global Forum, "In our medium, people cannot skip the advertising." Companies are also working on ads integrated into digital television broadcasts, so viewers might be cued to pause the action in a scene to find out about a Dell computer on the table or be shown targeted "smart ads" tailored to their specific interests. The decline of one mental model opens the way for others.

# A GLOBAL BRAIN

The changes in advertising are insignificant compared to broader shifts driven by technology, globalization, and other forces. We are on the cusp of breakthrough events in the Web which will have profound implications for individuals, businesses, and society. Networks are increasingly working like global brains in which individuals have become synapses that can fire in different patterns to create fresh ideas. Individuals are connecting with other individuals in incredible ways. The sheer scale, connectivity, and speed of these connections are unprecedented, stretching our old ways of thinking about the world to the breaking point. These changes challenge our mental models and our decisions about how we will organize and structure companies. How can we get our heads around these shifts? How should companies look at new product development? Is the IT department a help or an obstacle in a networked world?

How we think about these changes will shape how we perceive the opportunities and threats. The world is reorganizing itself on the fly. More than ever, we need a systematic approach to recognizing, assessing, and applying our mental models. This is the approach offered by our book.

In an interlinked world, ideas can come from anywhere and go to anywhere. For example, we received an e-mail message from a reader in Singapore with a note about an aspect of our book. The note concerned a study we discuss in the opening of the book in which subjects were shown pictures of tourists shaking hands with Bugs Bunny in Disneyland. Many subjects subsequently recalled a personal experience of meeting the rabbit in the Disney theme park. We point out that the Warner character wouldn't be caught dead at the Disney property. But in his e-mail to us, Cornelius Reiman of Singapore noted that in the 1988 film, *Who Framed Roger Rabbit,* Warner and Disney characters did appear side by side. It required a bevy of lawyers to make it possible, of course, and the producers had to assure the temperamental Bugs Bunny and Mickey Mouse that they had equal screen time.

The tourists in the study still could not have had the experience that they recalled, but we were surprised by how we received the information about the film. *Who Framed Roger Rabbit* was made more than a decade ago in the U.S, but the note came from an individual on the other side of the world. This is the way knowledge flows in our world. It is challenging our mental models and changing the way we think and work.

## UNINTENDED CONSEQUENCES

This is just one of the ways that the world is being turned on its head. Company-led models are being replaced by customer-led models. Top-down is being overwhelmed by bottom-up. But this shift is more than giving "power to the people," just as democracy was more than turning monarchy on its crown. It is a different way of looking at the world, a different mindset. We are seeing self-organizing systems for collaboration that challenge our conventional models. Complexity theory is moving from an arcane scientific topic to an ever-present reality. Mainstream news broadcasters such as Dan Rather have been humbled by independent bloggers engaging in "personal syndication." Programmers who are creating software such as Linux and Apache through open-source networks are challenging powerful companies such as Microsoft. In addition, encyclopedias such as Wikipedia are being created through collaboration by non-experts. This is giving new meaning to Jung's concept of tapping into the "collective unconscious."

The implications of these shifts are just beginning to dawn upon us. The Internet has been around for decades and has been in the public consciousness for many years. But its potential was not widely realized until recently because of prevailing mindsets. Initially it was used only in military defense and academic circles. Then, it was adopted for one-to-one communications such as sending e-mail. It then moved to one-to-many communications with web browsers and finally to many-to-many interactions through filesharing, blogs, and other networks. Pioneers such as eBay, Amazon, and Google could see its potential before anyone else and created businesses to act upon it. Other companies had access to the same technology, but did not have the same flexibility in thinking about it. This was where the real opportunities were created.

eBay, Amazon, and Google have all gone through continuous changes in their mental models and business models throughout their brief but profitable existences. eBay has added fixed-price sales to auctions and is selling products such as cars and houses. Second-hand cars now account for 30 percent of eBay's sales. In addition, 30 percent of sales on the world's best-known *auction* site are at fixed prices. Amazon has moved beyond books and now sells many other products. It also brokers used books for individuals. Google has leaped from searching the web to searching desktops, taking it into Microsoft's backyard. Google has also become a leader in online advertising. Many of these innovations were driven by the market rather than the companies themselves. At each step in the growth of these companies, managers have had the flexibility in thinking to recognize the next opportunities and seize them.

We live in a world in which the people who make equipment often cannot anticipate how it will be used. When Apple invented the iPod, for example, the creators saw opportunities that were not apparent to incumbents in the music industry. But once consumers had the hardware and software in their hands, they came up with their own innovations. One of these is the rise of "podcasting," independent radio programs broadcast on the web and downloaded to individual iPods. There is no need for a broadcasting studio, no need for an FCC license, no need to purchase a specific frequency. The program can go directly from the producer to the listener, although often through an intervening blog.

The spread of broadband Internet access also has had other unintended consequences. The emergence of Internet-based, voice-over IP systems as a viable alternative to traditional telephone land lines has shaken the foundations of telecommunications, driving the price nearly to zero with services such as Skype.com. Now cable companies and other players have entered the competition for telephone service. Ubiquitous wireless Internet connections are changing the way we live and work. Lawsuits against file sharing have led to more creative workaround systems, as innovation is driven by a sense of injustice. These shifts have created tremendous opportunities for emerging companies and threats for incumbents. But to see these impossible attacks or impossible new advantages, we first need to be able to engage in impossible thinking.

A bottom-up, consumer-driven approach can unlock the creativity necessary to produce dramatic results. For example, a study at 3M found that product ideas from lead users generated eight times the sales of ideas generated internally—$146 million versus $18 million a year—in part because lead users were more likely to come up with ideas for entire new product lines rather than minor improvements on old products. This is a transformational approach to innovation and collaboration based upon the emergence of a unique mental model. As the 3M study shows, the potential benefits for companies that embrace this new model can be huge. There is great power in this impossible thinking.

## ROSE-COLORED GLASSES

The return of the Internet is all the more surprising after the dot-com bust. By the end of the 1990s, it had seemed to some that it was all over. We saw the apparent triumph of the Microsoft Internet Explorer browser over Netscape. We witnessed the success of record companies in shutting down Napster. There was a general perception that the Internet had lived through its glory days. As return on investment (ROI) reasserted itself with a vengeance, there was little talk about eyeballs. There was a feeling that the original innovation and breakthrough thinking of the Internet had been spent.

But, as Mark Twain might say, the rumors of its death were greatly exaggerated. Just as the euphoria of the dot-com bubble blinded people to its risks, the pessimism about the Internet was blinding people to its potential. The rose-colored glasses were replaced with dark glasses. What we need to recognize is that we see everything around us through the filter of our mental models. These filters may make things rosy or dark, but until we recognize the lenses we use—our mental models—we can't begin to understand the possibilities for changing our views. When we see these filters, we have the power to change them. This is the power of impossible thinking.

We don't have to choose either one set of spectacles or the other. As Ben Franklin discovered, sometimes the best solution is bifocals, to see the world through different lenses simultaneously. The new mental models for collaboration haven't eliminated the old. They exist side by side. As we point out in the book, "paradigm shifts are a two-way street." We still have network news, proprietary software, and Encarta, along with blogs, open source, and Wikipedia. Revolutions are not absolute, so we need to keep a portfolio of models and choose the one that works best for a given situation.

## POWER OF INTUITION

Since the original publication of our book, additional attention also has been given to intuition. As we noted, intuition informed by experience can be a powerful way of accessing mental models. Malcolm Gladwell's recent book *Blink!* (Little, Brown, 2005) highlighted the power of such intuition by art experts who can instantly spot a fake that months of research hadn't revealed, and researchers who can predict fairly reliably that a marriage will fail by watching a few minutes of videotaped conversation between spouses. As we note, these insights often cannot be articulated (which can make them difficult to transfer to others), but they can tap into deep experience very quickly. We need to be careful that our intuition still fits with the realities of a rapidly changing world. By recognizing the mental models that underpin our intuition, we can better make this assessment. But intuition supplies an important mechanism for accessing and applying our mental models quickly. This is more important than ever as we live in a world of compressed cycle times.

The world continues to move in fast-forward. To take advantage of changes, we need to be prepared to think differently. This involves more than keeping an open mind. We need to actively identify our mental models, challenge them, and act on these new ways of seeing the world. We need to understand the usefulness and limitations of our mental models. We need to be able to creatively explore alternatives. Understanding and managing our mental models is more important than ever.

## CHALLENGING OUR THINKING

We have been grateful for the strong response to the publication of *The Power of Impossible Thinking*. We have had an opportunity to discuss these ideas in many sessions in different parts of the world. We also have heard from many readers about how the book helped change the way they thought about not only business but their personal lives—from making a career choice to selecting a partner for life to improving a golf game. With each new headline, we also see the implications of mental models for broader challenges facing society, from rethinking intelligence gathering for recognizing terrorists to seeing opportunities in serving the poorest of the poor, as discussed in CK Prahalad's *The Fortune at the Bottom of the Pyramid* (Wharton School Publishing, 2004). Different mental models change the way we look at and address these challenges. We have learned from our interactions with readers. They have helped to test and challenge our own mental models. These readers continue to confirm the central importance of understanding mental models in order to make transformations in business, personal life, and society.

We are now very pleased to be able to share our insights on mental models and the power of impossible thinking with a broader group of readers through this paperback edition. We hope it will help you *think* the impossible so you can *do* the impossible in your own life and work.

Yoram (Jerry) Wind

Colin Crook

# 1

# RECOGNIZE THE POWER AND LIMITS OF MENTAL MODELS

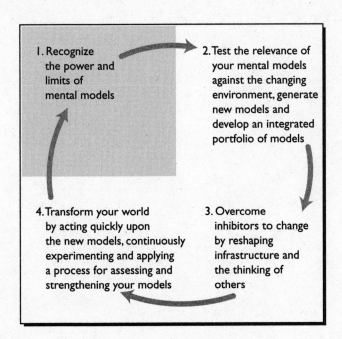

1. Recognize the power and limits of mental models

2. Test the relevance of your mental models against the changing environment, generate new models and develop an integrated portfolio of models

4. Transform your world by acting quickly upon the new models, continuously experimenting and applying a process for assessing and strengthening your models

3. Overcome inhibitors to change by reshaping infrastructure and the thinking of others

# 1

# OUR MODELS
# DEFINE OUR WORLD

*In the old world, managers make products. In the new world, managers make sense of things.*

—John Seely Brown[1]

## It's midnight, and you hear a loud radio in the apartment downstairs.

Last week the quiet old man who lived there passed away, and you've been concerned about the arrival of the next tenant. You never know who might move in, and you've heard some real horror stories from your college friends. In an apartment house, the wrong neighbors can make your life miserable.

Now your worst fears have come true. The rock music plays on and on. You toss and turn, looking at the clock. At 12:30 a.m., you decide to wait just a little longer. Even if your new neighbor is a jerk, you are reluctant to turn your first meeting into a fight. At 1:00 a.m., the radio is blaring just as loud. What kind of party are they throwing down there? You've got to get up for work tomorrow. How can a person be so ignorant? So you walk down to lecture this idiot on common courtesy. You knock heavily on the door, and it swings open.

You are surprised to find the apartment completely bare. There is no sign of your new neighbor. There isn't even a sign of furniture. So you walk in. In the back room you find some drop cloths and paint cans. Plugged into one wall, you see a boom box cranked up full.

There is no neighbor, just a careless painter who left the radio on when he left for the day. The new tenant hasn't even arrived yet. The ignorant neighbor that you invented based on the noise vanishes into air, but the anger and other emotions you felt are still very real. You have trouble settling

3

down and going back to sleep because you are still angry at this neighbor, a neighbor who exists only in your mind. You created this evil figure to explain the loud music, and he took on a life of his own. If you hadn't gone down and knocked on the door, you might have lived with this illusion for days.

Your mental models shape the way you see the world. They help you to quickly make sense of the noises that filter in from outside, but they can also limit your ability to see the true picture. They are with you always and, like your neighbors, can be a great help or can keep you up at night without reason.

What are mental models, and how do they shape your understanding and define the world you live in?

---

**Can the wrong mental model kill you?** Over the past quarter century, more than 150 children have died in the United States after their parents chose not to provide medical treatment because of their religious beliefs.[2] The parents belonged to one of some 20 religious groups whose teachings deny the use of traditional medical care, relying instead on faith healing. The results are often tragic.

In April 1986, two-year-old Robyn Twitchell died of a bowel obstruction in Boston, Massachusetts. His parents, Christian Scientists, took the boy to a church practitioner who prescribed only prayer. The child's condition worsened. He had difficulty eating and sleeping. He was shaking and vomiting. Five days after the onset of the illness, he became unresponsive. The parents and the practitioner continued to trust in prayer up to the time of his death. The parents were convicted in July 1990 of manslaughter.

Experts testified that the condition could have been treated with a simple operation to remove the twisting of the bowel, an operation that would have very likely saved the child's life. This procedure, based on a surgical model of treating disease, was not considered by the boy's parents because of the mental model they held about the causes and treatment of disease. In a certain sense, the boy's death was due to the way they made sense of the world.

This story is not presented to pass judgment on the parents for their tragic decision or criticize their religious beliefs. It does offer an example of a single decision that is viewed through divergent models—the parents' beliefs and the medical perspective that the courts used in ruling on the case. In the court's opinion, the outcome of following the parents' model was very likely much worse than the outcome that could have been achieved from following a medical model.

While their impact is rarely so sharply defined as in this case, our mental models can affect our lives, careers and relationships; the prosperity of our businesses; and the quality of life in our societies. Almost every aspect of our lives is shaped in some way by how we make sense of the world. Our thinking and our actions are affected by the mental models we hold. These models define our limits or open our opportunities. Despite their power and pervasiveness, these models are usually virtually invisible to us. We don't realize they are there at all.

We believe that what we see is reality rather than something we create inside our heads. The parents of Robyn Twitchell believed that prayer alone was going to cure him. For them, this was reality. The surgeons who could have treated the child saw the case through a completely different set of eyes, as did the criminal justice system. We might think of mental models as something abstract or academic—to be studied and explained like optical illusions—but in this case and many others these models clearly are anything but academic. They not only shape what we see and how we understand the world but also how we act in it. In a real sense, what we think is what we see, and what we see is what we think.

How do the models you use to understand your life keep you locked in certain patterns of thought or prevent you from seeing solutions that are right in front of you? What are the potentially negative effects of your current models? How could you change your models to improve the quality of your life?

## Rethinking IBM's Research Model

Models also limit or open new opportunities in business. In the early 1990s, the head of research at IBM, Jim McGroddy, came to visit one of the authors (Colin Crook), who was then chief technology officer at Citicorp. McGroddy faced a serious challenge. IBM was losing billions of dollars every year. How could the research program help turn this situation around?

Crook discussed the information-technology value chain that was guiding IT development at Citibank. This value chain had three basic levels: at the bottom were atoms and basic math; in the middle was technology, such as storage, displays and chips; and at the top were customer solutions. What was really important, he said, was the work on these customer solutions, and that was where Citicorp was differentiating itself from rivals.

McGroddy realized that this focus on customer solutions had been largely ignored by IBM Research. Most of the company's attention was on basic research at the bottom level or on technology in the middle. The company had become insular and product-focused, losing touch with its customers. This realization led to a reorganization of IBM Research and the creation of a new strategic area focusing on services, applications and solutions. IBM's successful turnaround was driven by research in that category, which increased from nearly zero in 1990 to more than 25 percent in 2001. This dovetailed nicely with the launch of new chairman Lou Gerstner's global services initiative, which became the fastest growing area for IBM.[3]

IBM may not have recognized it, but its research had been driven by a technocentric mental model. When this model was recognized and challenged, new opportunities could be seen, the organization could be redesigned and the business could be transformed (a transformation that was, of course, much broader than R&D). What looked like an R&D problem could be rethought from the perspective of the market. What looked like a difficult technological problem could be reconsidered as a challenge of business design.

## Compartmentalization of Business and Personal Life

We recently spoke with a successful manager who remarked that when she needs to hire a new employee, she inevitably turns to a headhunter. But in her personal life, she trusts to chance to find a life partner. It is a similar challenge of finding the right person with the right characteristics and chemistry, but she applies a completely different approach because she has a different mental model for her personal and business life. She would never think about going into a single's bar and hoping to stumble across the perfect vice president of marketing, but she will in her personal life. Because of this artificial wall, she was much less creative in thinking about her personal life (and less successful in filling the position for a life partner) than in her business life where she routinely found great people to fill key positions.

One of the limiting frames we have is the separation of business and personal life, even as these two worlds are merging together. Look at how many TV entertainment programs have a work setting for portraying stories of personal lives. As the lines between business and personal lives blur, there are opportunities for shifting our thinking within business and personal life and across the two. We can borrow mental models from one area and apply them to the other to change the way we see both aspects of our lives.

## Domestic Emerging Markets

To take another example, consider how most companies view inner-city markets. These markets tend to be areas with low incomes, high crime rates and other risks or costs—in short, they are seen as a marketer's nightmare. Even as major companies are waking up to the potential of emerging markets around the world, inner-city markets are still largely neglected. Yet, as Michael Porter has pointed out, these markets have distinctive advantages and hidden opportunities if we look more closely.[4] While income may be lower, population density is much higher so "spending power per acre" is comparable to more affluent parts of the city. These markets are in strategic locations and often present demographics segments that are crucial to future market growth.

If we were to reframe the inner city as "domestic emerging markets," what new possibilities would this open? What strategies that are being used to address emerging markets in China and

India might be applied in the cities of the United States and other developed nations with good effect? This simple shift in the way we view these markets could open new possibilities for strategies and new potential for growth.

How do your models for your industry and business prevent you from recognizing opportunities and realizing the full value of your organization?

## THE PARALLEL UNIVERSES IN OUR MINDS

The brain, weighing on average just around three pounds, has a complexity of structure and function that we are only just beginning to understand. Estimates vary, but we have around 100 billion neurons, which communicate via perhaps several hundred trillion synapses. The whole brain is awash in a swirl of neurochemicals, and lightning storms of electrical activity flicker across it, as millions of sensory signals from the eyes, ears, nose, mouth and skin are thrown into the mix.

It is a wonder we can even think. And yet we do. A linear processing machine bombarded with this flood of stimulation would probably shut right down. The brain is quite different. It somehow makes sense out of the welter of flashing signals. The human mind engages in daily magic tricks that make David Copperfield look like a parlor act. Studies in neuroscience indicate that the sense we make of external things is based in small part on what we see outside and in large part on the patterns located in our minds.

### MKANIG SNESE FROM NSOSNESE

As Lewis Carroll demonstrated in the "brillig" and "slithy toves" of his poem *Jabberwocky*, it takes only a little bit of context for our marvelous sense-making abilities to draw meaning from absolute gibberish. With a little effort, the following statement, circulating online, should make this point clear. While neither the study nor the university are formally identified, the words, however garbled, speak for themselves:

Aoccdrnig to rscheearch at an Elingsh uinervtisy, it deosn't mttaer in waht oredr the ltteers in a wrod are, olny taht the frist and lsat ltteres are at the rghit pcleas. The rset can be a toatl mses and you can sitll raed it wouthit a porbelm. Tihs is bcuseae we do not raed ervey lteter by ilstef, but the wrod as a wlohe.

Ask yourself: Does the rest of your life have this many holes that you are not seeing?

The mind appears to do this, in part, *by choosing to ignore some of the external world.* American neurophysiologist Walter Freeman discovered that the neural activity due to sensory stimuli disappears in the cortex. Our eyes and ears are constantly gathering information, but our mind is not really processing all of it (see sidebar, "Mkanig Snese from Nsosnese"). This stimulation flows into the brain, where what seems to be an internally related pattern appears, which the brain uses to represent the external situation.

The brain takes in the information about the world through the senses and then discards most of it, using it principally to evoke a parallel world of its own. Each brain creates its own world, which is internally consistent and complete. Perception is not a linear process of information reception, processing, storage and recall. Instead it is a very complex, interactive, subjective and evocative process.

It is as if a visitor came to the front door and rang the bell, and the person inside, by a quick glance through the fisheye peephole, formed a complete profile of the person outside, without opening the door. We know from experience that we have the ability to form snap judgments about people immediately—and that these judgments are sometimes wrong. Yet this process is extraordinarily efficient and effective, which is why there are peepholes in doors in the first place. Unlike a baby first learning about the world, we don't have to try to make sense of every new piece of information. Given a few lines, we can fill in the entire image. This ability to respond intuitively to what we see is crucial to quick thinking and action. (In Chapter 10 we discuss the power and limitations of intuition.)

## Building Our Brains

The brain has developed and changed throughout human evolution, and its layered structure clearly shows this, starting deep within with the oldest "reptilian" part and moving out through the "limbic" system to the "neocortex," the seat of rational behavior.

Our own brains change and evolve over time, with neurons constantly dying and being recreated, synapses being destroyed and created anew. The brain selects and reinforces or weakens certain synapses to forge the complex neural structures that determine our thinking. Then we reshape these neural "models" through experience, education and training.

The newborn child has a fundamental but only rudimentary capacity to make sense of the signals, probably derived from genetic instructions. Subsequent experience works upon this genetic foundation. The child's first, urgent task is to quickly develop the capacity to make sense of all these confusing signals. Within the first two years, most children appear to develop this capability. The process involved is to understand where the stimulus comes from and then categorize the signal as some specific case of a more general pattern. A mix of shadows and colors is recognized as a ball. The face hovering above the baby is recognized as the mother—but then all similar faces are also seen as mother until the model is refined. The child is able to form a holistic sense without getting bogged down in the details. This categorization is key. These experiences are also retained in the form of memory—complex patterns spread across the brain that are not representational but are evoked by other patterns and external stimuli.

As the internal worlds in the child's mind become richer, the external world recedes. Freeman's experiments show that the balance tips from the outside to the inside. The brain's own models replace the input signals from external sources. When the brain confronts a new experience, it calls up a complex neural activity or "mental model" that seems to be its nearest equivalent. We see the absence of these models in the child's wonder at the simplest of experiences. We feel their presence when we express regret about the familiar routines and ruts that sometimes determine our lives in adulthood. The development of mental models is, in a certain sense, a demarcation line between childhood and maturity. We increasingly live in a familiar world that can be considered as a benign illusion—benign, because it helps us move through the world efficiently, but an illusion nonetheless.

We eventually lose all awareness that these "models" are in fact internal illusions. We accept them as external reality and act on them as if they were. If they are good models, in most circumstances they more than adequately permit the mind to handle external reality. But here a danger creeps in. When the world changes in important ways, we can find ourselves with a model that is completely irrelevant to the current situation. We find ourselves wearing our street clothes when we are thrown off the deck of a ship. What we need at that point is a wet suit and lifejacket.

## WHERE "MODELS" COME FROM

Constant training shapes and refines our "models." A jazz musician or modern artist probably has a very different view of many aspects of the world than, say, a scientist or engineer. Even training doesn't fully explain our models. Not every musician or engineer will look at the world in the same way. A breakthrough thinker like Albert Einstein might have much more in common with a modern artist than with some of his colleagues in science. Some individual scientists may creatively push the limits; others may work in a well-defined area of study. Some CFOs may be risk averse while others are daring to the point of danger. Their approaches are shaped by their personality (genetics), education, training, influence of others and other experiences.

We can gain insights into our "mental models" by looking at where they came from. There has been a long debate about the influence of nature versus nurture in shaping our thinking. At the moment, it appears increasingly likely that nature, in the form of genetics, plays a significant role in determining who we are. Many of the basic capabilities of the brain, such as language, appear to be predetermined at birth by virtue of the genetics we inherit.

Clearly we are born with some hardware and hard wiring that influences the way we see the world. Mood disorders offer an extreme example of how these chemical and genetic differences can color the way we see the world. While genetic research and pharmaceutical interventions are offering new ways to change the structure and chemicals of our thinking, their exact impact on mental models is unclear. As much as we might like to find one, there is no pill or genetic therapy for changing our mental models, although at some point in the future development of science it may fall within the realm of possibility. There also seems to be considerable flexibility in the human mind in overcoming the limitations of nature.

Genetics appear to provide the fundamental basis of who we are and what we can do, and then experience plays a major role in shaping these capabilities, strengthening some and weakening others. Thus a number of forces of "nurture" shape and reshape our "mental models," including:

- *Education.* Our education shapes our mental models very broadly and forms a foundation that molds our world view. A scientist learns to approach the world in a different way than a jazz musician. This broad education is often the least visible force shaping our mindset. We surround ourselves with people of similar background. A liberal arts education aims in many ways to give people a common language and world view from which to operate, so it is very easy for this educational foundation to blend into the environment like a chameleon on a rock. While deepening knowledge in a subject area is one kind of learning, learning about mental models represents a second kind of learning (see sidebar, "A Second Kind of Learning").

- *Training.* Related to education is the specific training we receive to deal with transitions or handle new tasks. A computer programmer might learn a programming language, or an artist might learn to work in metal sculpture. This training is more specific and more visible than education, and more easily changed. Still, we often get into a rut in our training that is very difficult to break out of, even when the world around us has changed significantly.

- *Influence of others.* We are all influenced by mentors, experts, family and friends. These individuals, their philosophy of life and approach to problems affect us deeply in how we approach our own challenges. We are also influenced by the books we've read. For example, a child who grows up reading all of H. G. Wells' novels might be influenced by this experience to become a scientist. We are influenced by people in our immediate environment—first by parents, friends and teachers and later by supervisors and coworkers—who push us in new directions or encourage us to achieve more, challenging our own views of ourselves. We also are influenced by broader trends in society, as were many people who grew up in the 1960s. Finally, we are influenced by mass culture in a world in which MTV can transfer fashion trends around the globe in a matter of hours.

- *Rewards and incentives.* Our mental models and actions are shaped by the rewards we receive for holding them. These rewards can be tangible, such as direct financial gain, or less tangible ones, such as social approval.

- *Personal experience.* Some artists and scientists are self-taught. They create their own style through personal experience, which makes it easier to think outside the mainstream. The tradition of apprenticeship is also based on a process of combining learning from both experience and a mentor or expert craftsman.

In addition to the specifics of what we learn in our education, we also develop capabilities for *learning how to learn* that help us to make sense of our experiences. Our own successes and failures can dramatically shape our view of the world. Personal encounters can have a major impact on how we view life overall or in specific areas. How we cope with mistakes and learn from our successes affects how we approach every new challenge. Severe ordeals, such as imprisonment in a concentration camp or traumatic childhood abuse, may affect our world view throughout our lives. Some people find their worlds crushed and limited by these misfortunes. Others respond by developing a determination and drive that carries them not only across their present hurdles but also to new levels of success.

Today's experience quickly becomes tomorrow's theology. This is why generals are often fighting the last war. They have shaped their policies based on their past equipment and military strategy, carefully learning lessons from debriefings on the last battlefield that may no longer be relevant on the current one (although post-mortems can be a valuable source of insights as long as we recognize that the world may change). Experience can be a double-edged sword.

## Models for the Moment

Some of our models are very broad, held by members of an entire nation, political party or religious group, while others are very localized and specific. A broader model such as a belief in democracy or communism affects the mental models of followers, influencing their beliefs and behavior as well as the entire structure of society and economic life. Not all our models are on such a grand scale. Our background and philosophical beliefs often affect how we see the world, but we also apply situation-specific models. A fire drill or airplane evacuation routine is an example of a situation-specific model. Whatever our backgrounds, training and experience, we all look for the nearest exit, put on our oxygen mask if it is deployed from the ceiling or inflate our life vests.

In this case, the goal is to give everyone a common model that seems to be best practice in responding to a particular emergency. But when passengers on the flights of 9/11 were faced with a situation that was not on the cards in the seatbacks, they needed to improvise and create a model based on their experience, drawing upon past experiences such as sports, military training, stories or movies.

In many cases, our background and experience determine how we will respond in a particular situation. When Johnson & Johnson made its famous decision to pull its product off the shelves in response to the Tylenol scare in 1982 (when an unknown tamperer laced the capsules with cyanide, killing seven people in Chicago), the company's actions were based on a firmly embedded set of values embodied in the corporate "credo." It set a course of action that was consistent with its core mental model—that if it put its customers and other stakeholders first, returns to shareholders would naturally follow.

Sometimes our responses to specific challenges ultimately transform our broader models. Consider the long-held opposition to big government by the U.S. Republican party. In the face of terrorist attacks and scandals on Wall Street early in the new millennium, the Republican administration expanded government staffing, budgets and powers to meet these new threats to national economic stability. The proponents of reducing government had actually expanded it. The specific actions, designed to meet the challenges of the moment, ultimately undermined the broader model.

This view of the application of models for the moment is in contrast to approaches such as Meyers-Briggs, which attempts to define a specific individual style of approaching decisions. While the recognition of the different cognitive styles (such as perceptive/receptive, or systematic/intuitive) is an important one, we are not necessarily static in how we apply these approaches. An individual may work through a variety of styles in addressing specific challenges or responding to specific situations.

## A SECOND KIND OF LEARNING

There is a lot of discussion about the importance of creating what Peter Senge and others have called a "learning organization." We recognize the importance in personal development of continuing to engage in what Stephen Covey refers to as "sharpening the saw."

But in the application of these ideas to our business and personal lives, we often fail to make a distinction about two kinds of learning.

The first kind of learning, which is far more common and more easily achieved, is to deepen our knowledge within an existing mental model or discipline.

The second kind of learning is focused on new mental models and on shifting from one to another. It is does not deepen knowledge in a specific model but rather looks at the world outside the model and adopts or develops new models to make sense of this broader world. Sometimes we don't need to merely "sharpen" the saw; we need to throw it out to pick up a power tool. If we are focused only on sharpening, then we might not see the opportunity to apply new technology that can radically change the way we approach the task. The sharpest saw in the tool box may be no match for a powerful new approach based on a new way of looking at the world.

This book focuses primarily on this second kind of learning. It is not just doing a better job at the current task but asking whether it is the right approach and how we might be able to change it. It is not the kind of learning that results from an engineer's taking the 100th course in engineering, but rather the kind that comes from her taking a first course in jazz, which allows her to look at engineering problems from a completely new perspective. Learning about new mental models is much more challenging and complex, but crucial in an environment of rapid change and uncertainty.

## AVOIDING OBSOLESCENCE

During the painful layoffs and restructuring at Citicorp in the early 1990s, we witnessed the following uncomfortable scene: A talented computer programmer in his forties, facing the loss of his position, was shocked to find that he was no longer needed because his skills in COBOL programming were obsolete. This bolt came totally out of the blue, because he was a good programmer. He just hadn't kept up. Not only this, but as he worked through outplacement, he discovered to his horror that his skills were no longer valuable to *anyone*. He had been cruising along in his career, unaware of the changes around him, and now he found that the road he was traveling led right off a cliff.

Could this programmer have been better prepared if he hadn't been locked in an outdated mindset? Even if he couldn't have prevented his dismissal, could he at least have been better able to move forward afterward?

If the world remained static, we might be able to remain blissfully unaware of our models. Like our primitive hunter-gatherer ancestors, our basic instinct and experience would serve us well from childhood throughout our relatively short lives. But today the world changes ever more rapidly, and we need to be able to recognize our own models, to know whether and how to change them, to act quickly, and to influence the models of others.

Like the programmer in the example above, we often don't see the need to change until we experience the pink slip, the divorce, the lawsuit or the heart attack. Then, if it is not too late, we wake up to see that our old mental models no longer work. (Surprisingly, even these shocks sometimes are not enough.)

It doesn't have to be this way. You can consciously change your mental models before the world forces you to do so. Some of the people at Citicorp, including many who ultimately survived the job cuts, made a conscious effort to immerse themselves in the outside world. They explored different aspects of technology, such as new programming languages and techniques, and brought these new perspectives to their work. They actively challenged their own mental models and those around them. They continued to develop new and useful mindsets that were valuable to the organization. They became leaders of the transformations that were needed to turn the company around.

At any given point, we have a choice in how we view the world. But we are not always aware of these choices. The models we have developed through our education and experience are often invisible to us until it is too late.

In a changing environment, we can either transform ourselves or be transformed. Every day individuals in their work and personal lives prove that it is possible to change before life itself gives them a painful wakeup call. But to transform our lives, we have to first transform our minds. Our mental models determine what we are able to see and do.

## THE CONSEQUENCES OF MODELS

We live in a world of great risk and great possibilities. We have unprecedented opportunities to blend the best of the old and new, to open up new perspectives and connect to different fields of knowledge, like sampling from a buffet. Yet it is a risky business to abandon our old views of the world. We have seen the traditional views of religion, family, institutions and belief in capitalism eroded in recent years, with some positive consequences but also some degree of chaos rushing into the vacuum. When we depart from the dry land in business or personal life, we are subject to the crosswinds and crosscurrents of whatever crackpot ideas and fads come toward us. If we can navigate this passage to new mindsets, we will have opportunities to discover new worlds with rich potential.

Our true work, as John Seely Brown points out in the quote that opens this chapter, is making sense. It is not just for managers in business but for everyone in business, politics and personal life. As in a detective story, we are in a race against time, against clever rivals who deliberately or inadvertently create decoy trails to throw us off the scent. In a world of deep complexity and extensive information, this work of making sense has never been harder—or more important. Unlike most detective stories, this one does not have a simple (The butler did it!) answer at the end, unless we discover it or create it. It does not even have an ending.

The world we see today could undergo a gestalt flip tomorrow. We can get better at this process of making sense—and the first step is recognizing that there is a process at all.

Some will argue that the world is already far too complicated for us to make sense of it. They act as if we need to just keep our heads down, focus on the track in front of our feet and keep moving. That may work for a limited time (until some freight train comes barreling down the track we're walking on). But our strength as human beings is our power to make sense, adapt to a fabulously complex world and quickly decide on a practical course of action. This is how we have survived and progressed since the age of the sabertooth tiger. It is how we can succeed in today's complex world.

In today's complicated and uncertain environment, the greatest dangers are not from beasts prowling around outside. More often than not they are in our own minds, our inability to see our own limits and to see things differently. It is these internal beasts that we seek to better understand—and learn to live with, if not to tame—in the pages of this book.

## IMPOSSIBLE THINKING

■ What are your mental models that shape your thinking? How are your models different from those of others?

■ What are a few recent decisions, personal or professional, in which you can identify the role of mental models in how you framed the problem or developed your solution?

■ How has your own education and experience affected your mental models?

■ What are the potential blindspots of your models and experience?

■ How can you seek out new perspectives and experience to help challenge or change your current models?

## ENDNOTES

1. Address to Complexity Conference in Phoenix, Arizona, February 1997.

2. "Death by Religious Exemption." *Massachusetts Citizens for Children.* January 1992. <http://www.masskids.org/pcama/religion_1cases.html>.

3. Thanks to Robert Buderi for reviving this example in "The Once and Future Industrial Research." *26th Annual Colloquium on Science and Technology Policy.* Washington, DC. 3–4 May 2001.

4. Porter, Michael E. "The Competitive Advantage of the Inner City," *Harvard Business Review* (May–June 1995), pp. 55–71.

# 2

# RUNNING THE MIRACLE MILE

Racing has always been more of a mental than a physical problem to me.[1]

—Roger Bannister

## You are running on the track.

You are exhausted. You feel you can go no farther. You're short of breath. Your lungs seem about to burst. But if you can keep up this pace a little longer, you can beat your best time.

Suddenly you think about an acquaintance who had a heart attack while jogging. It's certainly not worth that just to beat your best time. So you slow your pace.

Was it your body that stopped you, or your mind? Are our greatest limitations physical or mental? Our models help us act in the world, but they also limit our actions. Like the idea of the flat Earth for early mariners, our mental models form the limits of our world. When we change them, we open up new possibilities for discovering new worlds.

Ask one of the legendary runners, Roger Bannister. He faced the seemingly impenetrable barrier of the four-minute mile, and raced past it. In this chapter we examine the power and limits of mental models.

Until 1954, the four-minute mile was something beyond human comprehension, and thus beyond human achievement. It was believed to be a real physical limit for a human being to run a mile in four minutes or less. "The four minute mile...was the goal that athletes and sportsmen had talked of and dreamt about for so many years," wrote British runner Roger Bannister. Like climbing Mount Everest before Hillary, Bannister wrote, runners "used to think it was quite impossible, and beyond the reach of any runner."[2] It seemed to be as absolute a limit as the waterfalls cascading off the edge of the Earth were to early mariners. And it proved to be just as much a mirage.

In May 1954, on an Oxford track, Bannister shattered this barrier, running the mile in 3 minutes 59.4 seconds. Two months later, in Finland, Bannister's "miracle mile" was again broken by Australian rival John Landy, who achieved a time of 3 minutes 58 seconds. Within three years, 16 other runners had also broken this record.

What happened in those three years? Was there a sudden growth spurt in human evolution? Was there a genetic engineering experiment that created a new race of super runners? No, the basic human equipment was the same. What changed was the mental model. The runners of the past had been held back by a mindset that said they could not surpass the four-minute mile. When that limit was broken, the others saw that they could do something they had previously thought impossible.

Where do the mental models come from that limit or accelerate our progress? In this case, there was a common knowledge among competitive runners about what was possible. The four-minute mile was seen as a human limit by most runners, but not by Roger Bannister. He brought something else to the table. First, he had a conviction that the four-minute mile could be broken. Second, as a medical student at Oxford University and later a neurologist, he took a scientific approach to training. He applied scientific observation and method to his own training. "Each race is an experiment," he wrote. "There are too many factors which cannot be completely controlled for two races to be the same, just as two similar scientific experiments seldom give exactly the same result."[3]

Bannister relied more on his observations of his own performance and insights of fellow runners than on professional coaches. "Running thrives in an atmosphere of interplay of ideas about training," he wrote. "Improvement in running depends on continuous self-discipline by the athlete himself, on acute observation of his reaction to races and training, and above all on judgment, which he must learn for himself."[4]

He applied and developed new training methods to improve his speed, using interval training to run four quarter miles separated by two-minute rests. In training for his record race, he and his teammates had driven down their quarter-mile sprints to 61 seconds when they stalled in their progress. They then stopped their training for several days of slow hiking and rock climbing and returned to run the quarter miles in 59 seconds.

Bannister's approach focused as much on conditioning his mind as on conditioning his body. "The mental approach is all important, because the strength and power of the mind are without limit," he wrote. "All this energy can be harnessed by the correct attitude of mind."[5]

Just as the mindsets of runners kept them below the threshold of the four-minute mile—and the new model created by Bannister liberated them to exceed it—our mental models limit or expand our world. The challenge for Bannister, as for ourselves, is to recognize these models so that we can continue to test their limits. We also have to be able to distinguish the soft and fleshy parts of our world view that can be reshaped from the underlying bone of reality beneath. The breakthrough of the four-minute mile didn't mean that humans were capable of running a one-minute mile, even if they had the right mindset, but it opened up many new possibilities.

Where in your business and personal life are there four-minute-mile opportunities that you just have not recognized are possible? How do models expand or bound your world?

## Flights of Fancy

As an example of the limits and opportunities created by mental models, consider how major global airlines have engaged in price wars that have brought many to the brink of bankruptcy (or sent them over the edge). How far could this price competition go? By conventional thinking, there has to be a limit, but not according to Ryanair Chief Executive Michael O'Leary, who envisions an age when air travel will be given away free. Building on Ryanair promotions that have offered thousands of free seats on flights, O'Leary said that by 2004, one flight in ten will be free, and the figure will continue to increase.[6]

Does O'Leary have his head in the clouds? No, he is simply breaking through the barriers of conventional thinking about pricing and the value of an airline flight. For example, one model he is pursing is the "multiplex" model, similar to how cinemas make most of their profits on drinks and popcorn at the refreshment stand rather than the movies on the big screen. The airline version of this would be to offer free seats on the flight but charge passengers for satellite television, games, Internet access and other entertainment offerings while they are buckled in. O'Leary also envisions a day when travelers will fly for free, with businesses and cities picking up the tab to promote tourism.[7]

Conventional wisdom might conclude that with all the free and discount seats it has already given away, Ryanair would be suffering. But the airline grew rapidly and actually outperforming rivals, with a 31 percent operating margin compared to 3.8 percent for British Airways and 8.6 percent for Southwest Airlines in the middle of 2003.[8]

## Shifting Models

There are many opportunities to shift mental models in business, and these opportunities are not just the result of technology revolutions. Many other key parts of business are undergoing fundamental review and possible transformation, as summarized in the accompanying table. Where inventory in the warehouse was once seen as an asset, the emergence of just-in-time delivery meant it could be considered a liability. The goal shifted from having strong inventories to keeping the supply chain as lean as possible. Where people were seen as an expense for an organization, in an age of knowledge workers people may be the most important asset. Technology assets are generally capitalized; but with change occurring so rapidly, many now think they should be expensed. Financial reporting is done quarterly or annually, but with new "virtual close" systems pioneered by Cisco Systems, it can now be done in real time. In all these cases, our models have constrained how we thought about these issues, and by shifting the model—like Bannister breaking the four-minute mile—we have been able to transform the way we think and act.

### Shifting Models

| | |
|---|---|
| Inventory is an asset | Inventory is a liability |
| People are an expense | People are an asset |
| Technology is capitalized | Technology is expensed |
| Reporting is quarterly or annually | Reporting is in real time |

Which models listed in the table above are the right models? The answer is: It depends. During the boom years at end of the 1990s, just-in-time inventory made perfect sense in an environment of steady or increasing orders. Just-in-time supply chains allowed companies to significantly reduce the costs of storing parts and components in warehouses. But a few years later, when the economy began to falter, these same systems suffered hiccups as a result of unpredictable order flows. Because they did not have sufficient inventories to draw upon, companies experienced long delays in delivering products to customers, or they needed to pay expensive rush charges to continue to deliver.

There is no absolute right model for all time, just the right model for a certain time. Even in the space age, as we'll discuss in Chapter 4, there may be times when you'll want to saddle up your horse.

## Models That Are Out of Sync with the Times

Problems occur with mental models when the environment changes in such a way that the old models no longer fit. Kenneth Olsen used a brilliant model for minicomputers to build Digital Equipment Corporation into a powerhouse in information technology. But he became so attached to this successful model that he was blindsided by the rise of the personal computer, which brought the company to its knees.

Our models are so powerful, invisible and persistent that when the old models no longer explain what is happening, we keep trying to make our experiences fit into them. These models die hard, sometimes only when the preceding generation of proponents passes away. Less often, the mindset can be changed without relying on attrition. When Bill Gates finally woke up to the potential threat of the Internet to his software business and decided to refocus, he made a videotape for his employees showing icons of business and culture such as Steven Spielberg and Charles Schwab saying how much they loved the Internet. This made it hard for anyone to dismiss the Internet as a fad or technological plaything of a bunch of college students. It was serious, and it had arrived.

# THE POWER OF MODELS

The Palm Pilot is a remarkable machine—not just because it is a wonder of technology and a phenomenal marketing success. It is most remarkable because its success represents the triumph of a new mental model.

When Apple CEO John Sculley first heralded the concept of the Personal Digital Assistant (PDA) with the introduction of the Newton in 1993, it was envisioned as the next generation of information technology—a tiny handheld computer that would serve as an assistant to keep calendars and contact information always at hand. But this captivating dream soon proved to be a technological nightmare. The technology was just not up to the hype.

The Newton handwriting recognition became such an object of ridicule that it was memorialized in a series of Gary Trudeau's popular *Doonesbury* cartoons, where the machine responded with bizarre interpretations of handwritten input. This is not the ideal way to draw attention to a new product. After spending $500 million on the Newton, Apple pulled the plug, helping set the stage for the company's subsequent near-death experience.

But Apple wasn't alone. A promising startup, GO Corporation, spent $75 million on launching a handheld before it pulled the plug. In all, companies spent an estimated $1 billion trying to bring the handheld market into being. Palm Computing was lost among the general rout with its large and overpriced flop called "Zoomer PDA" that was launched in 1994.

Palm learned important lessons from the experience, however, that allowed it to create its Pilot PDA based on a very different model. First, instead of developing complex software that would be able to interpret all kinds of different handwriting styles, Palm took another approach. Company founder Jeff Hawkins, who had spent his career studying human cognition and learning, realized that it would be easier to train the human operators to communicate with the machine than to prepare the machine to understand all the different variations of handwriting by users.

"People are smarter than appliances. They can learn," he said. "People like learning."[9]

He created Graffiti, a handwriting recognition program that requires operators to make modified characters with a single pen stroke. The alphabet can be learned quickly by humans and makes recognition much more efficient and accurate for the machines. Hawkins and his team also emphasized size and simplicity, rethinking every aspect of the device and shaving down the cost.

What is the value of mental models? Palm spent just $3 million to launch its new Pilot, less than one-hundredth of what Apple reportedly had spent on the Newton. Yet the Pilot became a product that would define and dominate the market for handhelds. In 1997, it won *Newsweek's* "High Tech Gizmo of the Year" award and *Information Week's* "Most Important Products of 1997" award.

By 2000, it was generating more than $1 billion a year in revenues for Palm. By January 2002, the company reported that more than 20 million devices using the company's operating system had been sold, accounting for some 80 percent of the market.[10]

By shifting his mental model from the technology of the machine to the interaction and learning between the machine and the human operator, Hawkins developed a breakthrough in thinking that created a breakthrough in the marketplace. Where many others had tried and failed, Palm had run the miracle mile. (And, like Bannister, the company then found itself facing many rivals with the same aspirations.)

The technology continues to evolve, and with each new generation there is a search for compelling new mental models. Companies are making attempts to merge the phone and PDA and to add features such as video. Devices with small keyboards such as the BlackBerry have extended the functionality of portable instruments in sending e-mail and other messages. These changes depend in part upon the evolution of the technology, but they also depend on our mental models. What is a phone? Is it something you talk on or something that you use to manage many forms of communication? What is a PDA? What is a computer? Each attempt to transform the way people use the technology begins with an attempt at transforming how they think about it.

# PERILS OF MODELS

Just as new mental models can propel companies such as Palm forward, outdated mental models can hold other companies back. The models keep these companies from running four-minute miles. The online music business demonstrates how the mindset of the old order attempts to hold back the tide of the new. Most large music companies are concerned about protecting their intellectual property from Napster and its file-sharing clones, using lawsuits and encryption to guard the crown jewels of their intellectual property (IP).

Consumers, however, don't hold this model. They are looking for better and more convenient access to music. They want to be able to take music from home and transfer it to a portable device or share new songs with friends. From their perspective, the music companies and their heavy-handed IP attorneys are just getting in their way.

Music companies see their customers as barbarians at the gate who are waiting to storm their castle and walk away with the crown jewels, so they raise the drawbridge and throw some more alligators into the moat. They have even *sued* consumers. This defensive mental model keeps them from adopting other approaches. The result is that they succeeded in killing Napster, but the Napster concept turned out to be a "cat" with nine lives. Other sites such as KaZaA and Grokster rapidly emerged to take its place. When one attack by peasants at the gates is repulsed, it just brings more attacks from different directions. The music industry cannot fight a war against its own customers without risking the further spread of the revolution. The industry said, like Marie Antoinette, "Let them eat cake." As history shows us, this is often the quickest way to lose one's head.

While the industry recognized that a revolution was under way, its responses were feeble, held back by the fears embodied in its old mental models. The industry launched subscription-based services such as Rhapsody and pressplay, but to protect IP, the music lasted only for the duration of the subscription, and it was difficult or impossible to transfer the music to a CD or portable player. Users never had the feeling of "ownership" of a purchased CD or of music from a file-sharing service. The subscription services attracted only an estimated 350,000 subscribers combined, compared to the more than 30 million users who have shared over 1 billion files through KaZaA peer-to-peer software alone. (Although the latter numbers are self-reported, they provide a sense of the relatively small scale of the subscription services.)

Clinging to the old model can exact a high toll. A study by KPMG concluded that the industry's focus on protection resulted in an estimated $8 billion to $10 billion in lost revenues annually for music companies. The study concluded that the industry needed to rethink its business model of encryption to thwart pirates and other restrictions and instead focus on meeting the demonstrated demand of consumers. Every new level of encryption just made it more difficult for consumers to access and transport their music and led to a new determination to crack codes, make digital copies and swap music through peer-to-peer sites. The 2002 KPMG study found that only 43 percent of the media companies made even *some* of their content available in digital form.[11] The rest made no attempt to respond to consumers. They were held back by their own mental models.

## Changing the Tune

While incumbents may be troubled by models that are no longer working, a window of opportunity is opened for upstarts. In April 2003, Apple launched a service based on a completely different model with its iTunes Music Store, built around the needs of consumers rather than copyrights. Even as the music companies were launching new lawsuits against college students sharing files, Apple created a system that allowed users to download individual songs for 99 cents a title from a library of more than 200,000. Once the songs are downloaded, they can be burned onto CDs and uploaded to other devices with little hassle and few controls beyond protecting against wholesale piracy. Although the service, when launched, was available only to owners of Apple Macintosh computers, users downloaded nearly half a million tracks in the first *two days*. Within about a week, users had downloaded more tracks than the more restrictive industry-backed services had distributed in *18 months*. In its first two months of operation, iTunes sold five million songs, and Apple announced plans to offer the service to PC users later in the year.[12]

Apple (as the manufacturer of the iPod digital music player) was a marginal player in the music industry, so it might have seemed disadvantaged in tackling a problem that topped the agenda of the recording industry. Apple's outsider status, however, gave it an independence of thought and action that allowed it to do what the insiders couldn't do—see and act upon a powerful new mental model. Apple CEO Steve Jobs realized that the old model of selling albums on CDs, which forced listeners to buy a whole package of songs to hear the one or two they liked, could be replaced with a customizable model of selling single songs. Jobs developed a model for distributing digital music that preserves the rights of owners and respects the needs of users. Apple had the ability, in the words of its advertising campaign, to "think different," and this allowed it to see profitable opportunities where others saw only new threats.

## Making a Segway: The Bumpy Ride to a New Model

While the music industry found itself trapped in outdated models, the slow progress of Segway people movers—the innovative super scooters that were intended to revolutionize transportation— illustrates another peril of new models: the idea whose time has not yet come. New models are difficult to advance in the world, and their progress depends in large part upon the perceived utility for the user.

This new invention, which carried users upright along city sidewalks, responding to their subtle body movements to change speed and direction, burst on the scene in a flurry of publicity. Talk show hosts rode them around on stage on national television; the super scooters made cameos on sitcoms such as *Frasier.* Charismatic inventor Dean Kamen envisioned his new product as a breakthrough in transportation that would fill the sidewalks of cities around the world. At the time of its public launch in December 2001, as what must have been the most hyped product of all time, Kamen forecast that by the end of 2002 he would be producing 10,000 machines a week. Investor John Doerr predicted that the company would reach $1 billion in sales faster than any other firm in history.[13] It didn't happen.

Others saw it differently. In fact, most of the world did. Sales stalled. Opposition mounted. Potential users, corporate and private, quickly lost interest in its gee-whiz design and took a hard look at its cost and utility compared with other forms of transportation. Public officials did not uniformly embrace it as a boon to urban life. They saw it instead as a potential hazard. Cities such as San Francisco banned the Segway from their sidewalks, considering the vehicle whizzing around at a top speed of 12 mph as a threat to pedestrians. Key initial adopters such as postal carriers found it heavy and expensive and complained about its short battery life. The cost was too high for all but the most avid adopters of new technology.

All these challenges are typical in the adoption of new technology, and particularly one that represents a new model for transportation. The first-generation products are always too expensive, too bulky, and too slow to be accepted. The ultimate success of a new technology, however, especially when it presents a new mental model, is its utility compared to other approaches. The Segway's slow progress raises some questions about the model upon which it is based. In addressing their transportation needs, the bicycle, scooter and travel by foot are among the most popular approaches for local travel. The automobile and airplane have greater utility for long-distance trips. The question is, among these options, where does the Segway fit? How will people make sense of it? In order to be a huge consumer product success, it needs to be seen as more than a technological toy. Can these mental models really be shifted in this way?

In Part 3, we consider some of the challenges of shifting from the existing order (such as the system of pedestrians and sidewalks) and the "adaptive disconnects" that slow the acceptance of a new model in the world. These issues affect the trajectory of a new concept such as Segway, but there are even more fundamental concerns about the utility of the model.

This case illustrates the challenges of using new models to change the world. Even stunning technology and bold vision do not always ensure a winning race. The one certainty, however, is that without the mindset that it is possible, the race cannot be run at all.

## THE HUMAN SPIRIT IS INDOMITABLE

In personal life, business and society, our models constrain our actions. The power of new models can lead to successes such as the Palm Pilot. The limits of old models can lead to lost opportunities, such as the intellectual property battles in the music business. The difficulty of changing models can constrain the spread of new ideas such as the Segway.

In our personal lives, the way we view diet, exercise and wellness can have a significant impact on our approach to the prevention and treatment of disease. The models that shape our relationships and our approach to our work have a great impact on the quality and direction of our lives. Our mental models about business issues such as growth or corporate governance will lead to very different sets of strategies for our organization. Our models about the role of government or the structure of the economy—free markets versus centrally planned, for example—can have dramatic implications for the prosperity of our citizens.

Transforming our world begins with changing the way we think about it. The more we understand the role of mental models in this process, and the better able we are to recognize these models, the better we can examine the strengths of our models and their limitations. We can sustain the models that allow us to act effectively in the world and get rid of those that constrain us unnecessarily. If Roger Bannister had accepted the barrier of the four-minute mile as a real, physical limitation, he might never have tried to surpass it.

Recognizing the models that shape our thinking is the first step in beginning to understand and, if necessary, change, our own mental models. If we can understand that the majority of what we are seeing and thinking at any given moment is coming from inside rather than from external stimuli, we make a great leap forward. As we become more conscious of our models, we can more easily recognize them for what they are. Seeing the little man behind the curtain may take away some of the mystery and magic of the Wizard of Oz, but it may also reveal new ways to provide the courage, knowledge, compassion or other qualities that we seek.

It often seems like an impossible challenge to understand our models and change them. But just as Roger Bannister overcame the mindset that prevented the four-minute mile, we have seen time and again how humans have been able to do the unthinkable—sailing across the flat Earth to reach the New World or crossing the daunting emptiness of space to put a man on the moon. It is possible to change our mental models. Time and again, humans have proven their ability to overcome seemingly insurmountable obstacles. As Bannister writes:

> The urge to struggle lies latent in everyone. The more restricted our society and work become, the more necessary it will be to find some outlet for this craving for freedom. No one can say, "You must not run faster than this, or jump higher than that." The human spirit is indomitable.

## IMPOSSIBLE THINKING

- What are the "four-minute miles" that hold you back in your personal and work life?

- How can you challenge them? For each limit, ask yourself: What possibilities would be opened if this barrier were no longer here? How can I get rid of it?

- Are there others who are already challenging the limits of these models, and can you follow quickly in their footsteps?

- What are the challenges and risks of adopting these new models? Is the world ready for them?

# ENDNOTES

1. Bannister, Roger. *The Four-Minute Mile*. Guildford: The Lyons Press. 1981. p. 210.
2. *Ibid.*, p. 184.
3. *Ibid.*, p. 133.
4. *Ibid.*, pp. 69–70.
5. *Ibid.*, p. 229.

6.  "Ryanair to introduce free travel in radical flight plan." *The Irish Examiner*. 15 May 2001. <http://archives.tcm.ie/irishexaminer/2001/05/15/story2863.asp>.

7.  "Hostess with the Mostest." *The Economist*. 26 June 2003. <http://www.economist.com/displaystory.cfm?story_id=1883740>.

8.  Capell, Kerry. "Ryanair Rising." *Business Week*. 2 June 2003. <http://www.businessweek.com/magazine/content/03_22/b3835074_mz014.ht>.

9.  Dillon, Pat. "The Next Small Thing." *Fast Company*. June 1998. p. 97.

10. Palm, Inc. "Palm Completes Formation of Palm OS Subsidiary as Palm Powered Devices Hit 20 Million Sold." *PR Newswire*. 21 January 2002. <http://www.palm.com/about/pr/2002/012102.html>.

11. Reuters. "Study Raps Media Focus on Piracy." 24 September 2002. *Siliconvalley.com*. <http://www.siliconvalley.com/mld/siliconvalley/news/editorial/4144704.htm?template=contentModules/printstory.jsp>.

12. Black, Jane. "Big Music: Win Some, Lose a Lot More?" *Business Week Online*. 5 May 2003. <http://www.businessweek.com/technology/content/may2003/tc2003055_8073_tc078.htm>. "How to Pay the Piper." *The Economist*. 1 May 2003. p. 70. Apple Computer. "iTunes Music Store Hits Five Million Downloads." 23 June 2003.

13. Rivlin, Gary. "Segway's Breakdown." *Wired*. March 2003. pp. 23–149.

14. Bannister, Roger. *The Four-Minute Mile*. Guildford: The Lyons Press. 1981. p. 249.

# 2

# KEEPING YOUR MODELS RELEVANT

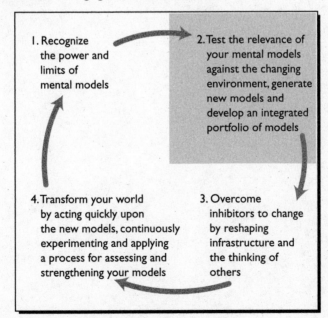

# 3

# SHOULD YOU CHANGE HORSES?

All growth is a leap in the dark, a spontaneous, unpremeditated act
without benefit of experience.

—Henry Miller[1]

## You have been carjacked.

You are now sitting in the passenger seat and a man in a ski mask is
pointing a gun at you while he drives your car. You have only a split second to
size up the situation. Does he intend to kill you, or will he drop you off
somewhere up ahead on the road? Your door is unlocked, so the thought
passes through your mind that you could jump out of the moving car onto the
street and run away. But would you survive the jump? Are you better off
staying in the car with the danger that you know, rather than making a leap
into the unknown?

How do you know it is the right time to give up the world that you know, even
when it has become dangerous, for something new?

In your personal and business life, you will often face such forks in the road.
They will not always be this dramatic, but the choices can be just as sharp
and the implications just as ambiguous. You will be faced with the choice of
holding onto an old model that may not be working or adopting a new one
with uncertain repercussions. If you are facing trouble in your marriage or at
work, do you abandon your model of family life or your model for a career, or
do you stick with the old model despite the problems? When do you need to
make the leap, and how do you do it? This chapter examines these issues,

beginning with the unfortunate story of Lord George Simpson, who perhaps should have looked a bit harder before he leaped.

---

Imagine you are Lord George Simpson, who took the reins of General Electric Company (GEC) in the United Kingdom (no relation to U.S.-based General Electric) in September 1996. Under the leadership of your predecessor, Lord Arnold Weinstock, GEC had risen to become one of the most powerful companies in Britain. It was an extremely successful money-making machine that dominated British defense, power and electronics.

Weinstock, who ran the company with an iron fist for 33 years, introduced an approach to operating the conglomerate in the 1960s that was radical for its time in the UK. He sat in his office and ran the corporation's 180-some companies based on a set of key financial ratios, firing managers when their ratios dipped below acceptable levels. He rarely walked into his own factories, but he watched the numbers like a hawk. And his managers trembled when they heard him on the other end of the phone line. He stripped away wasteful overhead and instituted strong controls. He added new businesses through major acquisitions.

While Weinstock indulged a personal passion for gambling on horses at the racetrack, he didn't leave anything at the company to chance. He created a model for running the business that was so successful, it became the standard for other large British firms.

While Weinstock's mechanical model and conservative strategy for the business were rewarded by strong financial performance, at least according to his measures, the low-growth approach was punished by the market in boom times. As Weinstock neared the end of his term in the mid-1990s, GEC's share price was languishing. Investors, who wanted growth, were rewarding GEC's rivals who entered microchips or consumer electronics. Weinstock and his managers were flogging performance out of existing businesses, but they were not aggressively pursuing the technology-driven growth that other competitors were achieving in computing and telecommunications.

As George Simpson, when you enter the building on your first day, you have inherited a very successful company, but one that is no longer the darling of investors. You are sitting on a pile of more than £2 billion in cash. As you walk into the stodgy offices in Hyde Park Corner and settle down into Weinstock's large chair under an oil painting of one of the racing horses he so much admired, you begin to consider your strategy. GEC is a solid warhorse, but it certainly can't keep pace with the nimble thoroughbreds running past it to the high-tech winner's circle. Is Weinstock's powerful organization finally losing its footing? The cozy political relationships that allowed for lucrative cost-plus defense contracts are fading fast. New technologies are transforming the competitive landscape and creating red-hot opportunities. Clearly, it seems, a different model is needed. Isn't it time to switch horses? Do you stay the course or put your own mark on the organization? What would you do?

Your choices at such forks in the road are often the most important decisions you can make. How do you know whether the old business model, and the mental model on which it is based, are worn out or just need to be reshod? How do you know that the new model will live up to its hype?

All the time that people are making such decisions about which models to bet on, the horses keep on running; there isn't a pause in the action. Not having much time to assess the situation, people tend to keep rolling over the same old bets, or to jump impulsively from horse to horse.

## Place Your Bets

There are no easy answers to the underlying questions. In making decisions about changing mental models—whether they involve a corporate growth strategy through acquisitions or a personal "antigrowth" strategy of diet and weight control—you face the danger of two kinds of serious mistakes:

- **Being left behind.** The first mistake is to stick with the wrong model and be left behind. You are backing an old nag that should have been put out to pasture long ago. You are running your business on an industrial model in an information age. You are eating a processed-food diet of the 1950s while knowledge of nutrition and exercise have moved forward. The rest of the pack, with better mental models, thunder by, and you are left in the dust. You fail to seek out something new until your losses accumulate or the horse you are backing keels over. Sometimes then it is too late. As Simpson took over GEC, he must have worried that the model that Weinstock had used to build the company was losing steam. It seemed that the time was ripe for a revolution, while the company still had the resources to pull it off. When you leave the safety of tried-and-true bets, however, you risk a second possible mistake.

■ *Backing the wrong horse.* In jumping to a new mental model, you might abandon a perfectly adequate one before it has been exhausted. An even more serious danger is that you might change to a model that turns out to be much worse. When Internet start-ups and venture capitalists convinced the world to look at eyeballs rather than ROI, they attracted big bets on a model that focused on how many users were looking at their Web pages rather than how many dollars were flowing into their coffers. A short time and billions of dollars later, many investors gave their heads a vigorous shake and were a bit shocked to see this same picture through very different eyes. They concluded that their bets, in many cases, had been unwisely made, based upon a vague and poorly understood model. As a consequence, there were big losses. This is the trouble Lord Simpson ultimately found himself in.

## A Wild Ride

Lord Simpson apparently decided it was time for a revolution. Weinstock had described his successor as "a man of vision," and he was right. Simpson moved the company out of its conservative Hyde Park headquarters to trendy offices on Bond Street and changed its generic name to the more nuanced Marconi, signaling his intent to concentrate on the hot-growth sector of telecommunications. The company sloughed off the old defense business to British Aerospace and drove full bore into telecom.

Marconi now had the kind of focus on growth that shareholders dream about. Lord Simpson had transformed the boring, old-fashioned conglomerate into a dynamic, sharply focused high-tech firm. As the bright red 1999 annual report gushed: "Our future... will be digital. We will lead the race to capture, manage and communicate information. We will ride the rising tide of demand for data transmission. We will be a leading global player in communications and IT."[2]

The dream was seductive. Despite signs that the telecom market was weakening, Simpson held to his view of the world. He had burned his boats to make a stand on this foreign shore and there was no way back. As competitors such as Nortel, Nokia and Ericsson warned of declining sales and profits in the first quarter of 2001, Simpson stubbornly clung to his view of telecom as a hot market. On May 16, 2001, he told shareholders: "We anticipate the market will recover around the end of this calendar year, initially led by European established operators ... we believe we can achieve growth for the full year, as a result of our relative strength supplying these operators."[3]

As commentator Frank Kane wrote in the *Observer* in August, while the rest of the world saw that Marconi's vision was collapsing, Simpson refused to give up on his view. He was, perhaps, too deeply committed. Kane wrote that "What might have been called brave determination a month ago has turned into willful stubbornness coupled with a blind refusal to see reality."[4]

The dream of Marconi turned to a nightmare as the company was swallowed up in the telecom bust, which left the global industry with a hangover of $750 billion in excess capital expenditure and debt. By September, Simpson and his top managers had stepped down from a business that was reeling. Marconi shed 10,000 employees. The more than £2 billion in reserves existing when Simpson took charge were gone, replaced by a crater of more than £4 billion in debt. The company's share price plummeted from a vigorous peak of £12.50 to the comatose level of four pence at the time of Lord Weinstock's death in July 2002.[5] He lived to see the once-great company he had built brought to the brink of bankruptcy. It was, in the words of the BBC, "one of the most catastrophic declines in UK corporate history."

How did this "man of vision" go so wrong? Marconi's business was built on a chain of assumptions. In 2000, when telecom operators were spending more than 25 percent of their revenue on expanding their networks, they had a voracious appetite for Marconi's telecom equipment and software. This spending was, in turn, based on projections of a rapid increase in customers and an insatiable demand for bandwidth. These projections were wildly optimistic and, as they collapsed in 2001, the industry suffered from overcapacity and quickly cut back on spending. During its acquisition spree, Marconi had paid top dollar to create end-to-end solutions for customers, based on a perception of continued growth in the sector. When these projections of growth collapsed, so did Marconi's business. All these changes occurred in the broader context of several decades of deregulation that had transformed the telecom industry.

The business models Lord Weinstock and Lord Simpson created were based upon totally different mental models. Lord Weinstock ran a business that was risk averse and very conservative, a vision that may have been shaped by his childhood as a poor Jewish immigrant from eastern Europe. He ran the business by the numbers. The affable Lord Simpson, a member of seven golf clubs, worked from personal relationships. He had built his career upon making deals. He had sold Rover to BMW and closed other major deals earlier in his career that helped in selling GEC's defense business and making a series of acquisitions to build Marconi's capabilities.

Both men had become successful based on their world views, and both in different ways were blinded by them. Lord Weinstock's reliance on financial controls over personal management may have led to his poor judgment in appointing Simpson as his successor. Lord Simpson's reliance on personal relationships and deal making may have blinded him to the importance of rigorous controls that are needed to run the business. As both men entered a process of establishing a new model for GEC's business, they made the dangerous move from their areas of deepest experience into new industries and ways of operating that were not familiar.

To institute a new order of things, leaders need to be able to persevere against the naysayers and rise above obstacles. They need to be able to overlook the limits of today to build the business for tomorrow. When does the "brave determination" that is needed to champion a new vision become "a blind refusal to see reality"?

There are several psychological forces that tend to keep people committed to a course of action long beyond the point when they should rationally quit. The first is the "sunk cost fallacy." This can be seen in the actions of the stock market investor who has watched share prices of a company plummet from $60 to $20. At this point, instead of objectively assessing the potential of the stock, the investor may hold onto this stock—or buy more shares—in hopes of regaining these "sunk costs."[6] But if the company is collapsing, there will just be more losses. Managers with deep investments in a given project, financial or reputational, will likely sustain it beyond when they should objectively pull the plug. This tendency to deepen commitment can also be seen in political commitments such as the U.S. involvement in Vietnam, where past investments made it very difficult to pull out.[7]

A related factor that clouds our judgment about when to quit is the escalation of conflict. In a competitive situation, investments in a given course of action can reach ludicrous levels. For example, in an auction game in which two competitors bid to win a dollar bill (with the winner paying the sum of the two final bids), bidding quite often ends with the winner paying three to five dollars to obtain a single dollar.[8] There are a variety of factors that drive this escalation. Initially, it might be a desire to make money or prevent a future loss, but as the bids mount, regaining losses or simply outdoing an opponent become more important.[9] In the dollar auction, the ridiculousness of such bidding is very clear, but the same effect can lead to overbidding for much higher stakes (such as the G3 wireless auctions in Europe) and a heavier "winner's curse." Once Simpson was committed to his course of action in transforming GEC, it became very difficult to pull back, despite the mounting losses.

This is not to say that GEC should have continued on the course set by Lord Weinstock. His model of centralized financial control of a conglomerate may have been too slow for the late 1990s. It was due for a change, perhaps, especially since the market did not value such companies highly. There are other cautionary tales from companies that changed too slowly—Xerox seeing its business undermined by Japanese competitors in the 1980s or, a decade later, IBM watching its business drained away by the PC and Sears seeing its department store whittled away by the rise of new retail formats. IBM was so focused on tracking measures for mainframes that it missed the fact that its total share of computing was declining. Sears was watching department store rivals so intently that it missed the rise of different niche retail formats that were taking business away in clothing or hardware. When the racing bell goes off, it is dangerous to stand still.

Simpson's tale of woe emphasizes the inherent difficulty of shifting mental models. If telecoms had fulfilled their outrageously rosy predictions, Lord Simpson would have been a visionary and a hero who had taken his company in a bold new direction. Instead, he walked away from the track in disgrace, having squandered virtually his entire inheritance. Other choices, however, had been open to him, other than betting the entire company on a new direction.

## KNOWING WHEN TO SWITCH HORSES

To their credit, Lord Simpson and Lord Weinstock did recognize that the world was changing and that GEC needed to change. This recognition is the first challenge, because it is often difficult to see there even is a problem with the old model until it is too late. While businesses can be destroyed by the race to new models, others are also destroyed by standing still. How do you recognize when you need to change your mental models?

- *When the old model dies, you have no choice.* The clearest sign that you need to shoot your old model is when the old nag stumbles and breaks a leg. When you face a serious crisis or failure of the old model, there is no question that you need to find a new one. If you have to shoot the current horse, you may find yourself on the side of the road with no transportation. When your old models in various areas fail, you risk losing your health, eroding the profits in a business or undermining the prosperity of society. You face dangers in waiting this long to act. How do you see the trouble coming before you encounter a full-blown crisis?

- *Pay attention to outliers and "just-noticeable differences."* In psychology there is a concept of a "just-noticeable difference." It is a change that could be noticed but is absorbed by the process of normalizing variance. When you see something that doesn't fit the current model, you make it fit. In the movie *The Matrix,* in which the characters are living in a simulated world that they believe is real, it is only through small glitches in the program that they are able to see beyond this illusion. Most of the time, people normalize the variations that they see, and this can get them into trouble. The temperature rises slowly in a room, and you don't realize the change until you break into a sweat. You dismiss chest pains or lack of energy until these symptoms turn out to be a serious medical problem. A company like Motorola is building analog wireless phones at a time when the industry is turning to a global digital standard, but because its current business is successful, it fails to recognize quickly enough that the world is changing. As a result, it is forced to concede significant market share to Nokia, Ericsson and others.

Often these small variations are truly insignificant, but they can sometimes turn out to be the tail that wags the dog. If you systematically pay attention to them, you can recognize when they should make you reconsider your mental models. The more hubris you have built up as an individual, an organization or a society, the more you need to be alert for these outliers and to look at them from different angles to see what they mean. As an

adult with many years of experience, you may need to deliberately take time to sit down with young people, read widely or otherwise seek out views that contrast sharply with your own. As a
mature organization, you may need to create processes for
reporting the information around the fringes rather than just
looking at the big averages or the statistics that you have always
tracked. These past statistics will tell you where you have been
but not where you are headed. You need to look for differences
that indicate your old model is not working or that the potential
for a new model has emerged.

- **Avoid cognitive lock.** Part of the challenge of seeing these
  small variations is "cognitive lock." People become so fixed in
  a single view of the world that they filter out all information
  that conflicts with this model and are unable to see another
  possible explanation. The problems with the O-rings on the
  *Challenger* space shuttle were apparent before the disastrous
  explosion, but they were attributed to quality control in the
  manufacturing process rather than to the effect of low temper-
  atures. Viewing the challenge through the lens of disciplinary
  training in manufacturing or engineering let the real problem
  remain unseen. If your education is in marketing, you'll tend to
  see problems as marketing problems. If your education is in
  finance, you'll see everything in terms of ROI and cash flow.

- **Create an early warning system.** One way to recognize small
  differences and avoid cognitive lock is to create systems for
  identifying specific changes in your environment. During the
  Cold War, when the United States and the Soviet Union had
  their fingers on the buttons of nuclear weapons aimed at one
  another, they developed sophisticated early warning systems
  to let them know when trouble was headed their way. These
  systems essentially were designed to signal that the deterrent
  model of "mutually assured destruction" (MAD)—a standoff
  where neither side moves because of the threat of annihilation
  from the other—had broken down. In this case a new model, of
  open nuclear war, would have been signaled, requiring a different set of actions.

You need to develop early warning systems so you know when to look more closely at your models. Robert Mittelstaedt, Jr., has pointed out that many serious disasters from airline crashes or nuclear accidents occur through a chain of multiple mistakes.[10] There is often time to recognize and address the initial mistakes, but they are overlooked until they become compounded. Chemical companies and other firms have found it very effective to conduct analyses of "near misses," instead of waiting for major catastrophes. The major accidents usually do lead to a thorough analysis, but the near misses often are overlooked. Managers wipe their brows and go back to work. By systematically identifying and making sense of these near misses, companies can achieve higher levels of learning and correct potential problems without the pain of very serious mistakes.

Early warning systems should be based on real-time feedback and have trip wires for action or more intense investigation. Any latencies or lags in basic control systems cause instability. The trip wires should be based on your understanding of your current models. If you know your models' limits, and the assumptions upon which your models are based, you can monitor when the limits have been crossed and the assumptions contradicted. A missile crossing into U.S. territory would have been a clear sign that the assumptions of the Cold War standoff were no longer valid.

These trip wires are not the kind of absolute cutoffs for ratios that Lord Weinstock monitored, but rather events that call for increased scrutiny in a certain area. For example, a credit card company set trip wires for a certain level of customer complaints, employee or customer attrition, reductions in average purchases or declining frequency of use of the card. Companies also set up trip wires for detecting fraud. If a customer uses a card outside his or her normal pattern or geography, the company will turn down the charge until the customer verifies it.

The problem with trip wires and warning systems is that they can sometimes blind you to larger changes in the environment. Trip wires are based on preconceived scenarios of possible events on the current model. Other events, which you may not anticipate at all, could sneak up on you from a different direction. The "digital dashboards" that are being developed to keep critical performance measures in front of managers in organizations tend to focus attention on a few key metrics. The U.S. and Soviet systems were designed to recognize a nuclear missile attack but would have been ineffective against a suitcase bomb or other terrorist act. Lord Weinstock's ratios were not what allowed him to recognize the changing terrain of investment and the telecom industry.

The more you rely on systems to guide your actions, the more you may erode the intuition to see something new. In addition to these more rigid systems for running the business, you also need to cultivate flexible metrics and monitoring. You need the tactile experience of your "hands on the wheel." The best race car drivers are not necessarily those with the best dashboards but rather those with the best feel for the road. You need to look up from the dashboard occasionally and peer out the front and side windows to ensure you are truly headed in the right direction.

■ *Look at the world through the eyes of customers.* One way to get a fresh view of your products or services is to look through the eyes of your customers. Too many companies are internally focused, so customers can offer a fresh perspective on the business.

■ *Recognize fads.* When people decide to abandon their old mental models, they become much more susceptible to the crosswinds of fads, pursuing mirages that appear just beyond the horizon. The assumptions can be wildly off, as was Simpson's view of the growth of telecom. Similarly, in personal life, when you set out to change your traditional diet, you can be swept into an endless series of fad diets, some with radically different mental models. Some are based on taking pills or fortified drinks to replace meals; some strip away almost all red meat and encourage high-fiber, low-calorie eating; while others, such as the Atkins diet, allow unlimited meats and cheeses while scorning carbohydrates. Barry Sears' 40/30/30 ZONE diet calls for a balance of 40 percent carbohydrate, 30 percent protein and 30 percent fat. Some diets are based on eating all you can of certain foods on certain days—or an unlimited quantity of a certain food such as cabbage soup—while others are designed around periods of fasting where you eat no foods. Some are based on one-size-fits-all approaches, while others, such as the plan proposed by Peter D'Adamo in *Eat Right for Your Type,* tailors the diet to your specific blood type—recommending a hunter-caveman diet for Type Os while Type As are to eat a more vegetarian diet. Can all these diets be right?

In assessing potential new models, you need to be rigorous in your analysis. What is the basis for the claims? Can the model really deliver on its promise? In what ways does this new mental model create a different set of blind spots and how can you protect yourself against these?

■ **Know yourself.** Depending on your own experience, you can face different kinds of pitfalls in shifting models. Very inexperienced people, in general, will tend to jump too quickly to embrace a new model. Most experienced people, in general, have a tendency to stick too long with the old model. By understanding ourselves, we can better avoid being blinded by either maturity or inexperience.

As illustrated in Figure 3.1, young people or start-up organizations have high differentiation (are able to see the world through fresh eyes) but have fewer capabilities for action.[11] As they age, they reach a prime state where they are both able to recognize new things and have the capabilities needed to act on these insights. Maturation follows, when they are still good at getting things done but increasingly are locked into their well-worn models and cannot recognize new things. They have accumulated considerable experience, which they tend to use to explain everything, whether the explanation actually fits or not. As differentiation and capabilities sink low, the individual or organization enters demise.

Flexibility and openness to new ideas, which are more common in young individuals and in start-ups that are still formulating their processes and mindsets, can lead to a tendency to run from fad to fad, chasing new models merely because they are new. On

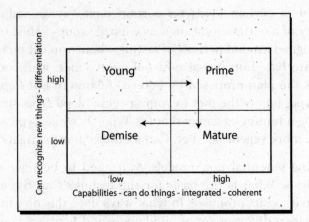

**FIGURE 3.1** Knowing yourself

the other hand, the status quo approach, which is more common in mature individuals and organizations, leads to a tendency to dismiss new opportunities and mindsets. This is the approach seen in Lord Weinstock, who stuck doggedly to his old models even as the world was changing around him. The danger if yours is a mature organization is that you will back the wrong horse, missing changes in your environment because all new information will be force-fitted into the old model. With maturity, you have considerable experience and a vast mental model repertoire, which have served you well but are both a blessing and a curse. Demise follows when the ability to get things done diminishes and new things are increasingly difficult to handle.

Individuals have little choice but to follow this path from youth to demise in their physical development, although many consistently reinvent themselves to stay young in their thinking. Organizations generally react to a perception that they are headed into decline by attempting to reinvent themselves and bring in new leadership, as GEC did with the arrival of Lord Simpson. This is a turning point for the organization, and a potentially dangerous one. It is like a heart transplant. In attempting the transition from the old to the new the patient may gain many more productive years of life—or may be lost on the operating table.

Some visitors to the racetrack will have a tendency to stick to the same horses and riders they have always known. Others will tend to jump from horse to horse, backing whatever hot new jockey or horse enters the starting gate. Both tendencies will lead to certain kinds of mistakes. Knowing how you approach the process of shifting new mental models can help you be more vigilant about errors.

■ *Beware of the midlife crisis from postponing change.* Because of this cycle, mature individuals and organizations sometimes hit a "midlife crisis." They avoid changes for a long while and then make a dramatic leap, often with very negative consequences. The impact of the corporate version of this process can be seen in Lord Simpson's decisions. This pattern can also be seen in the wholehearted embrace of the Internet in the late 1990s by companies that had long dismissed it. In the more personal version of this crisis, the protagonist may give up the minivan for a sports car, abandon a marriage of many years to revisit the bars and dating of his youth or give up a stable career to launch a new business venture. Some people use this route to successfully reinvent their lives, but many destroy their family relationships and their careers in the process, with little to show for it at the end. They become frustrated with their old mental model and essentially throw it out to adopt a new one.

■ *Use experimentation to avoid a leap in the dark.* One way to avoid the "midlife crisis" and minimize the need for dramatic leaps is to engage in continuous adaptive experimentation. (We'll discuss approaches in Chapter 7.) Though Henry Miller contends that leaps in the dark are necessary for growth, they are not always necessary and they don't have to be *in the dark.* People often present options in the form of stark, binary positions (staying or leaping, resting on GEC's laurels or reinventing its future), but usually there are many more options. The fork in the road presented by a new mental model is more complex, as illustrated by Figure 3.2. At these decision points, you could decide to keep your existing model without changing it; throw out the old model and adopt a new one, as Lord Simpson appeared to do; or conduct experiments, monitor and modify or adapt your model as needed. Unless an extreme shift is needed, this third approach is very attractive. With more experimentation, Lord Simpson might have discovered the weaknesses of his model at a lower cost. You do need to beware of using "experimentation" as an excuse to avoid courageous changes that are needed. In many cases, however, as Shakespeare put it, "discretion is the better part of valor." Why take a big and dangerous leap when you can design experiments that offer you insights with a lot less danger?

In reality, there are even more degrees of freedom than are suggested by Figure 3.2. You may not need to choose rigidly between the old model and the new. Instead you can develop a portfolio of models and apply the one that works best for the specific situation. Simpson didn't have to abandon Weinstock's old ratios and controls. They embodied quite a bit of wisdom that might have served the new organization well, even as it created new models and moved into new directions. In this way, paradigm shifts are not absolute and irrevocable, but rather "a two-way street," as discussed in Chapter 4.

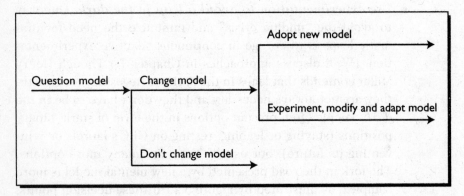

**FIGURE 3.2**   Choices for change

# OFF TO THE RACES

The horses are already out of the starting gate. Your life and your business continue to race forward. You have placed your bet on a given model, and it has probably served you well up until now. Is it time to change horses? How do you avoid making the mistakes that GEC made in shifting its business and mental models? How do you know when to switch horses? How do you avoid backing the wrong horse or making a series of bad leaps?

Even under the best of circumstances, not all your bets will pay off. The story of Lord Simpson's decisions in this chapter, with the benefit of 20/20 hindsight, is not intended as a personal critique. Everyone has made similar—although perhaps less dramatic—mistakes. The important question is: What can you learn going forward?

Given that mental models determine your reality, it is your understanding of your mental models—and knowing when to change them—that determines your opportunities for success and your risks of failure. The chapters that follow discuss this process of building bridges between old and new mindsets, engaging in adaptive experimentation and managing the challenge of complexity. Through these and other approaches, we can recognize the need to change and move in directions that are neither a leap nor in the dark.

## IMPOSSIBLE THINKING

- In what ways are your current mental models working? In what ways are they failing? Do you need to switch horses?

- What are some new models you might adopt to rethink your business or personal life?

- What are some low-cost, low-risk ways to test these models through experimentation before adopting them wholeheartedly?

# ENDNOTES

1. Miller, Henry. *The Wisdom of the Heart*, ©1960 by Henry Miller. Reprinted by permission of New Directions Publishing Corp.

2. GEC Annual Report and Accounts. 1999.

3. Randall, Jeff. "Where Did Marconi Go Wrong?" *BBC News*. 5 July 2001. http://news.bbc.co.uk/1/hi/business/1423642.stm.

4. Kane, Frank. "Steer Clear Until Simpson Goes." *The Observer*. 19 August 2001. http://www.guardian.co.uk/Archive/Article/0,4273,4241635,00.html.

5. "Obituary: Lord Weinstock." *The Economist*. 27 July 2002. p. 85. Heller, Robert. "A Legacy Turned into Tragedy." *The Observer*. 19 August 2002. http://observer.guardian.co.uk/business/story/0,6903,776226,00.html.

6. Staw, Barry M. "The Escalation of Commitment to a Course of Action," *Academy of Management Review*, Vol. 6, No. 1 (October 1981), pp. 577–587.

7. Staw, Barry M., and Jerry Ross. "Commitment to a Policy Decision: A Multi-Theoretical Perspective," *Administrative Science Quarterly*, Vol. 23, No. 1 (March 1987), pp. 40–64.

8. Shubik, Martin. "The Dollar Auction Game: A Paradox in Noncooperative Behavior and Escalation," *Journal of Conflict Resolution*, Vol. 15, No. 1 (March 1971), pp. 109–111.

9. Teger, Allan T. *Too Much Invested To Quit*, New York: Pergamon Press, 1980, pp. 55–60.

10. "Want to Avoid a Firestone-like Fiasco? Try the M3 Concept." *Knowledge@Wharton*. 28 September 2000. <http://knowledge.wharton.upenn.edu/articles.cfm?catid=2&articleid=242>.

11. This is based on an interpretation of the work of Nobel-prize-winning biologist Gerald Edelman.

# 4

# PARADIGM SHIFTS ARE A TWO-WAY STREET

All movements go too far.

—Bertrand Russell

## You check your email.

Then you print out a few messages, putting ink on paper to form words. Your basic approach and typefaces date in principle back to the presses that Gutenberg used to revolutionize communication in the 15th century. Even so, your desk does not always reflect this paradigm shift of more than half a millennium ago. You rummage through your top drawer, past the pencils and the ballpoint pens, to find your fine fountain pen that was a gift from your daughter. You write out a note of thanks on a small card of heavy paper, an innovation dating back to a breakthrough in China in A.D. 105, or even earlier. You affix a stamp and go to the post office. On the way out, you pick up your newspaper at the end of the driveway and flip on the radio to hear the latest news. When you return home at night, you'll also watch television or a video, read books and surf the Internet or you might decide to go out to a movie.

What's going on here? When each of these paradigm shifts in communications occurred, there were some who predicted a revolution that would overthrow the old order. Yet the old order survives—like traditional Amish farmers keeping up the old ways in the midst of a modern world. Why? Because the old approaches have some value and utility. Sometimes you may look at paradigm shifts as absolute and irrevocable revolutions—a one-way ticket to a new order of the world. As examined in this chapter, paradigm shifts are often a two-way street.

---

Pity the poor buggy whip and harness makers when the automobile came in, right? They were dinosaurs after this quintessential "paradigm shift" from the old model of horse-drawn transportation—supported by blacksmiths, horse dealers and buggy whip makers—to a new model of automobiles, paved superhighways and gasoline stations. The old horse economy packed up and left town, right?

Not so fast. There was a dramatic shift in transportation, and a shift in the role of the horse, but the old model of horseback riding didn't cease to exist. The horses were not all sent out to pasture as one might have expected. Their uses changed, but the clatter of hoofs continued to echo across the land. The primary use of horses was changed from more functional work to recreation—yet in a few places even now "workhorses" are still required. In fact, the Barents Group in Washington estimates there are 6.9 million horses in the United States, and the horse industry directly or indirectly involves 7.1 million Americans and contributes billions of dollars to the U.S. economy.[1] All of which means there are still a few people making harnesses and buggy whips.

In addition to recreation, there are certain areas in which the horse outperforms other forms of transportation. For example, it is often the preferred mode for ranch and farm work or police patrols through city streets and parks where motor vehicles might be too loud or dangerous. Horses also have nostalgic or emotional appeal, as seen in the horse-drawn carriages at royal weddings or the horse that rode with boots reversed in its stirrups during the funeral of President John F. Kennedy.

In the U.S.-led war in the rugged and hostile terrain of Afghanistan in 2002, U.S. special forces soldiers and Afghan allies took to horseback to move at night along perilous mountain trails. From their saddles, they used hand-held computers to help direct the precision-guided munitions of their air force to their targets on the ground. U.S. Defense Secretary Donald Rumsfeld called it "the first cavalry charge of the 21st century."[2]

This is not to say that horses will ever make a comeback on our superhighways, but rather that the old model of horseback riding continues to be viable, even in the rocket age. If the military planners didn't know about this model, or consider it, they would have had fewer options to choose from in planning their war.

## SOMETHING OLD, SOMETHING NEW

Rather than an absolute and irrevocable shift from one paradigm to another—which is the way revolutionary advocates of new paradigms often paint the picture—new paradigms and the old exist side-by-side. If we recognize this, we can take a pragmatic approach in choosing from the new and the old paradigms in addressing any given problem. Where a motor vehicle works best, we use one. Where a horse solves the problem better, we are willing to go back to the old model. We are neither Luddites, who have a dogmatic *objection* to the new, nor revolutionaries having a dogmatic *attachment* to the new. We look at all the models and select the one that works best.

In this way, paradigm shifts are a two-way street. We can move back and forth between the old and the new, as can be seen in many areas (see sidebar, "Two-Way Streets").

### TWO-WAY STREETS

*The Internet.* During the onset of the dot-com revolution, there was a sense that this revolutionary new channel would obliterate the old ones. Financial service firms were shaken to the core as upstarts like Wingspan promised to eradicate branch banking, booksellers worried that their stores would crumble into the expanding jungles of the

Amazon, and grocery retailers watched in horror as companies such as Webvan proposed that pushing a cart through the aisles of a supermarket was a quaint anachronism. The reality was that the Internet was integrated into a comprehensive set of channels of a "call, click or visit" approach. Successful companies such as Barnes & Noble, Tesco or Schwab brought powerful online capabilities to their physical outlets, but customers were given the choice of interacting according to the old paradigm, the new, or a mix of both. While most of Schwab's customers conduct transactions online, the majority prefer to set up their accounts and turn over their hard-earned dollars in a physical office.

**Paperless office.** Our "paperless" offices are churning out more paper than ever. In an age of bits and bytes, the American Museum of Papermaking reports that each person in the United States consumes about 675 pounds of paper per year, and together we read over 350 million magazines, 2 billion books and 24 billion newspapers a year—all printed on paper.[3] We are still writing with cartridge pens and pencils, even though we have ballpoints, roller balls and all kinds of other innovations in writing instruments. All these different models live on because they are preferred by certain users or in certain situations.

**Television.** The revolution of television was expected to eliminate the need for radio. Why would people want to just *listen* when they could see at the same time? While the radio may have been bumped from its central throne in the living room, the old model of radio listening continues to be a viable solution to challenges such as connecting to the world while driving in the car or in other situations where visual images might be a distraction. The old models also find new life as they continue to evolve and mutate. Digital satellite radio is offering national coverage and large content selection, based on minimal advertising and a subscription model. Similarly, the reports of the death of the movie theater with the development of the home video player were greatly exaggerated. Books and newspapers also are still alive and well.

**Analog and digital.** The rise of the digital watch did not eliminate the analog watch face with hands. This may just be tradition, but it also reflects different ways of looking at the world and different preferences. The two models exist at the same time, and different people choose to see time displayed in different formats in different situations. In automobiles, for example, most clocks are digital, probably because they are easier to integrate into the dash and easier to read while traveling at high speeds. Most speedometers, on the other hand, are analog rather than digital (although there are digital ones), perhaps because the sweeping needle is a better way to visually show acceleration. The digital and analog models continue to exist side-by-side, and designers of cars, clocks and other applications can select the one that seems to work best for a particular application (or give the end user the option of deciding). Even some apparently analog speedometers are controlled digitally, allowing the driver to switch from miles per hour to kilometers per hour with the flick of a switch (without requiring the usual double scales on the speedometer). This "two-way-street" solution combines analog and digital as a way of resolving another set of dual models—the English and metric systems—that stubbornly persist despite efforts to create a uniform model.

**Airlines.** Discount airlines such as Southwest, EasyJet and Ryanair are challenging old models of air travel. With stripped-down amenities and routes, the "glorified bus services" are able to offer much lower fares than major airlines. While these companies have been very successful, the major airlines haven't stopped flying. Both models exist side-by-side (at least so far), and travelers can choose one or the other depending on their own preferences or the situation. Ryanair has also reduced its overhead by moving 96 percent of its bookings to its Web site rather than booking through travel agents. Customers might choose to fly a traditional airline for business but use a discounter for personal travel. Air travelers also have a wide variety of ways to book their travel, including travel agents, Internet sites such as Travelocity or name-your-own-price sites such as Priceline.

**Protecting privacy.** During the McCarthy hearings and Red Scare in the 1950s in the United States, people were willing to compromise individual protections and privacy to address the perceived threat of the "Red Menace." With the end of the Cold War, protecting personal privacy again became a new priority, but since the 9/11 terrorist attacks, privacy is again being compromised to address the threat of terrorism. We move back and forth between views—on the one hand, that individuals have an absolute right to as much privacy as society can give them, and on the other, that security concerns supersede the right to privacy. These different views will continue to shape debates in the future.

**Ventilation systems.** When the Rocky Mountain Institute worked on renovations to the White House and Executive Office Building in Washington, DC, they reopened parts of an original ventilation system that had worked very well but had been discarded. It didn't fit the prevailing model of air conditioning systems, which required tightly sealed buildings and central air conditioning and heating units. The Rocky Mountain Institute designers, seeking to create environmentally friendly "buildings that breathe," challenged these prevailing models. They saw that there was quite a bit of genius in the old systems.[4]

**Married life.** When couples marry and have children, they give up the model of single life and adopt the new mental model of parenthood. Suddenly they begin driving minivans and worrying about getting their kids into the 92nd Street Y preschool. This doesn't mean, however, that their old model of individual, single life is totally discarded. The members of the new partnership may still have some of the same interests and hobbies that shaped their single lives, and they might take time for a romantic dinner or a night out with friends, even while adopting the new mindset of parenthood.

**Management fads.** As discussed in Chapter 3, every new fad seems to be an absolute revolution, but usually it turns out to be less than absolute. Total quality, process reengineering and other models for what makes the business tick all have some truth, but not *all* truth. Companies that pursued these approaches with a revolutionary zeal often were disillusioned by the poor results that followed. In reengineering, some companies threw out the old models, such as a focus on human resources and motivation that recognizes that employees are not just cogs in the wheel of a process. These companies then had to go through the painful process of rediscovering the old principles. Sometimes the most successful implementations have been less about revolution and more about integrating the new mindset into the current organizational thinking.

**Medicine.** Treatments and research change so quickly that one doctor and teacher has said that half of what they teach in medical school today is wrong.[5] While the use of beta blockers to treat high blood pressure by slowing heart rates was initially thought to endanger the lives of patients with heart failure, a decade later new research indicated that these beta blockers could *reduce* the risks of death for patients who suffer heart failure. Ancient remedies such as leeches have been brought back to treat the pain of arthritis.[6] As streams of medical research have rapidly emerged, with studies and counterstudies, the models of medicine continue to evolve.

# THE SEQUENCE OF SCIENTIFIC REVOLUTIONS

Thomas Kuhn is usually credited with fathering of the concept of the "paradigm shift" in his famous book of the 1960s, *The Struc-*

*ture of Scientific Revolutions.* He introduced the idea that science sometimes advances not through evolutionary progress in a given framework but through sudden leaps to a new model for viewing the world. Periods of "normal science" are broken up by a crisis when the old theories no longer fit or internal contradictions among theories are identified. For example, the failure of Newtonian physics to explain the motion of light led to Einstein's development of the theory of relativity as a new paradigm.

The "paradigm" that Kuhn discusses is similar to what we have called a "mental model." It is a pattern or model that attempts to explain what we see or seek to understand, especially in intellectual activities. Kuhn and his later followers, however, often portray these paradigm shifts to new mental models as one-way, absolute and irreversible. Unlike the gestalt flip of an optical illusion (where you see first the young woman and then the old woman and you can move back and forth between them), Kuhn says that scientists *cannot* switch back and forth between two ways of seeing. As a result, this revolution, as Steven Weinberg comments, seems "more like a religious conversion than an exercise of reason."[7]

In fact, scientists do switch back and forth between different ways of seeing. In introductory physics courses, professors teach Newtonian mechanics and James Maxwell's field theories because they continue to have value in explaining phenomena in the world. The different models exist side-by-side and can be used by students and researchers to address specific problems.

While new models are usually adopted and applied based on their utility—the car is far superior to the horse for transportation—this one-way "religious conversion" can lead to zealous applications of the model beyond the point of true utility. For example, once people adopt the use of motor vehicles for transportation, they begin driving cars a few blocks to the store—or even driving 20 minutes to the fitness center to walk on a treadmill. They stop looking carefully at the true utility of the model, often because the paradigm shift is seen as one-way. They give up the old paradigm for the new, rather than incorporating the new into a portfolio of possible models.

Perhaps Kuhn has himself fallen into one of the oldest paradigms of human thinking—the need for a black-and-white world. If there are two choices, we want to choose either A or B as superior—not live with both of them. We want a clear winner and are very uncomfortable with ambiguous situations such as the recent U.S. presidential election, which left voters uncertain about whether George W. Bush or Al Gore had been elected.

The desire for certainty often leads to a process of "conversion" from the old mindset to the new, and the converts become the new model's most fervent advocates. This happens with many management fads, where the organization takes a full left rudder into a new approach, forgetting its past wisdom or failing to take a broader view of the organization. Instead of considering the new model as a valuable tool for addressing organizational challenges, they hold it in hand like a hammer and see every problem as a nail.

The goal is not to overturn the old order. Some advocates of change, whether it is the proponent of the next great management fad in the boardroom or the political revolutionary in the street, emphasize only the danger of sticking to our current mental models. In this book we take a more pragmatic view. We need to recognize our mental models for what they are, so we can tell when they serve us and when they let us down. We need to understand the old order and explore new orders that might work better or fit better with a changed environment. While revolution always has its appeal, it often entails a danger as great as, or greater than, that danger of sticking with the status quo.

## SOMETIMES WE GO ONLY ONE WAY

We want to be careful to avoid this trap of absolutism ourselves. While it is important to recognize that paradigm shifts are often a two-way street, this doesn't mean that we move along them in both ways. Sometimes we only go one way, from the old paradigm to the new. E-mail is a better solution to many communications needs today, but we are better off if we don't forget that pen and paper exist and can consider whether they are a better solution to certain communications needs. Models do not go away, but they can fall out of use.

The paradigm of treating illness by driving out evil spirits, while not completely gone from modern life, is not a well-trodden path, given the demonstrated success of modern medicine. Even so, it is important to see that this old mental model exists and that we can still return to it. Even with the dominance of Western medicine, we have seen the rise or revival of alternative therapies such as vitamins and supplements, homeopathy, acupuncture and chiropractors, based on a very different view of treating illnesses. Marginal models may later be revived as a dominant mindset on the basis of their utility or the perceived danger of the current model (such as serious side effects from traditional medical treatments), or these models might become dominant within a particular segment in a heterogeneous population.

The approach of "complementary medicine" or "integrative medicine" recognizes this two-way street, combining ancient healing traditions with modern scientific medicine. Some may adopt alternative treatments as the dominant approach, using pills and surgery as a last resort, while others might use alternative treatments only for very minor ailments. The perceived utility of each approach differs across these different segments, but the people who are at the extremes—dogmatically opposed to alternative therapies or absolutely opposed to Western medicine—have limited their options as a result.

Changes in public opinion and regulations can mean the death knell for certain behaviors or mental models. In the 1950s, tobacco smoking was socially accepted, with movie actors and actresses puffing on cigarettes on and off screen, but it has grown increasingly less acceptable, backed up by strong regulations prohibiting it from airplanes, restaurants, offices and other public places. This trend seems unlikely to move in the opposite direction, although there has been increasing interest in certain types of tobacco smoking, such as the emerging popularity of cigar bars.

Restrictive regulations such as those imposed during Prohibition may eventually result in backlash and repeal. Of course, regulation itself can be a two-way street, as we have seen in waves of regulation and deregulation.

Even such discredited and destructive mindsets as Nazism or white supremacy continue to live on in small pockets, where proponents accept these views and follow them. As much as many of us might like to block off these two-way streets, traffic continues to move in both directions. We find such models reprehensible, yet some people continue to see them as the best way to make sense of the world.

Like matter and energy, no mental model is ever really destroyed. It is just ignored. If we walk one-way from the old paradigm to the new, that is a choice we make to turn our back on the old. It doesn't mean the old model disappears. But if we recognize that it exists and we look back at it once in a while, we may recognize that it has more value than we had expected. We can then journey between a variety of different mental models to gain new perspectives on our challenges.

## THE PARADIGM SWING: LIVING IN ST. PETERSBURG

Sometimes paradigm shifts move back and forth, like a shifting population. St. Petersburg, for example, founded in 1703 by Russian Czar Peter the Great and richly adorned with palaces and public squares, became the most Western of Russian cities as Peter sought to bring Western culture and technology to Russia. This port city on the Gulf of Finland offered a window on the larger world. After the Russian Revolution, and upon the death in 1924 of V. I. Lenin, founder of the Soviet Communist Party, Communist leaders renamed the city Leningrad. The new name symbolized a major paradigm shift away from the Western-looking origins of St. Petersburg to the more inwardly focused Soviet society. In 1991, as the Soviet Union collapsed and Western influence grew, the residents of Leningrad voted to rename the city St. Petersburg again.

When Communist leaders named the city Leningrad, they clearly felt that they were signaling a dramatic and permanent paradigm shift in politics and outlook. Yet the Winter Palace (Hermitage Museum), the Cathedral of St. Isaac of Dalmatia and other key features of the landscape were unchanged from the old St. Petersburg. In fact, the change was not so dramatic as expected. And the idea of St. Petersburg as a window on the West continued to resonate with its people, so when they were given the opportunity to choose a new name for their post-Communist city, they returned to St. Petersburg.

Sometimes our paradigm shifts are temporary. We think we have changed everything—moved to Leningrad—and wake up one day to find we are back in St. Petersburg. The pendulum swings from the old paradigm to the new and then back again. The new thinking is short-lived in its dominance. It doesn't actually go away. The idea of Communism is still there. It just falls out of favor and becomes less widespread and dominant in shaping our thinking.

The focus on building market share that drove the investments in the Internet was replaced by a more intense focus on ROI and cash flow. This doesn't mean that market share goes away as a concern—it just becomes more of a recessive gene for a time.

When democracies go to war, they are often willing to put up with more draconian measures usually associated with totalitarian states. In World War II, the United States moved Japanese Americans into internment camps. With the demand for factory labor, the Americans and British immediately brought large numbers of women into their factories to continue wartime production. We are willing to change our mental models, even strongly held ones, for the sake of utility.

In our personal lives, we have seen the pendulum swing from a traditional view of marriage toward the idea of no-fault divorce and open marriage in the 1960s and 1970s, based on the value of personal freedom. We now see a revival of more traditional views, based on studies that indicate the utility of marriage for partners and their children, but also many different paradigms for marriage and family.

Companies have moved from rigid hierarchical organizational charts to flatter, matrix structures. They have moved to greater global integration and then back to a more regional focus. Governments have run from nationalization or tight regulation to privatization or deregulation, and back again. Regulations are relaxed when the government is focused on the utility of promoting innovation and efficiency. Laws are tightened when the public is concerned about industries run amok, and utility is found in protecting investors and customers from perceived corporate abuses of power.

The question of utility is always: Utility for whom? A shift in the prevailing mindset is often preceded by a shift in *who* defines the utility or the basis of its definition.

## PARADIGMS WHOSE TIME HAS NOT YET COME

In addition to using old mental models to address current problems, we also can develop new models for addressing future challenges. Science fiction is filled with outrageous ideas for travel through space that were not possible at the time they were written. With breakthroughs in technology, these became possible. These were paradigms whose time had not yet come. By exploring these potential future paradigm shifts, we can better assess their impact, prepare for them, and recognize when they are unfolding.

Take, for example, the view that hydrogen will replace petroleum as the primary source of power in the world within a matter of decades. This view could have far-reaching implications not only for the oil industry but for global economics and politics. As author Jeremy Rifkin postulates in his book, *The Hydrogen Economy,* the shift to hydrogen, using an energy source that is far less concentrated in a few hands, could lead to a much wider distribution of power (both electrical and political).[8]

Adopting this view of the world wholeheartedly might lead to serious strategic mistakes. There is some question whether British Petroleum, with its "Beyond Petroleum" campaign, has moved too quickly in embracing alternative technologies in its branding. On the other hand, a company that ignores this view of the world may be left behind. By looking at the world through both this new mindset and the old one of a world based on fossil fuels and other traditional power sources, managers can switch between the two and select the one that makes the most sense at any given time as the world changes. If managers are not open to the idea of an economy based on hydrogen or other power sources, they might not be able to see it, even if it begins to emerge. Companies need to be able to view their actions through an environmentalist mindset to see possible objections to their business that might not be visible through a strictly performance-oriented mental model.

While some of these models may at first seem outrageous, there may be parallel developments that might make them possible. For example, a big question of the hydrogen economy is where the electricity comes from to produce the hydrogen in the first place, and whether it can be done in a way that it is cost effective. Genomics scientist Craig Venter has proposed a different way of producing hydrogen other than using electricity—a totally synthetic microbe that liberates hydrogen. Several research groups are now looking into this. He and other scientists are looking for microbes that liberate large quantities of hydrogen as a byproduct of their natural biological processes. Dr. Venter is also looking at creating a synthetic microbe specifically designed for this task. Shifts in one area, genomics, can affect the viability of a new model in another area, energy production. Because of these complex effects, it may be dangerous to reject any new model out of hand. We need to look at its value today and under possible futures, continuing to reevaluate its potential as the world changes.

# SEEING IN BOTH DIRECTIONS

How do you decide whether to add a particular model to your active portfolio or to abandon it? There are a variety of strategies for making this decision:

- **Consider the utility.** Is the old model useful to achieve a particular goal or facilitate a particular activity? Can the new model do this better? Pay attention to subtle differences. For example, while the computer may be able to crank out a mass mailing much more efficiently, a letter handwritten with a pen may be more likely to be opened. (In fact, some nonprofit organizations switched from machine-printed labels to hand-lettered envelopes for direct mail solicitations because the latter stood out from the reams of junk mail and were more likely to be noticed.) If you were to evaluate handwriting only on the basis of efficiency, you would miss the personality and warmth that also are of value to the recipient.

- **Look for new uses.** Many people involved in raising horses or in related industries probably quit the business after the rise of the automobile. But others saw that while horses' utility for transportation might be declining, there were other potential applications. What are the new uses of the old models?

- **Put away the old models.** Keeping too many models in your active set of tools can be confusing. It will slow your reaction time and force to you to rummage around for the right tool. It can also be expensive to keep every option open. It is very costly, for example, to keep a horse in a stable just on the off chance that other types of transportation might fail. If you are not using a model now, set it aside so you can apply the remaining models more effectively. Consider the costs of keeping a model active and the costs of switching between models. There may also be rare occasions when the costs of keeping a model alive are so much greater than any potential benefits that you retire the model completely.

- **Don't trash your old models, archive them.** Even when a model has no current utility today and is not included in your active portfolio, it might turn out to be useful to solve some unsolvable problem tomorrow. While you may not leave your fountain pen on your desk, you should keep it in your drawer. When you run into a difficult problem, like the U.S. Army's challenge of guiding missiles in the mountains of Afghanistan, it may be that one of your old models will offer a solution.

■ *Avoid going over to the dark side.* Once you can see the world through a different mindset, it is often difficult to go back to your old way of thinking. You become a complete convert to the new way of seeing things and can no longer see the world in the old way or communicate with your former friends and colleagues. We may view these different mindsets like the struggle between Luke Skywalker and Darth Vader in *Star Wars*. Vader tries to bring his son Luke completely over to the dark side, and the younger Skywalker tries to bring his father back to the forces of good. The problem is that to communicate with one another, each needs to be able to see the world through the others' eyes. At the same time, they cannot completely go over to the other view of the world without giving up connection to the old view. If you either reject the new mindset out of hand, or accept it completely, you lose the ability to choose different ways of looking at the world and you erode your ability to convey the new mindset to the folks back at home.

■ *Create an inventory of potential new models.* When you have a new model such as hydrogen power, keeping it in a conscious inventory can help you be aware of it and look for ways to apply it. Even science fiction may offer models that could have some practical purpose at some point in the future. The more you can be conscious of these different models and actively consider them, the better you will be at recognizing that their time has come.

■ *Draw together diverse perspectives.* In addition to the models you assemble in your own head, you can also ensure a diverse set of mental models by bringing revolutionaries to the table to offer different views. If you have horseback riders in the room, they will actively be looking at ways to use horses in developing new solutions, but if no one at the table has that background, the use of horses is unlikely to be seriously considered. Even though most of those present know of the existence of horses, they might not actively consider how horseback riding might be used to solve a current problem. If these different views can be heard, the organization will have access to a much richer set of options in addressing its challenges.

- *Create a tool box of models.* The goal of this process should be to create a portfolio or toolbox of models that are most useful to you. The models will vary from individual to individual—the plumber's toolkit will be quite different from that of the electrician. In this sense, the toolbox is a metamodel that contains a variety of other models. By assembling this set of models, you then have the freedom and flexibility to quickly access those that can help most in addressing a particular challenge.

- *Learn how to be comfortable looking wishy-washy.* Embracing a diverse set of models based on utility can make you look as if you feared commitment to a single model. Some proponents of a given view could feel that by embracing everything, you don't embrace anything completely. This will make them nervous or even angry. You need to be comfortable working with coexisting models that provide utility in different circumstances.

Mental models are tools that you can use to make sense of the world around you, solve problems, and act. To be able to put down a current model and pick up a new one, you need to have a certain level of detachment. Even as the toolbox of a modern handyman still contains hand tools as well as power tools, the minds of effective problem solvers contain a variety of models, old and new. Each one might come in handy some day.

As much as possible, you need a systematic process—both in your own mind and in your organization—to gather up all these mental models. This process can be deliberate, such as the way the legal system adds new models through case law and legislation, but also builds upon core principles such as the national constitution and past laws. A learning organization builds upon its past knowledge to accumulate new wisdom from its experiments and share fresh approaches and perspectives from inside and outside the organization.

You need to keep your drawers stocked with pencils, ballpoints, fountain pens, writing paper, a phone at the ready and a computer and printer, wired to the Internet. With all these options available on your desk and desktop, you are not a prisoner of a certain world view—locked in the castle of a particular paradigm surrounded by a moat to prevent attacks. Instead, you give yourself a passport to travel freely among different paradigms, seeing the sights, crossing back and forth along the bridges, gaining new perspectives and choosing the best path to your goal.

## IMPOSSIBLE THINKING

- What is your current portfolio of mental models that you use to address challenges?

- Look at some of the old mental models that you have discarded. What is their potential value, and where can they best be applied? (For example, if you are sending all your correspondence via e-mail, when would a personal note be more effective?)

- What are the strengths and weaknesses of each model? How could the abandoned models still be used in new ways?

- How can you expand your portfolio by adding new models?

# ENDNOTES

1. The Horse Council. "Horse Industry Statistics." *American Horse Council.* 1999. <http://www.horsecouncil.org/ahcstats.html>.

2. "Satellites and Horsemen—The War in Afghanistan." *The Economist.* 7 March 2002. p. 28.

3. "Paper in Our Lives." *The American Museum of Papermaking.* 2002. http://www.ipst.edu/amp/collection/ museum_paper_lives.htm.

4. Lacayo, Richard. "Buildings that Breathe." *Time.* 22 August 2002. p. A36.

5. Sanders, Lisa. "Medicine's Progress: One Setback at a Time." *The New York Times Magazine,* 16 March 2003. p. 29.

6. *Ibid.*, p. 29.

7. Weinberg, Steven. "The Revolution that Didn't Happen." *New York Review of Books,* 45:15. 8 October, 1998.

8. Rifkin, Jeremy. *The Hydrogen Economy.* New York: J. P. Tarcher/ Putnam, 2002.

# 5

# SEEING A NEW WAY OF SEEING

O brave new world that has such creatures in it.

—William Shakespeare

## Don't look up from this page.

Describe the room you are in. Describe the artwork that is on the walls. Describe the color and pattern of the walls and furnishings. What is the view from the window? What color is the chair you are sitting on? If you are in a public place, who else is with you? Pick one person and try to describe his or her hair color, eye color and other features without looking up.

If you are at home or another familiar place, you might have a fighting chance. Maybe you purchased the furnishings or artwork. (If you do have a "home court" advantage, you might try this again sometime when you are away from home.) If you are on the road, at an airport or hotel, you have to be pretty observant to be able to answer these questions.

Think about a recent transaction at a retail store or ticket counter. What did the person taking your cash or tickets look like? You probably didn't interact with him as a person—just as a ticket agent or cashier—so there was no reason or time to notice the details.

How do you find new ways of seeing? How do you begin to see beyond the limits of your own sight and pay attention to new details that might lead you in a new direction? You don't notice everything in the room because you have decided what is important based on your mental models. This is efficient as long as you don't miss important things. How do you recognize when you are missing something critical? How can you see the parts of the world that you have ignored?

---

When Richard Stallman spoke to researchers at IBM in the 1990s, he must have seemed like a drop-in from another planet. The bearded MIT hacker who founded the Free Software Foundation was invited in to speak about his radical ideas on software development. In his "GNU manifesto"—which created the foundation for work on GNU, an open-source alternative to the UNIX operating system—Stallman envisioned a world in which "everyone will be able to obtain a good software system free, just like air."[1]

The problem was that Microsoft, IBM and other companies had built their software businesses on a very different model. Their software was not open, but proprietary. That meant that the source code was developed by internal programmers and locked as tight as a safety deposit box. Sharing software was the same as stealing it, a point that software companies hammered home in their licensing agreements and through the pit-bull growls of their attorneys. The company that sold the software held the code, and users paid for licenses for every breath of this "air." At the point when Stallman made his first presentations, even the "crazies" in IBM's research labs couldn't see a way to build a business model around this extreme view of open source. It was a totally foreign model.

"We had been following what he had been doing ever since I was in research," said Daniel Sabbah, Vice President of Application and Integration Middleware Development at IBM. "But there was no business model."

At the same time, IBM researchers recognized the benefits of the open-source model. The software was created by a community structured as a meritocracy, in which developers competed to add source code and users fixed bugs so that the system was self-correcting. Distribution was easier because it was free, and the community that created it helped to spread it. IBM continued to watch this new development and think about it.

Ultimately, this radical idea would transform the way IBM approached its software development. The shift came as IBM was fighting an uphill battle to market its Domino Go software for Web servers based on a traditional proprietary model. By the mid-1990s, Microsoft had captured more than a quarter of the HTTP Web server software market, while IBM had only about 2 percent—a serious concern for a company that was increasingly building its future around e-business. But while large companies battled it out on proprietary server software, an open-source alternative called "Apache" had quietly captured about half the market. The open-source model had moved from a radical idea to a force to be reckoned with, and IBM had no choice but to pay attention. "The horse was already out of the barn," said Sabbah, who is a Wharton Fellow.

Yet, the next act was far from certain. The company could have dug in its heels and fought for the old model of proprietary software. Instead, it transformed its entire thinking about software development. IBM developed a less extreme open-source model than Stallman's, allowing for the creation of a profit-making business model. Still, the biggest challenge for IBM was overcoming legal concerns. The lawyers objected, "If you don't control it and don't own it, we don't want to do it." They pointed out that, as a deep-pocketed player, IBM faced significant risks by climbing into the sandbox with the open-source community. Instead of accepting the objections as a reason to reject open-source, open-source proponents within IBM engaged in rigorous due diligence about licensing agreements and even the origins of the code.

IBM developed a business model based on building more advanced software and service contracts on top of the open-source code. Apache creates the "ecosystem" in which IBM and other companies can build their businesses. Apache creates a standard foundation for the house, making it easier for IBM to build the roof.

"The biggest objections were legal objections, and there were business risks. But in order to be a viable business, you take risks and sometimes those risks pay off," Sabbah said. The move to

Apache also meant walking away from investments in IBM's proprietary Web server project. "If you are going to love every single one of your children to the point that you never give them up, you are not going to have a successful business," Sabbah said.

It turned out to be a win-win situation for both IBM and the Apache project. IBM contributed equipment and programmers, giving the open-source project added credibility and the service support to increase the comfort level of large clients. At the same time, IBM now had solid software and an easy distribution platform for basic server software, which was never going to be a high-margin business anyway. By early 2003, Apache was running on more than 60 percent of all servers[2] and IBM had launched other successful open-source-based projects such as WebSphere and Eclipse.

How did the recognition and transformation to this new model take place? First, the research division was constantly looking for new ideas.

"We have a vital and vibrant research division," Sabbah said. "And they listened to us 'crazies.'"

The project also had support from the company's leadership, people like Sabbah's boss, Steve Mills, "who ran interference with the critics and was actively egging me on." It also helped that IBM had such a small position in the proprietary market that it had little to lose. Still, there were many opportunities for second guessing along the way, as they bet a significant part of the business on this new model.

"Now, you tend to forget all the isolated times along the way when you wondered if you were right," Sabbah said.

---

# HOW TO SEE DIFFERENTLY

Most of the time we ignore so much of the world around us. We are sleepwalkers in our own lives, relying upon crib sheets and lecture notes in place of the full spectrum of experience. We walk through the world and don't pay attention to it. We see without seeing. We quickly classify others as "others" and don't see them as individuals. We classify new ideas as "crazy" and don't give them a second thought. We tread the same old paths and don't look to the left or right. Like the magician's daughter Miranda in Shakespeare's play *The Tempest,* we are prisoners of our own islands of thought until some foreign intruders come to our shores. Then we realize the wonder and perils of interacting with this "brave new world" outside the scope of our former mental models.

How do you cultivate the ability to see things differently? How do you remove your own blinders and come up with new perspectives? How do you take these perspectives seriously enough to transform the way you see the world, but not so seriously that you lose touch with your past or your current reality? How does a company like IBM adopt an open-source mindset without losing its focus on making a profit? This chapter examines a variety of approaches to broadening your thinking.

- ■ *Listen to the Radicals.* You need to be able to listen, as IBM did, to the radicals and look for the wisdom and opportunities within their "bizarre" ideas.

Although Canon President and CEO Fujio Mitarai is the nephew of one of the company's founders, he has a reputation for thinking very differently than his Japanese peers.[3] After working 23 years for Canon U.S.A., Inc., he was able to blend Japanese and American approaches to business challenges, so he was neither a gaijin (foreigner) who would be rejected out of hand nor a traditional Japanese executive. This hybrid approach helped Canon bring radical ideas and approaches into the executive office and achieve record profits at a time when its Japanese peers were faltering.

Who are the radicals in your world and what are they saying to you? What are they seeing that you don't see? What can you learn from them? Is there some wisdom in their ideas, and how can you bring it into your life in a way that won't appear quite so bizarre to those around you?

■ ***Embark on Journeys of Discovery.*** At age 22, Charles Darwin embarked aboard the *HMS Beagle* on a five-year circumnavigation of the globe. There were other sailors aboard, but Darwin was the only one who saw the journey through a distinctive perspective. For the young man, this was a journey of discovery and adventure, a rite of passage, a coming of age, a nineteenth-century scientific "grand tour." To spend five years of his youth sailing around the world was a stupendous investment of time and energy. From the Amazon jungle to the now-famous Galapagos Islands to the Blue Mountains of Australia, sailing across vast distances in the Pacific, Indian and Atlantic Oceans, Darwin was exposed to an unbelievable number of new experiences.

Beginning his *Beagle* voyage as a doubting creationist, Darwin subsequently became a firm evolutionist. His training as a geologist had left him pondering the conflicts between the creationist view and the geological evidence. The *Beagle* voyage and its associated expeditions and scientific activities gave him an immense amount of stimulation and intellectual material. He was a powerful observer and kept meticulous and detailed notes of just about every experience. A combination of keen observations and novel experiences provided Darwin with raw material for his subsequent grappling to make sense of what he observed. This whole process yielded one of humanity's greatest intellectual achievements—evolutionary theory.

Interestingly enough, Darwin never left Great Britain again after returning from the *Beagle* voyage, but because he was open to the experience, his mind was stretched in ways that not only transformed his own thinking but also transformed scientific theories more broadly.

It is not just where you go but how you see the experience that counts. Darwin would have been merely a tourist had he not recorded and thought deeply about his new adventures. Beyond that, if he hadn't brought a Western scientific perspective to his travels, he might never have extracted new insights from them.

Journeys that could offer new ways of looking at the world might be into new lands but also could be into areas such youth markets or video gaming. Listening to the emerging segments of consumers, employees and investors can offer fresh perspectives on your organization or industry.

Where do you need to travel to see new ways of seeing? What journeys of exploration can you embark on? In what places are the new ideas emerging? What perspectives do you need to bring along to make sense of what you are seeing?

■ *Look Across Disciplines.* The University of Cambridge's Laboratory of Molecular Biology has produced many leaders in the field of biology, with a dozen Nobel Prize winners including DNA pioneers James Watson and Francis Crick. Part of the genius of its original thinking was that the lab "welcomed researchers who wandered across disciplines and then encouraged them to interact closely."[3] This interdisciplinary reach and collaboration has made the laboratory a center for a series of key advances—from identifying the structure of myoglobin and other proteins to developing a method for making monoclonal antibodies.

Similarly the legendary medical treatment of the Mayo Clinic is based upon the insights of teams of physicians, facilitated by a culture, an incentive system and interactive technology that support collaboration. The organization pulls together the expertise it needs from various perspectives and clinic sites to address a patient's specific problems.[3]

Part of your own familiar territory is your education and training, and you can make new discoveries when you cross these borders. Education and training create communities that have an approved way of seeing and understanding the world. This shared view makes it easier for community members to work together. Doctors have a common mindset and language that facilitates working with others within their professions.

Medical doctors and chiropractors, on the other hand, live in separate universes. They often don't have this common education and training, so they inhabit separate, and often mutually exclusive, worlds.

A student of physics or medicine will approach the world in a very different way than a student in the philosophy department. How often will these two be found conversing with each other? Eventually, in fact, they may lose the common language they need to communicate at all. As the two students pursue doctoral degrees, they may become so immersed and concentrated in their respective disciplines that they actually inhabit separate worlds. One of the perils of specialization is this isolation.

Some of the advances in physics or medicine, however, have a direct impact on philosophy, and vice versa. For example, researchers are using magnetic resonance imaging (MRI) and other scientific tools to assess brain activity while addressing ethical dilemmas that have long been a concern of philosophy. With genetic research and other innovations, many of the breakthroughs in biology depend upon computer science or engineering. Biology has been transformed in the process. Its approach, once very "soft" and qualitative, has become much more "hard" and quantitative. But these types of connections will only be recognized if the students have access to one another's worlds.

While business schools have historically been organized based on academic disciplines (such as management, marketing, finance, etc.), management problems cut across disciplines. The Wharton School has reshaped its MBA program to create a much deeper interdisciplinary approach. Today's students are empowered to develop more creative solutions to problems by looking at the same challenges from multiple perspectives.

A lot of the progress in different fields is at the intersection of other disciplines. How can you cross the boundaries of your education or practice to see the perspectives from other parts of your organization or other disciplines?

■ *Question the Routine.* Like ocean waves against the beach, routines can lull you to sleep. How did the corporate boards of Enron and other companies that experienced corporate disasters miss the glaring problems in front of them? Like many organizations, they had a certain routine or cadence that took the place of active engagement in looking at their own mental models.

Board meetings can become a predictable and formalized process that is repeated each time the board assembles. It is a ritual dance and the CEO leads it. The steps are well rehearsed, and the board has little choice but to follow. Unless someone is bold enough to question the process itself, the routines take on a life of their own and tend to block out active questioning.

Research on marketing— for both industrial buying and individual consumer purchases—shows that we are often on autopilot in making our buying decisions. Consumers usually engage in a "straight rebuy" decision. You might like a particular type of instant coffee and, having settled on that brand, you don't look at anything else on the supermarket shelf. There is no decision. You walk by, find the product and drop it into your cart.

Marketers have spent quite a bit of time trying to find ways to break through these patterns and encourage consumers to try alternatives. Some consumers have a natural proclivity for "variety seeking" and like to try new things just for the pleasure of it. But most of us need a good reason to try something new. If our traditional product is not available, we are forced to try something different. For example, if you are in another part of the country or the world where the product selection is different, you will need to look at alternatives. Or if the risk and investment in the decision are increased somehow—for example, if you have to buy coffee for a small army—you might look more carefully at price and other factors.

Routines and cadence are important in the life of organizations and in your own personal life, but you need to be alert for times when they might lull you to sleep. Are you vigilant enough? What are you taking for granted? How are other people handling similar routines?

You can also break your own routine deliberately to force yourself to look at the world differently. Try experimenting with your own routines—from the way you structure your day to your path into the office to your interactions with colleagues or family. Be aware of the new insights you gain. If you take lunch at that same place and time every day or hold a regular staff meeting that has become tired and predictable, make a simple change in your routine. Companies that took the simple step of introducing "stand up" meetings, where employees gather together but don't sit, found that this fairly simple change made the meetings shorter and more focused, altering their whole character.

You need to pay attention to how much you pay attention. Be aware of when you and your organization are on autopilot. If you think about it, you probably know how it feels. Engage in the exercise presented at the opening of the chapter to quiz yourself about simple aspects of your environment. Are you really paying attention? Are you awake to the possibilities around you? If not, do something to disrupt your routine, even in a small way.

- **Recognize the Barriers.** You also need to be aware of those around you who prefer that you don't reconsider your decisions and current models. In marketing, the "in" supplier in a straight rebuy decision is making every effort to make you feel comfortable and reinforce this automatic behavior. The "out" supplier, on the other hand, is trying to challenge you and make you modify your behavior.

In accepting a model, ask yourself about the motivations of those supporting or attacking it. Particularly if you are surrounded by defenders of the status quo, you will have a much harder time moving in a new direction. In the rise of open-source software, the lawyers may have been much more committed to the idea of proprietary software, and this became an added obstacle to adopting a new way of seeing.

What barriers in the world around you lock you into your current view? What inhibitors and blinders keep you from seeing new models? How can you overcome these obstacles or look over these fences to the world beyond?

- **Practice "Flying Upside Down."** Routines are reinforced by education and training, but this makes you less prepared for outlier experiences. Airline pilots, for example, were routinely trained to fly under normal conditions and even to deal with a range of expected problems, but they didn't have the experience of adapting to serious malfunctions such as the plane losing control or flipping over. Airlines are expanding the range and accuracy of simulations to adapt to the wide range of "loss of control" events, which were identified as the second highest source of airline fatalities, ahead of fire, sabotage or collision.[4]

A NASA-funded study tested how prepared first-year pilots were to deal with eight loss-of-control crash scenarios that were deemed recoverable. While the young pilots were able to recover from the problems they had been trained to deal with or that had straightforward solutions—such as wind shear or nose-low spirals—they were unprepared to deal with six of the eight more difficult scenarios. The best responses to these problems often conflicted with the recovery techniques for problems with a similar feel but very different causes. For example, the generic solution of "powering out" of a stall by using a nose-high attitude may be the wrong technique if the cause is due to an icing situation. Airlines and government officials are looking at expanding the range of pilot training and the accuracy of flight simulators in presenting more diverse scenarios.

What are the equivalents to "flying upside down" in your personal life or career? How can you prepare for events that are far outside your normal experience and require different responses than "flying upright"? How does your current education or training prepare you for these events? How can you expand your education or thinking to see these outrageous scenarios and prepare for them?

- *Engage in Gradual Immersion.* Gradual immersion is an important principle in absorbing a new mental model. It takes time to get used to a new way of looking at the world, and sometimes you have to follow the logic from the old world to the new. Consider the work of modern artists such as Ryman and Reinhart, who created monochromatic canvases. Many visitors to museums look at these works and shake their heads. They figure they could easily have painted something as good. This challenge is explored in the successful play ART, which is centered on reactions to a totally white painting.[5]

If you can follow the progression of artwork from the realistic to the abstract—through the many stages of development of contemporary art, particularly the evolution of conceptual and minimal art—the white canvas begins to make sense as part of this evolution. You begin to train your perception to be able to see how this piece of art fits into a broader story and so it makes sense—not from the perspective of your instinctive reaction but from the perspective of your new knowledge. It is an acquired taste, like drinking scotch.

For a new model that appears as inviting as ice water, how can you gradually immerse yourself to slowly adapt and better understand it?

- **"Destroy" the Old Model.** While you ultimately will create a portfolio of models, sometimes you need to "destroy" the old model to make space to see the new one. "Idealized design," pioneered by Russell Ackoff, starts with a desired state and then works backward to the steps necessary to bring the world from its current "mess" to that state.[6] For example, one morning in 1951, the head of Bell Labs assembled all his top researchers and told them the entire telephone system in the United States had been destroyed overnight. He said: *We have to design it from scratch right now.* He challenged the researchers to fill the void. Once they recovered from the shock—and realized that he was neither telling the truth *nor* joking about the destruction of the current system—they began to fill in this blank page. Out of that challenge to see the world differently came innovations such as the Touch-Tone phone, Caller ID and cordless phones.

  What would happen if you set aside your current model? Without the burden of these "legacy systems," what could you create in their place?

- **Envision Multiple Futures.** Scenario planning, popularized by the work of Royal/Dutch Shell and many leading practitioners, works from the other direction, examining the trends and uncertainties of the current environment and the way these drivers might play out in a set of potential scenarios for the future.[7] For example, in the IBM software case, there might have been a scenario at the start of the open-source movement in which the whole world moved to open-source and another scenario in which the movement failed to take off and software remained largely proprietary. At that point, no one knew which direction the market would go, so rather than betting everything on one model or the other, scenarios allow managers to plan for different worlds that might emerge.

What are the potential future worlds you might live in? What mental models will be needed to succeed in each of these future worlds?

■ *Take a Devil's Advocate/Contrarian Perspective.* Creating a formal process entailing a "devil's advocate" or "contrarian perspective" can encourage different ways of seeing and bring them to the fore in organizations. These alternative views of reality are often suppressed as a result of pressures such as "groupthink." By creating a role of "devil's advocate" (a term which, surprisingly, came out of the Catholic Church), we can encourage the expression of these contrarian and even heretical views without the proponents having to fear torture for blasphemy. For every major new proposal or mental model, appoint a specific person or team to represent the opposing view. If someone proposes X, the devil's advocate will argue for "not X." In this dialectic and debate, the strengths and weaknesses of each model can be explored more fully, and new models might emerge.

How can you create a devil's advocate role in your organization and in your personal life? How can you raise such questions in your own discussions to surface new ways of seeing the world?

In addition to these approaches, paying attention to the weak signals from the environment and creating early warning systems (discussed in "changing horses" in Chapter 3) and the use of post-mortems to learn from past mistakes (to be considered in our discussion of R&D of the mind in Chapter 7) are also valuable in generating new ways of seeing. The strategies for addressing "adaptive disconnects," to see the world through others' eyes or bring them around to your view, as we will discuss in Chapter 9, can also help in "seeing a new way of seeing."

# NEW MAPS

The strategies described in this chapter can help you find new ways of looking at the world, but you still are challenged to know when to look seriously for new models. It took a lot of energy to set out on the journey of discovery that Charles Darwin made in the *HMS Beagle*. It took great time and energy for a company like IBM to put structures and business models in place that allowed it to embrace open software. You can sometimes recognize the need for this type of change by paying attention to the parts of the world that no longer fit your mental models and that help you see when your models no longer work. If you think about optical illusions, before you make the shift from one view to another, you usually focus on specific details of the picture—which then lead to a shift in view.

New models very often emerge from a crisis. Yet if you keep an open mind, become more aware of the limitations of your existing models and actively set aside time to explore other models, you can recognize the need sooner and respond more quickly and effectively in seeing a new way of seeing. If you keep a set of different models at hand, you can try out different ones in solving problems, experimenting with new approaches to see if they might work better than your existing ones.

## IMPOSSIBLE THINKING

- Where can you look to find new models and fresh ways of viewing the world?

- How can you step out of your routine to engage in journeys of discovery (even via a brief trip to an art museum or a scientific lecture)?

- Who are the radicals or unheard voices in your organization and outside, and how can you start paying attention to them? What new models do their insights suggest?

## IMPOSSIBLE THINKING

- What can you learn from listening to young people in your family or your organization?

- How can you keep your mind open so that, like Darwin, you can use your experiences to come up with a different way of viewing the world?

# ENDNOTES

1. Stallman, Richard. "The GNU Manifesto." *GNU Project.* 1993. <http://www.gnu.org/gnu/manifesto.html>.

2. February 2003 Netcraft Survey Highlights." *Server Watch.* 3 March 2003. <http://www.serverwatch.com/news/article.php/1975941>.

3. Holstein, William J. "Canon Takes Aim at Xerox." *Fortune.* 14 October 2002. p. 215. Kunii, Irene M. "What's Brightening Canon's Picture." *Business Week.* 21 June 2002. <http://www.businessweek.com/technology/content/jun2002/tc20020621_9093.htm>. "Hard to Copy; Canon." *The Economist.* 2 November 2002. p. 79.

4. Pennisi, Elizabeth. "A Hothouse of Molecular Biology." *Science*, 300 (2003). pp. 278–282.

5. Berry, Leonard L., and Neeli Bendapudi. "Clueing In Customers." *Harvard Business Review.* 81:2 (2003). pp. 100–106.

6. Croft, John. "Taming Loss of Control: Solutions Are Elusive." *Aviation Week & Space Technology.* 157:9 (2002). p. 50.

7. Hughes, Robert. *The Shock of the New.* New York: Knopf, 1981.

8. Ackoff, Russell. *Re-Creating the Corporation: A Design of Organizations for the 21st Century.* New York and Oxford: Oxford University Press, 1999.

9. See, for example, Schoemaker, Paul J. H. *Profiting From Uncertainty: How To Succeed No Matter What the Future Brings.* New York: The Free Press, 2002.

# 6

# SIFT FOR SENSE FROM STREAMS OF COMPLEXITY

We are drowning in information but starved for knowledge.

—John Naisbitt

## Are French fries carcinogenic?

A Swedish study reported in 2002 that starch-based foods such as French fries, potato chips, rice and cereal contain acrylamide, which was linked to cancer in lab experiments. Did you stop eating these foods as a result? If you had, you'd have been surprised nine months later by a follow-up study. It found that these foods, while they do contain acrylamide, do not appear to cause cancer.

And the whipsaws continue: "Fried Food Ingredient Mutates DNA, Study Finds," proclaims a Reuters headline on June 17, 2003, above a story noting that acrylamides damage DNA by causing mutations. A few weeks later, however, on July 5, another Reuters headline reports: "Study Finds No Link Between Cooked Potatoes, Cancer."

Do you eat potatoes or not? Or do you just stop reading the newspaper? How do you sift through this kind of complexity?

After years of suffering through meals with low-fat and fat-free foods, you read a recent finding that trans-fatty acids, not saturated fats from food, increase our risks of heart disease and cancer. These researchers are recommending adding back in unprocessed fats such as olive oil and butter—and even lard. So why have you been suffering with margarine on your bread all these years?

What new studies will appear tomorrow? How do you sort out the facts from the fiction? Should you just stop eating altogether? Should you take up smoking? After all, there might be a study someday that shows it's really not so bad.

We are bombarded with advice, research and streams of information. How do you tell what is important and act upon it? How do you recognize the information that means you need to change your mental model and your behavior and filter out the steady stream of other data without being overwhelmed? In this chapter we explore strategies for making sense from these streams of complexity, including a process of zooming in to see detail and zooming out to see context.

---

We are drowning in information. An ongoing research project at the University of California, Berkeley, estimates that the world produces between 1 to 2 *exabytes* of information per year. That is $10^{18}$ bytes, or roughly a personal burden of 250 megabytes for every man, woman and child on the planet. E-mail is flowing at an annual rate of about 610 billion messages. By 2000, there were about 21 terabytes of static HTML pages, growing at a rate of about 100 percent per year.[1] More people are writing daily "blogs"—online journals with their daily observations on life—and making them available to millions. Who has time to read them all?

Richard Wurman points out that a weekday edition of *The New York Times* contains as much information as the average person was likely to come across *in a lifetime* in seventeenth-century England.[2] Knowledge is doubling every 10 years, and more new information has been produced in the last three decades than in the last five millennia.

This complex flood of information can quickly overwhelm our ability to make sense of the world. We need to get better at sifting for sense from the streams of complexity. In this chapter we explore a process that helps us see both the detail and the big picture.

## What Is Knowledge?

The meaning of "knowledge" itself is changing. We all know how to create encyclopedias. First, you assemble thousands of the world's leading experts on different topics and ask them to share their knowledge in their areas of expertise. The *Britannica* 11 (11th edition, published in 1911) is regarded as the best example of assembling the world's best experts to produce an encyclopedia. It was perhaps the last time all the world's knowledge could be assembled in such a way. It contained, in the words of the publisher, "the sum of human knowledge—all that mankind has thought, done or achieved" or "a cross section of the trunk of the tree of knowledge." This was an age when people could truly envision knowledge as a tree rather than the modern tangled jungle with shifting sands and thickets crawling with variegated species of plant and animal life. (It was a just a little over a decade earlier that the U.S. Patent Office had recommended to Congress that the office should be closed to save money, because everything that could be invented had been invented.)

This "sum of human knowledge" is created by adding together the entries of experts on specific topics. A leading historian writes the entry on the American Revolution, an art historian authors the essay on Michelangelo and a physicist pens the section on Newton's Laws. With the help of editors, these authors create concise entries that assemble huge troves of human knowledge into a shelf of books or a CD-ROM. This is the way in which for generations we've been creating these great books that codify and organize the world's knowledge into a tight and useful package.

But now consider a very different model presented by the Wikipedia (www.wikipedia.com). There are no distinguished experts who sign their small entries in the book. The project is a grassroots, self-organizing system in which individuals—anyone—can add entries and connect them to other entries. If the entries happen to be wrong, temporarily, the idea is that someone more knowledgeable will come along and correct them. There are basic ground rules for contributing, but the system is totally open. The contributors, all of whom remain anonymous, share their collective knowledge. Over time, the product becomes richer, more complete and more accurate. The links are created within this Web-based system.

Similarly, search engines such as Google have moved from using machines to find information on the Web, to using teams of expert humans to make sense of the sprawling Internet, and now to using a diffused approach based upon volunteers keeping track of one small area of knowledge. The "Open Directory Project" (http://dmoz.org) is creating a human-edited directory of the Internet based on a global, volunteer community of individual editors who have an interest in particular subject areas. In contrast to commercial directory sites with relatively small paid staffs trying to keep pace with an ever-increasing number of pages, the volunteer project harnesses the passion of many individuals. It "provides a means for the Internet to organize itself."

These are completely different views of organizing information. Which one is better? From the perspective of a traditional encyclopedia editor, the Wikipedia's approach is unfathomable. How can you trust information without an expert source? From the perspective of the Wikipedia project, large numbers of people poring over such material will inevitably find and correct errors more quickly. And, in a world in which knowledge changes very rapidly, in which even top experts are sometimes biased and history can be rewritten, the Wikipedia approach may be the most flexible in adapting to change, reflecting the most diverse views and creating a broader and richer knowledge base. These different approaches to gathering knowledge lead to different outcomes.

For example, in defining the word "community," Britannica's 15th edition focuses on the biological definition of the word, where the Wikipedia, as an online community, takes a broader view. Its set of definitions includes subsections on topics such as "agents" and "virtual communities." On the other hand, the Wikipedia definition of "transformation" is focused primarily on the precise terms used in molecular biology and mathematics and not on the application of the term to describe business or personal change. While the *Britannica* has an entry for "insight," there is no specific entry in the Wikipedia; each has its own blind spots and both fail to specifically address the concept of "mental models" at all. To be fair, we should also note that we are comparing the online version of the Wikipedia against the paper version of the *Britannica*, so we need to recognize that the format for the information also changes the way we interact with it. An online version, for example, is in general much easier to use for a specific search, while a print version is often more convenient to browse through.

There are other approaches to organizing and making sense of knowledge. The *Oxford English Dictionary* looks at the evolution of the meaning of words over time, citing their actual usage in written works. (The *OED* also used a development process similar to the Wikipedia, in which entries were sent in by many volunteers, one of the most prolific of whom was actually a convicted murderer who was an inmate at a British asylum.[3]) An online project called WordNet, developed by Princeton University Psychology Professor George Miller, based on his studies of memory processing, takes a broader view than the average dictionary or thesaurus.[4] Besides listing definitions (it has eight for "community"), synonyms or antonyms, WordNet also assembles "hypernyms" or the classes of things to which the word belongs (for example, a dog is a kind of canine, carnivore, mammal, animal, organism), "hyponyms" or specific examples of the word (such as pooch, lapdog, pug, Dalmatian, Newfoundland), and "meronyms" or parts of the word ("flag," referring to a dog's tail, for example).

These variations give the word context, which is valuable for humans and particularly important for machine translations. Without such context, computer translation programs have been known to commit classic gaffs, such as turning the phrase "the spirit is willing but the flesh is weak" into the translation "the vodka is good but the meat stinks." The implications of the former statement differ sharply from those of the latter.

The way we make sense of words and other information powerfully influences our perceptions and actions. The encyclopedia, Wikipedia, *OED* and WordNet offer different models for gathering and organizing knowledge. Since there are many ways to look at the same data set, the way we sift, sort and shuffle it has a dramatic effect on what we see.

Although experts, like journalists, are expected to be unbiased, they invariably share the systemic biases of the disciplines and cultures in which they work. Journalists try to be fair and objective by presenting all sides of a particular issue. Practically speaking, however, it is about as easy to present *all* sides of an issue as it is to invite candidates from all political parties to a presidential debate. Some perspectives ultimately are not included.

The culture even biases our definitions of words. When one of the authors asked students to look up definitions of terms such as "democracy" in the encyclopedias of different nations, the results, as might be expected, reflected widely varying concepts of the same word.

---

# THROWING A DROWNING MAN ANOTHER MEGABYTE OF DATA

Information has not only increased, it flows in different ways. With 24-hour global news organizations, we have shared global experiences with billions of people around the globe, such as the September 11 terrorist attacks, the death of Princess Diana or World Cup soccer. Companies want 24/7/365 employees wired into the network with pagers, BlackBerry handhelds, e-mail and cell phones.

We may have reached the limits of our ability to absorb this information—let alone *make sense* of it. The finite capacity of our attention is shown in our remarkably constant *consumption*. The time the average U.S. household devoted to media (TV, radio, recorded music, newspapers, books, magazines, home video, video games and the Internet) increased only 1.7 percent between 1992 and 2000, hovering around 3,300 hours per year. This may suggest that we have reached our limits. Still, in 2000, the average household took in through various channels 3.3 million megabytes of information.[5]

Many of us have already exceeded our limits. This "data smog" has lead to a phenomenon that British psychologist David Lewis has called "information fatigue syndrome," as information overload interferes with our sleep, our concentration and even our immune systems. It has been linked to physical ailments such as indigestion, heart problems and hypertension. A more pervasive effect is paralyzed thinking or flawed decisions.[6]

Complexity quickly leads to confusion. A study at the Oak Ridge National Laboratory, sponsored by the U.S. Department of Transportation's Intelligent Vehicle Initiative, exposed test subjects to various gadgets that are invading our automobiles. As drivers made their way down a test track, they were bombarded with automated directions, cell phone calls and Internet news broadcasts. At the same time, researchers posed simple math problems: If your car gets 12 miles per gallon, how many gallons will you need to travel 96 miles? One in six drivers missed their turn, some didn't answer the cell phone and many failed to answer this elementary math problem. Mercifully only two or three of the 36 test subjects went off the road during their 45-minute drive, but many more of them saw their thinking "crash" along the way.[7]

## Knowing More, Knowing Less

The effect of information in the past was to decrease uncertainty. Now sometimes the more information we have, the less we understand. Reports come from many sources, with widely varying characteristics, and we need to determine how reliable the information is. The interpretation is shaped by the agendas of the parties that are presenting it and receiving it. Rapidly changing information makes predictions about the future more difficult. A networked, nonlinear world of constant change—the global village—is also a turbulent world of transient fads and enduring truths.

The real challenge is not just to survive this onslaught of information but to make sense of it. How do we take this complex sea of information in which we live and extract the salt of truth from it? How do we find the pearls that are hidden in its depths, without drowning?

## Swallowing the Sea

Some would take the approach of the Chinese brother in the old story, who had the ability to swallow the sea. He could consume the entire sea and then take his pick of the fish left on the bottom. An example of this "swallowing the sea" approach is the U.S. Defense Department's plans to spend $240 million to develop a Total Information Awareness (TIA) system. The project would swallow the data from every American's bank accounts, tax filings, driver's license, airline and travel bookings, credit-card purchases, medical records, phone and e-mail transactions and anything else available in a massive sea of disparate information. The government could then move through this ocean looking for patterns or potential correlations that indicate signs of trouble.[8]

Setting aside concerns about individual privacy, TIA appears to represent a brute-force solution to dealing with information. Many experts think that this massive, heterogeneous, unwieldy and constantly changing database is unlikely to produce original insights. Once terrorists understand what is being tracked, they can try to develop suitable countermeasures. Corporations already have much experience of the benefits and limits of so-called 'data mining,' which serves as a cautionary tale. An alternative model uses distributed defenses that work like an immune system, seeking out threats and responding to them. This system is less labor intensive and expensive as well as more difficult for "hackers" to outmaneuver.

It is tempting to think that some supercomputer can crank through all the data in the world and derive an original understanding. Assembling great quantities of disparate data, though, doesn't necessarily lead to better insight. It can actually render making sense more difficult and can be overwhelming. Powerful information systems and data mining need to be linked to a process for making sense within a narrowly defined area of interest.

This accumulating of data without sense making was wonderfully satirized in the book *Funes, The Memorious,* by Jorge Luis Borges. The title character, Ireneo Funes, is blessed (or cursed) with a perfect memory of anything he has ever seen in his life. He remembers every minute detail. He can identify the exact second at which the sun set on a particular day long ago, and every gradation of color in its setting, but he cannot change anything from this perfect memory. He cannot think any new thoughts because he is overwhelmed by all the past information. Through this story, Borges highlights the distinction between the accumulation of raw data and the creativity needed to *make sense* of it. We need to avoid using our technology to become like Funes and, instead, focus on processes that allow us to sift the gold nuggets from these torrents of knowledge.

## IT'S ALL ABOUT CONTEXT

We cannot just collect mass quantities of information and expect the sense to appear. What we sometimes fail to see about the nature of information is that it usually cannot be understood independent of its context. When we harvest packets of information and throw them into large baskets, we can make it harder to understand what they mean because we separate them from their context.

What we see often depends upon where we see it. For example, what do you see in Figure 6.1?

Some people will see a "B" while others will see the number "13." Is it a number or a letter? Now consider the same lines in context. In Figure 6.2, the context directs us to see a "B." In Figure 6.3, it directs us to see a "13."

Is it a number or a letter? We often treat such questions as if there were one right answer. The answer depends not only upon what we see, but upon *how we make sense* of what we see. The way we make sense depends not only on the character itself but also on the context in which we find it.

**FIGURE 6.1**
It's all about context!

**FIGURE 6.2**
Effect of a context of letters.

To make sense of this image, we first focus on the individual character (13 or B). Next we step back and look for the context. Then we can zoom back in again. With our vision, we do this instinctively as we go through life. We focus on details, step back to look at context and then focus on details again. Zooming out allows us to avoid getting so focused on the minutia that we become *confused* and cannot act. Zooming in helps us avoid getting so *diffused* that we cannot take specific action.

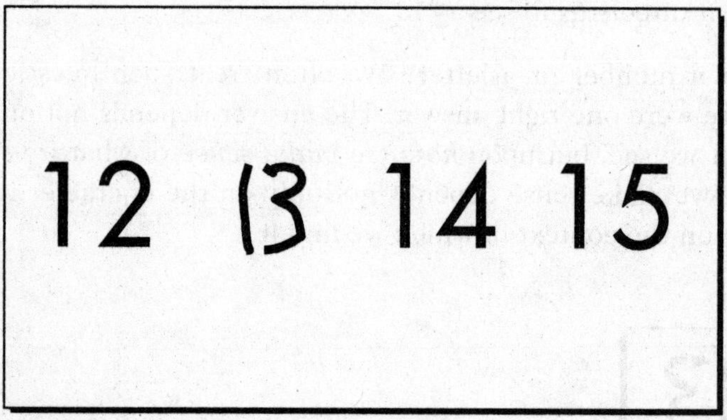

**12  13  14  15**

**FIGURE 6.3**    Effect of a context of numbers.

## Zooming In and Out

As with our physical vision, the key to navigating the complexity of our current information environment and making sense of it is to cultivate a process of zooming in and out. Through this process, we can counter a natural tendency to be either too nearsighted or farsighted. It is like the eye exercise of looking away from your computer screen at regular intervals to avoid the fatigue and fixation of staring.

Given that we make sense generally by using only a small portion of the available external sensory stimuli to construct a coherent picture, we face several challenges in sifting through an avalanche of information. The first is to make sure we pay attention to the *relevant portion,* so our perspective is not built upon shifting sands or the wrong information. We do this by zooming in and examining interesting details closely. This helps us identify disconfirming information that should cause us to challenge our broader models. The second challenge is to make sure we can gain sufficient perspective to create a coherent picture at all. We do this by zooming out and looking at the big picture.

If we stay "zoomed out," we can quickly become overwhelmed by all the data. A person trying to listen to every conversation in a crowded party ends up hearing nothing. If the partygoer stays "zoomed in," he might be so intently focused on a single conversation that he fails to notice the arrival of an important associate. By moving back and forth between these two focal points, we are like the driver checking the dashboard and then looking out at the road. We can see both the details and the bigger picture we need in order to make our way down the highway.

A mouse approaching a piece of cheese might sniff it closely to see if it is edible or has gone bad, as illustrated in Figure 6.4. This process of zooming in is necessary for action. But the mouse also needs to consider the context for this decision. If the piece of cheese is on a dinner table, the mouse can then zoom back and proceed to eat. But if the piece of cheese is found in the context illustrated in Figure 6.5, the best course of action is quite different.

**FIGURE 6.4**
Zooming in to see the detaiL

We must have a coherent process of examining detail, which allows us to act quickly, but at the same time we need to retain an overall picture so we can make sense of the context. Like an artist painting a picture, we need to be aware of the overall plan for the canvas even as we focus on applying paint to one small leaf.

We need to engage in a continuous process of zooming in and out, each time shifting the area of focus onto the next interesting thing. At points along the way, we need to pull back from our current focus of attention and take a broader view. We reconfirm the context and make sure things have not changed. Life is far too complex to think that: "only one thing matters." It is highly unlikely that there is only one first-priority thing in your life, unless it is of course some dire emergency. It is all a question of balance and constantly moving across all the issues in your life, focusing on the next interesting thing, selected by zooming out and looking at the overall context and then zooming in. However, once you zoom in, it is crucial to decide, take action and then zoom out.

The old-fashioned "To do" list, with a set of absolute and unchanging priorities, if slavishly followed, can represent a fixation on zooming in. You work your way down from your "level A"

**FIGURE 6.5**
Zooming out to the see the context

priorities in an orderly fashion, but what happens if the world changes in the meantime? Are you able to look up from your list and recognize this, or do you keep cranking along even when the problem has changed? You might be better served by a process of perspective and context. You zoom in, focus, take action, zoom out and check context. This can help ensure that you not only finish your top-priority tasks, but that they are the *right* tasks.

# THE PROCESS OF ZOOMING IN AND ZOOMING OUT

How do you engage in a continuous process of zooming in and out? You need to look carefully at the detail of a flower in the garden—identifying what species it is, its color, whether it shows any signs of disease or needs care, whether encroaching weeds need to be pulled out. Then you can zoom out and look at the whole garden. What is the overall effect of all the flowers there? Is there the right balance or mix of individual flowers? Is the whole garden healthy? Is one wilting flower an isolated problem or part of a bigger pattern of failure? This process is repeated as you move your perspective out and then in.

Which comes first? It depends on the problem at hand. Some challenges, with very technically complex issues, begin with a zooming-in process. You might face a specific crisis, such as an operational failure or severe medical condition that needs immediate attention. You focus exclusively on this specific challenge for a short period of time. After addressing the serious medical crisis, you might then look at broader issues such as diet and exercise that may have contributed to it. Other challenges start with the broader context, maybe a vague sense that something is wrong with your health, or an awareness of falling sales or of slowly declining outputs from a factory. Having this big picture, you start to delve into the details to see what is going on.

## Knowing Where You Stand

The order of the processes is not as important as the ability to move back and forth between these two perspectives. You generally start at a particular vantage point, so the first question to ask is: Where am I standing in relationship to this challenge? If you are at a detached distance, then you may need to zoom in to examine the important details. If you are right up against the details of the problem, drowning in its complexity, you need to pull back and look at the broader context. Once you know where you are, you can adjust your perspective to avoid it becoming too fixed.

You also need to know what you are looking for. When you walk into a restaurant or conference room, you don't usually spend a lot of time observing every aspect of every piece of furniture, painting, or lamp or the view from the window. Instead, you classify the environment as a restaurant or conference room and focus on the person you are about to meet. You may miss a lot of detail in this process, but you stay focused on the important detail. On the other hand, if you are an interior designer meeting with a client to discuss the redesign of the room, then you *should* attend to all these details of your environment. In this case, your classification of rooms and decorations will be much richer and you will need to be much more precise in identifying the decorating style, color schemes and other factors. Your perspective shapes the context, and that shapes the information that you pay attention to.

If you know where you are standing in relation to a particular issue—close to the details or at a detached distance—you can better decide what you need to do and begin the process of moving in closer or moving out. How do you engage in this process?

## Zooming In

The process of zooming in is to focus more intently on the details of the situation. It means leaving the comfort of the detached context and getting in up to your elbows in the swamp. Several approaches facilitate this process of focusing on detail without being completely overwhelmed by it, including rigorous analysis and categorizing. Note that these approaches will not help you *change* your mental model, since your focus is based on your current model. They will only help you cut through the clutter of a complex environment. When you step back and zoom out to a broader perspective, you can then better understand your current mental models and see the possibilities for new ones.

- **Engage in Rigorous Analysis.** Mark Twain tells the story of a cat who sits on a hot stove and wisely learns not to sit on a hot stove again. But the cat also avoids the cold stove as well.

  You need to be careful not to overreact to small pieces of information that might alarm you. A U.S. government recommendation in early 2003 to purchase duct tape and plastic sheeting in case of chemical or biological attacks led to a run on duct tape and rolls of plastic in hardware stores. A day later, commentators inside and outside government characterized the run on duct tape as an overreaction. In this case, there was no harm done, but other overreactions are not so benign. You need to be careful to engage in rigorous analysis to explore the risks and rewards of different approaches.

  Rigorous analysis helps to focus on understanding the details. For example, Citibank realized that the mountains of credit card data it gathered from users were meaningless unless the company could pose focused business questions. For example, when you have a customer on the line at a call center, what are the best cross-selling opportunities? This is a question that you can actually test against the data set. Without the right questions, analysis and perspective, no matter how large your collection of trees, you won't be able to see the forest. A rigorous process of formulating hypotheses and analysis helps guide the process of zooming in on specific information.

  Analytical tools such as "meta-analysis" can take this rigor to a higher and broader level. In meta-analysis, researchers look across a wide range of studies to extract insights. For example, instead of reviewing the one latest study on fatty foods and cancer, as is often done in the media, meta-analysis would consider all the similar studies, assess their results and rigor, and draw general conclusions from the entire sample.

  This rigorous analysis should pay particular attention to the outliers and inconsistencies. These can be the small splinters of truth that throw the old model into question or take you in a new direction. For a specific challenge, ask yourself how you can engage in more rigorous analysis. How can you test assumptions, develop hypotheses and pose clear questions? How can you focus in on the detail in a way that allows you to experiment and learn?

■ **Categorizing and Prioritizing.** Having a framework for new information makes it easier to focus on details without becoming overwhelmed. A scientist who discovers a new species of bird already knows the new bird fits among warm-blooded vertebrates and birds. The scientist can compare it with other existing species to make sure it has not already been discovered. If it is not distinct, the bird can then be placed into an existing classification. If it is distinct, a new place must be made for it within that context. You can use a similar approach for dealing with the information that wings its way into your life.

There are many ways to categorize. One common way is by proximity. For example, card players organize cards by suit and number in bridge and by scoring category in gin rummy. Or, to take a very simple example, a cook washing vegetables might make a dirty pile on one side of the sink and a clean pile on the other to better keep track of which ones have already been cleaned.[9] Here are some other bases for categorization:

– *Similarity:* How similar the items are.

– *Common fate:* Whether the items move together, like components of a car or students in a single grade in school.

– *Continuation:* Whether they fit into a smooth, continuous line. This is the type of categorization used in putting together a jigsaw puzzle to distinguish the pieces that fit into a specific part of the picture or in choosing parts for a product on an assembly line based on whether they fit the plans. Also, if we arrange our information chronologically or alphabetically, this mode of continuation offers a natural way to access it.

– *Surroundedness:* Whether they can be seen as a closed form, and whether they stand out together against a background.[10]

In addition to more intuitive categorizing, several statistical tools can be used to create and fill categories. Tools such as clustering and multidimensional scaling (MDS) can help to identify relationships and categorize large bodies of information from consumer marketing research or other sources. These tools can help to sift though large sets of data and extract new insights.

Prioritization is one important way to categorize and filter information. What is most important, and how does it relate to other points of information? This can be done informally by identifying a set of key metrics or decisions that need to be an object of focus. It can also be accomplished through a more formal approach such as the Analytical Hierarchy Process (AHP). An important caveat, however, is that this set of priorities is generally based upon a given view of the world, so it is still important to step back periodically and see whether the priorities still fit with the current realities.

How can you best categorize the information coming into your life? What frameworks and systems can help you organize and keep track of it so you are developing a complete body of knowledge rather than random bits of information? Be aware that in the process of using categorization to zoom in, you initially will apply categories that are based on your current mental model. You will see the detail better, but you will still be viewing it through your current lens. Look for different ways of categorizing based on other models.

■ **Avoid Being Paralyzed by Too Broad a Context.** You also have to watch out for too broad a focus that overwhelms you and leads to inaction. To see everything is to see nothing. Be aware when your context is too diffused to let you come up with specific solutions to the problem at hand. Up to a certain point, this is a positive process of looking for new information, particularly disconfirming information. But it can lead to procrastination that can be an excuse for not taking action. When you feel yourself being paralyzed by too much data, it is time to zoom in for more detail.

Paralysis can also come from fear of looking at new information. In a Charles Schwab television advertisement that aired during the 2003 Super Bowl, an investor was shown running away from the mailman who was delivering another set of poor financial statements. The company realized that the biggest hurdle was not just in getting investors to switch to Schwab but to get them to look at their investments at all. Schwab addressed this challenge by offering to switch all of an investor's accounts over to Schwab for a $95 fee to "start fresh" with Schwab. Schwab recognized the need to break the paralysis of inaction and fear before the investor could even begin to try to make sense of the current market conditions and develop a sound strategy.

While you need to be open to different models, and even to look at situations through the lenses of different models, you also need to avoid being paralyzed by this process. After considering different options, you need to choose a view and act upon it. You don't want to be in the middle of the track if a train is bearing down on you. One side or the other may be better, but standing in the middle is certain death. If you reach this point, choose a specific position or perspective, even if it turns out to be the "wrong" one. As discussed in Chapter 10, intuition can be a powerful way to break through "paralysis by analysis" to think and act quickly.

## Zooming Out

The process of zooming out lets you look at the bigger picture. This involves recognizing the limits of your field of vision, avoiding cognitive fixation, understanding your context, stepping out of the stream, using multiple approaches and collaborating with others.

- **Recognize the Limits of Your Field of Vision.** Makers of over-the-counter (OTC) analgesics were so focused on other OTC competitors that they were surprised by a decline in overall use across all competitors. What was causing it? The competition was coming not from typical rivals but from substitutes for headache relief such as prescription medicines (more attractive to individuals because they are covered under health plans), nutriceuticals, massage, homeopathic medicines or acupuncture. These companies needed to look more broadly to make sense of what was going on. To do this, however, they first had to recognize the limits of their field of vision.

Look for disconfirming evidence. Step back and consciously enlarge your field of vision. How can you define your competitive space differently? Where do you draw the lines in your personal thinking, and how can you step over these lines periodically? Are you too narrow either geographically or in focusing on a specific discipline? If you can define more clearly the inside of your field of vision, you can then begin to look outside more systematically.

■ **Avoid Cognitive Fixation.** Just as you need to pay attention to when you are paralyzed by too much information or too broad a view, you also need to be wary of the problem of cognitive fixation.

It can be dangerous to be too fixated. A pair of young lovers staring into one another's eyes across a romantic dinner, for example, will be in grave danger in their self-absorption if they fail to notice that the building is on fire. You need to be able to pull back and take the larger view, or something may suddenly enter your field of vision that you wish you had recognized earlier.

When you stare so intently at one point in space, or one particular problem, that your eyes glaze over, you have probably lost your sense of perspective. There may be no formal warning light for this problem, but if you pay attention, you can often sense when you have reached this glazed-over state. Sometimes, your first reaction might be to focus even harder on the problem at hand. The best response, however, might be to consider stepping back. This is the time to zoom out.

■ **Appreciate the Context.** A brilliant environmental scientist who was very concerned with energy conservation once was touring a nuclear aircraft carrier with a respected admiral. As they walked through the rows of churning motors and equipment, the scientist was looking at the entire picture through his conservationist view. Partway through the tour, he turned to the admiral and told him that the whole aircraft carrier could be organized much more efficiently, saving a lot of energy. The admiral turned a cold eye toward him and said: "I have two nuclear reactors in the basement. Conserving power is not a concern for me."

The scientist had analyzed all the information around him and reached a brilliant conclusion. But the conclusion was irrelevant, because he didn't understand the context, as the admiral did. The scientist was looking at the big picture, but he did not fully appreciate the context of energy conservation on a nuclear aircraft carrier.

The power of making a shift in context can be seen in Coca-Cola's colorful 1997 annual report that proclaimed "one billion down" and "47 billion to go." The report pointed out that even though the company sold 1 billion servings of its products in that year, there were still an estimated 47 billion servings of other beverages consumed around the world (including water, coffee and tea). Instead of defining its progress within the narrow confines of soft drinks, where it was engaged in a long-standing ground war with archrival PepsiCo, the report expanded the context to include all beverages. This view immediately suggests a new set of opportunities for growth in a mature market.

In business, you often see a manager who is wrestling with a complex problem suddenly light up and say, "Ah, I see, it is a marketing problem." Or maybe it is a "pricing problem" or an "operations problem." Depending on the specific manager's courage and predilection, it will very often be a problem that is directly within her realm of expertise (I can save the day) or completely outside it (it is not my problem). This recognition is the ability to match the problem to a specific context.

What is the context of the current decision you are making? What assumptions have you made about the context, and how do these need to be challenged?

■ **Step Out of the Stream.** It is impossible to swim forever without taking a rest. You need to step out of the information stream periodically and create space for reflection. You also need to be aware of times when you are drowning in information. At such times you may be tempted to swim faster, but you may be better off stepping out of the stream instead of stepping up your pace.

How can you set aside time during the day or the week for contemplating and thinking more broadly? How can you periodically step out of the stream of data and information to reflect upon it?

■ **Use Multiple Approaches.** You can ensure a broader context by using multiple approaches. You need to develop multiple sources of information and use different analytical methods to validate your information. This process allows you to see the same issue from multiple perspectives, giving you more context for making sense (as long as these multiple perspectives don't add too much to the confusion). You can cultivate multiple perspectives by bringing diverse groups of people to the table or by synthesizing diverse studies into clear and coherent empirical generalizations.

What are the current approaches you are using to understand the world? How can you add to them so that you can use multiple perspectives to broaden your thinking?

■ **Collaborate with Others.** It is difficult for individuals to hold all the relevant information or to create their own context. Traditionally, newspaper editors, TV news anchors and other "talking heads" or "wonks" have provided value by their efforts to sort through the plethora of information and provide structure and interpretation. This worked reasonably well in the past when life was "simpler." Today, it is well nigh impossible for even the most frenetic information junky to comprehend and interpret all there is to know in the world. Even within specific disciplines of science, it is proving difficult for specialists to talk to each other.

Through collaboration technology, individuals can now contemplate making sense of specific things and sharing this with others. This process is already well in hand on the Web, where vast numbers of people have formed innumerable interest groups and work together to interpret new developments or events. These groupings tend to share a common mental model set, so that cooperation is possible. They range from the conspiracy theorists all the way through to groups dedicated to helping each other handle difficult and esoteric diseases such as trigeminal neuralgia.

Within these communities there exist "thought leaders" who exhibit particular competence or wisdom and garner a following. The emergence of this global phenomenon is starting to help both communities and individuals make better sense of the world. Indeed it is not only "making sense" that occurs but also "taking action." Today we see action groups able to initiate global demonstrations on specific issues of concern. A set of bloggers (web log authors) drew attention to the racist comments of Trent Lott that led to his fall from power. Of course this same process permits the emergence of global fads, urban legends and damaging rumors.

Sometimes you can look to thought leaders to help make sense of the information. When you find reliable guides, editors, sages, or mentors, they can help you process these vast flows of data to fit into your mental models, so that you can act upon it. Given the incredible reach of modern technology, they can gain an enormous influence and increasingly shape perceptions. You, of course, need to be open to their ideas and new ways of looking at the world, but avoid becoming locked into their models.

Sometimes, instead of putting your trust in individuals, you can create platforms for sharing collective knowledge. A community of people with shared mental models can come together and work on making sense of things, as in the Wikipedia or Open Directory Project discussed earlier. There are also more structured communities such as the Wharton Fellows program, an ongoing decision support network of executives around the world that combines formal programs with access to a network of Fellows, faculty and other experts.

# EXTREME THINKING: SIMULTANEOUS ZOOMING IN AND OUT

While we have presented the process of zooming in and out as sequential, which is the way it usually must be done by an individual, zooming in and out could be more simultaneous, particularly when two or more people are working together. A powerful innovation in computer programming shows the possibilities.

One of the core practices of "Extreme Programming" (or XP)[11] is "pair programming," in which two programmers work together at the same computer to create software. The key is the definition of tasks for each programmer. One person, the "driver," is zoomed in on the details of the development of the code, while the other, the "navigator," is zoomed out, looking at the big picture as the programming is moving forward. This helps avoid the problems of well-written code that misses the bigger picture or becomes detached from user needs.

The entire XP approach is beyond the scope of this book, but it offers a powerful model for the process of zooming in and out. Suppose, for example, that an organization developed a paired approach to strategy development. Instead of periodic retreats to zoom out and look at the big picture, separated by stretches of operational zooming in, one person would keep an eye on the big picture while the other would drive the operational progress. We see this informally with the Office of the President or the separation between the CEO and COO, but roles are not always so clearly defined as "navigator" and "driver," and they often have clearly demarcated responsibilities. Extreme Programmers also have a way to build perspective and their working relationship: they exchange roles.

On the face of it, the "pair programming" approach appears to be highly inefficient, sending two people to do the job of one, but proponents say it produces significantly better software more quickly. It does this by avoiding the big-picture errors that so often slow down a software project. Among the well-known companies using XP methods are Ford Motor Company, Daimler Chrysler, UBS and First Union National Bank.

How can you create roles in your organization of "navigating" and "driving" through the complexities of your decisions? How can you think differently about your own approaches to these tasks?

## AN APPLICATION: DO YOU WANT FRIES WITH THAT?

Suppose you've read about that Swedish study mentioned at the opening of this chapter, which says French fries and other foods are carcinogenic. You now need to decide how to act upon this information. Should you change your view of these foods? Should you change your diet and behavior? Should you cut back? Eliminate them?

In this case, since you are presented with a specific piece of information that might challenge your current model, you might begin by zooming in:

■ *Engage in rigorous analysis.* Look a little deeper at the assumptions underlying the analysis and the disclaimers in the original research that may have been lost in the media. What is the strength of this study? How many subjects were involved over what periods? Should you believe it or wait for more information?

■ *Avoid paralysis.* When people see conflicting health studies, they sometimes throw up their hands and assume they can't trust anything. This mistake allows them to reject other studies that could save their lives. They throw out the baby with the bathwater. By examining the specific information at hand, you can avoid the paralysis of focusing too broadly.

■ *Classify.* You need to see how this piece of information relates to other information. What other research has been done in this area, and what does it show? If you classify this as a preliminary study, you will likely give it less weight than longer-term studies and insights based on multiple reference points. You might classify this as an interesting study to watch but decide it doesn't warrant a change in diet.

You then might want to zoom out to consider the broader context:

- **Collaborate or use guides.** You could consult your own doctor or a nutritionist to assess the research. You also could turn to respected online sources or news sources to evaluate the strengths of the claims, or to friends or colleagues. You could look at the actual studies in more detail to see what they represent and assess the quality of the news sources reporting them.

- **Understand your perspective.** You could consider your own point of view on the issue. Are you someone who typically suspects scientific studies reported in the press and so might tend to discount the results of such a study? Are you predisposed toward organic and whole foods, so that you might tend to give too much credibility to a study that is in sympathy with your view? What are your own biases that affect how you process this information?

- **Consider the context.** Next, you need to consider the broader context. What are the other risks you face from your food, and how does this risk stack up? Is it more dangerous to get behind the wheel of your car to drive to the fast-food restaurant than it is to consume the French fries? How much time do you have to devote to considering your diet, given all the other things you need to think about?

At the end of this process, you need to zoom back in and act (or decide on a course of inaction). You can decide to wait for more evidence before changing your diet, or you can change your diet immediately to be on the safe side, avoiding suspect foods. But if you stop eating altogether until you sort out the research, you could starve to death before getting a satisfying answer. You need to make a decision quickly.

# ZOOMING

The pace of information shows no signs of slowing down. It comes in an amazing variety of types from an amazing variety of global sources. Without a process for addressing it, you may become overwhelmed and then ignore most of it. Or you may focus on some familiar part of the landscape and ignore the rest. Both of these approaches have dangers.

By zooming in and out, you can gain a better understanding of the context and the specific information you need in order to act. You can see the piece of cheese and recognize that it is sitting in the middle of a trap. Both perspectives are needed to make effective decisions, particularly in a world of relentless information flows and great uncertainty and complexity.

Cultivate a process of zooming in and out as you look at any given challenge. Learn to recognize and be aware of when your vision is pulled back and focused so you can consciously change your focal point. Don't be afraid to jump out of the stream when necessary to take a needed step back, or to plunge into a particular detail to get the specific knowledge you need in order to act. Think about ways to establish a team for a "pair programming" approach, so you can engage in zooming in and zooming out simultaneously. By means of this process, you can see where you are going and the path to get there.

## IMPOSSIBLE THINKING

- In what areas of your life, personal or professional, are you overwhelmed with information? How can you zoom out to look at the broader context?

- In what areas of your life are you limited by too broad a perspective? How can you zoom in to examine the details more closely?

- How can you create routines and structures in your daily life and in your organization to encourage this process of zooming in and zooming out? Can you designate some parts of the organization to zoom in and others to take the big-picture role of navigation?

- Pay attention to your own feelings. When are you suffering indigestion from too much data? When are you feeling hungry because you don't have enough information? What do you need to do to respond to these feelings?

# ENDNOTES

1. Lyman, Peter, and Hal R. Varian. "How Much Information." *University of California, Berkeley, School of Information Management & Systems.* 18 October 2000. <http://www.sims.berkeley.edu/research/projects/how-much-info>.

2. Wurman, Richard Saul. *Information Anxiety.* New York: Doubleday, 1989.

3. Winchester, Simon. *The Professor and the Madman.* New York: HarperCollins, 1999.

4. *WordNet—A Lexical Database for the English Language.* Cognitive Science Laboratory, Princeton University. <http://www.cogsci.princeton.edu/~wn/>.

5. Lyman, Peter, and Hal R. Varian. "How Much Information." *University of California, Berkeley, School of Information Management & Systems.* 18 October 2000. <http://www.sims.berkeley.edu/research/projects/how-much-info>.

6. Murray, Bridget. "Data Smog: Newest Culprit in Brain Drain." *APA Monitor.* March 1998. <http://www.apa.org/monitor/mar98/smog.html>.

7. "High-Tech Cars Could Bring Cognitive Overload." *Access ITS Intelligent Transportation Systems.* 23 January 2001. <http://www.itsa.org/ITSNEWS.NSF/a619bd3fc912d6f38525658d00073cd1/4d4a2ccf01557420852569dd00517abe?OpenDocument>.

8. Black, Jane. "Snooping in All the Wrong Places." *Business Week.* 18 December 2002. <http://www.businessweek.com/technology/content/dec2002/tc20021218_8515.htm>.

9. Kirsh, David. "A Few Thoughts on Cognitive Overload." *Intellectica.* 2000. <http://icl-server.ucsd.edu/~kirsh/Articles/Overload/published.html>.

10. Kirsh, David. "The Intelligent Use of Space." *Artificial Intelligence.* 1995. < http://icl-server.ucsd.edu/~kirsh/Articles/Space/AIJ1.html>.

11. Extreme Programming was developed by Kent Beck. Its name perhaps draws inspiration from "extreme" sports. It has no relationship to Microsoft XP except for the shared consonants. For more information, see *Extreme Programming,* 26 January 2003 <www.extremeprogramming.org> or Brewer, John, and Jera Design. "Extreme Programming FAQ." *Jera Design.* 2001. <http://www.jera.com/techinfo/xpfaq.html>.

# 7

# ENGAGE IN R&D OF THE MIND

All life is an experiment. The more experiments you make, the better.

—**Ralph Waldo Emerson**

## Your brake pedal sinks to the floor.

You are in an old car at the top of a bridge across a large river. Ahead, at the end of a steep descent, is a line of cars at a tollbooth. You push the brake pedal, and nothing happens.

Up until this moment, when you pushed the pedal, your car slowed. Now the pedal is on the floor and your speed is unaffected. You have only seconds to figure out what is wrong and do something about it before you slam into the cars at the tollbooth.

What is going on here? Is your brake line broken? Are you out of brake fluid?

You make a quick experiment. You pump the pedal a few times—and the brakes come back. What a relief!

But will they work next time you need them?

You continue on, with one hand on the emergency brake, ready to use this crude alternative model if necessary to stop your car. You put a bit more room between you and the car ahead to give you more space to experiment. Each time you try to brake, your foot sinks to the floor without effect, but after a few pumps, the brakes come back. Slowly you make your way to a service station.

Their diagnosis is that the seals in your master cylinder have given out. No fluid has been lost, but the pressure is no longer transferred from the pedal to the brakes without pumping.

Even before your old models begin to show signs of failing, you need to experiment with new ones. You need to test and understand the new reality of your situation and come up with effective models to deal with it. Unlike most scientific experiments, this process doesn't occur in laboratory conditions. Your experiments are conducted in the messy, real-world situations where you must continue to take action even as you experiment.

How can you become more conscious of this process so you can conduct ongoing experiments without taking your hands off the wheel or your eyes off the road? How can you derive the most understanding from the experiments you do conduct? This chapter explores the process of "R&D of the mind" by which new models are discovered, tested and refined.

---

Adopting a new mental model is often envisioned as a leap to a new way of thinking, a sudden conversion or flashing breakthrough. But as master experimenter Thomas Edison has observed, genius is only 1 percent "inspiration." The other 99 percent is "perspiration." The perspiration is the hard work of experimentation, trying new things and seeing if they work. It is the relentless pursuit of knowledge by testing new ideas and approaches.

Experimentation is seen in the thousands of materials that Edison tested for filaments in developing the first practical incandescent light bulb. He tried metals and fibers from all over the world before settling on carbonized sewing thread to create a bulb that would burn for 40 hours and illuminate Menlo Park. He then developed the electrical infrastructure that was needed to generate and transmit electricity.

This was where his openness to new ideas broke down. He became a fierce proponent of direct current (DC), battling the competing model of alternating current (AC). The latter model ultimately proved to be the more effective, but it needed to overcome Edison's opposition. Through the experiments of others, the AC model was proven to be superior and became dominant.

Experimentation is not just a plodding process of testing and discovery. It is also the creative identification of new questions and hypotheses, the establishment of new spaces or the recognition of the value of serendipitous observations that take us in new directions. It is also the creative leap of establishing something new, like Edison's development of the phonograph.

Adjusting and adopting new mental models is like sailing a boat. As conditions change, we need to raise and lower our sails and change direction to make the best use of the shifting wind and currents. It is a dynamic and ongoing process, not a one-shot shift. There are broader changes we can make, such as changing the design of the ship—or our models—but once we are on the open seas, the process is a set of tactics for testing and adjusting to the current situation in which we find ourselves.

## THE NEED FOR EXPERIMENTS

In the course of our childhood, our parents and teachers give us mental models to view the world by. We are constantly experimenting with these models. We are told not to lie, but what happens if we do lie? We are told to stay on the sidewalk and pay attention to our teachers, but we might test these instructions before accepting them. Children very often share their parents' views of politics and religion until they reach adolescence or adulthood, when they begin to question these models. As we grow up, we absorb additional models from our schools, work and culture. We are given social norms and expectations for work, family and conduct. We also learn formal approaches such as scientific method and then test their effectiveness.

Some people continue to test these models on an ongoing basis. This is particularly important when we are engaged in creating revolutionary product breakthroughs, such as Edison's inventions, or we are adapting to a changing environment. We also need to engage in more experimentation if others are experimenting and are developing a better set of models. A candle-maker in Edison's time would have done well to pay close attention to his experiments. In this process of experimenting, we create the opportunity to recognize new models that might work better for a particular situation.

There is a Darwinian evolution to mental models. We try new approaches, and the successful models emerge. Once their success is evident, they become widely adopted. Early pioneers of the total-quality movement succeeded in improving processes and products, leading to the wide adoption of their approaches. Early users of computers showed the power of these machines in business, and then they were widely adopted. Over the past few decades, we have experimented with a wide range of models for structuring relationships and families—creating diverse alternatives to the traditional model of marriage and children.

Individuals experiment with various diets and note the empirical results before sticking with them or moving on to others. These experiences are usually set up as experiments. First we are drawn to the diet by empirical studies (such as those produced by Dr. Atkins), anecdotal evidence ("Sally lost 20 pounds in three weeks on this new diet"), or recommendations by friends or physicians. Then we conduct our own experiments with the diet to see whether this model works for us. We measure our weight at the beginning and we step on the scale through the course of the diet, noting improvement. We accept or reject the diet based on this personal experimentation.

An inherent problem with these individual experiments is that they lack a control. We don't know what our experience would have been if we had *not* gone on the diet or we had tried another diet. Thus, how can we know whether diet X is actually best for us?

If we fail to engage in these continuous experiments, we may find ourselves in a painful situation or suffer the traumatic failure of our current model. If we do not periodically test the strength of our relationships, we might be surprised by the sudden failure of a marriage. If we don't experiment with new ideas and pay attention to the feedback from peers and supervisors at work, we may find ourselves out of a job. We need to test the relevance of our current models and assess the efficacy of potential new ones.

This is done through a process of R&D (research and development) of the mind.

## CONDUCTING COGNITIVE R&D

We all are familiar with the process of experimentation in the laboratory. What is the process at the personal level? Is it one big experiment or a series of little experiments?

This R&D approach is to regard the external world as not totally understood and constantly changing. Our mental models are treated as hypotheses. We need to either confirm the value of our existing mental models or to postulate new ones and carry out experiments to validate them. Either way, the external world is always regarded as an experiment. When things are not quite right, experiments or "probes" are sent out to investigate. This approach should not create an excuse for constant uncertainty or doubt or paralyze our ability to make decisions. It is the basis for remaining aligned to the reality of our world in order to maintain our competitive position. And experiments are a way to establish causality.

We can take three approaches to experimentation:

- **Planned Experiments.** From our scientific training, this is what we usually think of when we discuss experimentation—a controlled and sharply defined study. We develop a hypothesis, design an experiment to test that hypothesis and then analyze the results to see whether they confirm or disconfirm the hypothesis. We begin to develop new understanding that might suggest a new hypothesis or further testing of the existing one. This method turns random experiences into systematic learning, but the experiments are often quite difficult and expensive to conduct effectively unless we have an environment in which we can control many of the variables.

- **Natural Experiments.** We can learn from natural experiments through the same discipline, but even more care is needed. Everyday life generates vast amounts of data, but we ignore or dispose of most of what we see or experience (except, of course, for Funes the Memorious, discussed in the preceding chapter, who remembered everything). Natural experiments go on around us continuously, although we seldom view them as such. If we adjust our viewpoint and regard them as natural experiments, we can exploit them by developing theories to explain events going on around us and then examine how things work out. The surrounding world may not have the controlled structure of a formal scientific experiment, but it can serve as an effective learning laboratory.

■ *Adaptive Experimentation.* The third approach, which can be used in conjunction with the other two, is to ensure that the process of experimentation is ongoing. As each experiment is completed and assessed, the hypothesis is adjusted as needed, and then the next experiment begins. Experimentation is not a one-time activity but rather a continuous process of trial and adjustment and a commitment to continue with the results.

We are beginning to see a major natural, ongoing experiment all around the world concerning the much-forecasted convergence of the personal computer industry and entertainment. An early example is the introduction of PCs that, by addition of a remote control to the traditional keyboard and mouse, operate like televisions. The hypothesis may be that the PC has run out of gas in its current form and that the market is finally ripe for convergence between the computer and television. The exact evolution and convergence of the two machines, and others, depends upon both technological changes and consumer behavior. Since no one knows the exact direction or timing of the technology, companies experiment with different combinations. Microsoft became involved in cable networks such as CNBC to experiment with content. Sony moved into computing and entertainment content. Companies such as Hewlett-Packard continue to develop new equipment to test whether the long-awaited convergence has arrived. The hypothesis might still be proven false, as it has been in years past, but experimentation continues with this new mental model for computing and entertainment.

Not every technological breakthrough represents a new mental model, but these technological changes offer opportunities to experiment with new models for thinking about our personal lives and business opportunities.

## Making a Leap

Sometimes we need to make a dramatic transformation, but it helps if we can do it as a result of careful experimentation with new models. IBM switched its focus from equipment to services, but the shift was undertaken via cautious experimentation.

In contrast, Monsanto's self-transformation from a chemical company to a "life sciences" company was based on extensive experimentation with the science involved but perhaps not enough experimentation with society's acceptance of the model itself. As it staked its future on genetically modified foods, it encountered more intense opposition than expected in Europe and other parts of the world. Opponents rejected this new mental model of agriculture. In their view, the techniques of manufacturing according to a genetic blueprint and using seeds as intellectual property were dangerous manipulations of the natural environment with totally unknown consequences.

Because what was involved was more a bet-the-company proposition than a small experiment, essentially staking the company's fortunes on the hypothesis that genetically modified foods would be well received, failure of the hypothesis was expensive. Opposition was so strong, in fact, that leaders in Zambia refused to accept the genetically modified foods for their starving populations, even though Americans had those same foods for breakfast every morning. Monsanto learned a lesson about public reaction at a high cost, because it had made such a strong commitment. There was a disconnect between the scientific community's view of the new technology (a major breakthrough with great benefits in reducing pesticide use and improving harvests) and the broader public's view (a dangerous experiment that could lead to unforeseen negative consequences).

## Challenges of Experimentation

A challenge in all experimentation, but particularly in more personal experiments, is to avoid the many biases that creep into our judgment about what happened. Our experiments with mental models usually do not occur in the context of pristine laboratory conditions. There are rarely opportunities to create double-blind studies with statistically significant populations. Accordingly, a variety of biases may develop, which we need to guard against as best we can:

- **A short-term bias.** Diets exemplify a weakness of all experiments. A difficulty in assessing the results of our experiments with diets—in personal or even in scientific medical studies—is assessing the long-term impact. Many diets produce a short-term improvement, which can be quickly lost as the individual loses interest. We need to take action in the short term, so it is not always possible to make a thorough assessment before moving ahead. But if there is background material from others on long-term implications of different models, we should try to find it. We should also do "thought experiments" to think through possible long-term implications of a particular model or approach. We might not have empirical evidence that a particular diet might result in recidivism in the long term, but we may be able to see that diets in general have this outcome. Then we can be much more critical in assessing the impact of the particular diet and the likelihood that it might suffer from a similar weakness. In general, a short-term view of experiments leads to an attempt at optimizing things for immediate rewards. This works well when things do not change, but when we increasingly optimize, we tend to reduce our flexibility for handling future change.

- **Lack of appropriate controls on variables.** Without appropriate controls on the variables of the experiment, other factors can affect outcomes and undermine the results. For example, there is the famous "Hawthorne effect" that experimenters found when testing the impact of lighting and other environmental conditions on factory workers. While improved employee productivity appeared to result from these changes in the environment, researchers concluded that it could be attributed to the extra attention the workers received during the study. With this in mind, researchers performing medical studies use a control group who are given placebos (or subjected to some other control), in order to take account of the effect that merely receiving a pill, with its implicit suggestions of benefit, can have upon the condition being studied, regardless of whether the pill contains medication or only sugar. Similar biases may creep into customer-satisfaction surveys of purchasers of new cars, where the experience of being asked about their purchase satisfaction actually improves the customers' satisfaction.

■ *Losing detachment from results.* It is very difficult to maintain an unbiased perspective. We often carry out experiments to prove a point, and we may shape things to make that point. For our R&D to be valuable, we need to be willing to detach ourselves from the results and take a cold look at the data, even when it makes us uncomfortable. If we can't do this publicly, because we have a particular position we want to advance in the world, we should at least cultivate the ability to do it privately. Only in this way will we be able to see the true implications of the experiments we conduct.

## When to Experiment: Weighing the Costs and Returns of Cognitive R&D

Adaptive experimentation requires time and energy. We cannot always be experimenting. If experimentation occurs aside from the action, it takes time and attention away from it. A passenger jet pilot who spends all his time in a simulator may be ready for anything but will make little productive contribution to his company. On the other hand, there are limits to how much we can experiment while engaged in life. A passenger jet pilot who is constantly experimenting in the cockpit with new ways of flying the plane will end up with angry passengers or even a crashed plane.

An executive who dabbles in many small business ventures or continual reinvention might lose focus on her existing business. A person who is constantly trying out new relationships won't be able to settle down into one stable relationship and develop it. A dieter who is always trying out the latest fad will expend dollars and time reading books and implementing new plans that might be better invested in exercise.

Experiments exact a cost in time, attention and physical resources. For cognitive or thought experiments, the primary cost is reckoned in time and attention. Experiments of other kinds require some commitment of staffing, funds and other resources to test a particular hypothesis. The point of doing an experiment is to keep these commitments small; but they can still be significant, especially when several experiments are undertaken. And no matter how small the commitment to the experiment, such investments in learning still detract from investments in operating under the current model.

How much time and energy should we devote to experimentation? Experimenting is not our only task. We have a life to live or a business to run. If we don't experiment at all, we may end up doing the wrong job very efficiently. If we experiment too much, we may not have time to do the job at all. We need to find the balance between performance and learning, between operations and R&D.

A conscious effort to devote a certain portion of resources to "cognitive R&D" can help ensure that we are at least thinking about our models and how they might be changed. Our choices about investing in monitoring, experimenting and developing new models will depend in large part on the importance of the decisions that face us or our organization and the risks of ending up with the wrong model. It is a complex calculus depending on a number of factors:

- *The importance of the decision.* Some decisions, like high-involvement consumer purchases, require a lot of research and attention. When consumers buy a car, they spend hours, days and weeks looking at models, conducting experimental test drives, and reading reports on various models and manufacturers. They are willing to invest this time because it is a high-involvement decision. In contrast, most supermarket customers don't spend more than a few seconds thinking about low-involvement purchases such as the choice of a roll of paper towels. Often they won't think about it at all, merely repeating the same decision they made the last time. But if they pay a little more attention to the environment, they may notice that another brand is on sale and experiment with that brand.

■ *The situation.* The situation we are in also affects the significance of a particular mental model. While we may spend less than a second selecting a soup for dinner at the grocery store, we might spend much more time if we were packing it for a trek up Everest. Similarly, if the situation makes the mindset important, we need to spend more time getting it right and more time exploring different models. We need to be aware when our external situation changes in ways that increase the risks of our mindsets. This is a signal that we may need to pay more attention to models we have accepted automatically.

■ *The utility of simpler approaches.* When is a merely adequate mental model enough? Newtonian physics, despite its limitation at the extremes, works reasonably well in explaining simple mechanics, without introducing the complexity of quantum physics. To find out quickly what will result when a car slams into a wall at high speed or a bowling ball is dropped from a roof, Newton's theories will serve pretty well and often will be more efficient.

At times we will naturally put additional energy into challenging our old mindsets or developing new ones—especially in fast-changing environments. Similarly, in our personal life, when we reach turning points such as the loss of a job or marriage, we will spend more time thinking about models and experimenting with alternatives.

Of course, this argument is based on the assumption that investing in cognitive R&D is a zero-sum game. In fact, not all experiments detract from our ability to focus on current actions. We might be able to live our lives as one big experiment, observing and learning while we continue to act. We can take the same route to work but pay more attention to the signs along the way. We can listen to a book on tape and learn about some new discipline while still making the same trip into the office. We can use a computerized trip planner to explore alternate routes in a much more focused way, so that a small investment in new thinking might lead to a much better route. In this way, we minimize the cost of experimentation and increase our ability to experiment.

## INTO THE LABORATORY

How can you apply this process of adaptive experimentation to the personal and professional challenges facing you? Here are some approaches that can promote ongoing experimentation and learning:

- **Conduct post mortems.** A common practice among surgeons is to assemble as a team once a week to discuss any complications or negative outcomes from their surgeries during the week. The chief surgeon and senior faculty are present and can offer insights on what went wrong and what lessons can be learned. Similarly, military leaders conduct "after-action reviews" to improve strategies and tactics. Professional football players watch videos of their past games to improve their play and understand why the crucial ball got away. By creating a regular time for studying these challenges and mistakes, these teams increase their learning from the natural experiments that occur in the course of their work. How often do you spend time understanding a lost contract or failed initiative? There are many opportunities to look at the charts or watch the video to create "backward looking" experiments. If you pretend that the initiative you just implemented was an experiment, what can you learn from it about the design of the experiment or your hypotheses?

- **Use simulations.** One way to gain experience without the cost in time and money that usually accompanies the process of making mistakes is through well-designed simulations. Simulations allow the participants to live through a certain experience and learn from it. The simulation—whether it is a simulated trading floor, a flight simulator or a war game—can help you develop a better understanding of the actual challenges you might face. While formal computer-based simulations or war games can be quite complex and expensive, simulations can also be done much more informally through "thought experiments" or role playing. Role playing, which can be used to test approaches and work out difficult interpersonal interactions, requires only one or two additional willing players (or even several chairs with a single player taking on all the parts). Thought experiments are even less complex to orchestrate, since they occur entirely in the head, as you envision taking a given action and then think through the consequences and outcomes. These simulations can push to the extremes of experience, packing a lot of challenges together and exploring possibilities that it might take many years to encounter in real life. In addition, by removing the severe consequences while still providing feedback on your actions, they can offer a chance to step back and look at the process as it unfolds, leading to a more scientific approach and analysis of your own mental models and actions. You can test them without the risks that are often involved in such experiments in the real world.

■ *Study natural experiments.* The U.S. Army gained powerful insights on tactical strategy from a free online computer game that was initially designed as a recruiting tool. It turned out to be a fascinating platform for a set of natural experiments on military strategy. Young players would go through a virtual boot camp and then be sent out on a variety of missions. The game's usefulness went beyond gauging the reflexes, resourcefulness and strategic thinking of potential recruits. Army strategists realized that when the pool of players had completed 100 million sorties, this archive of virtual experience offered a tremendous laboratory for studying new tactics and approaches. Looking at the unconventional strategies of successful players offered a window into unexpected maneuvers and approaches that might be applied in the field. What began with a game imitating life ended up with life imitating the game. To take advantage of such experiments, pay attention to those that may be going on around you and study them from new angles.[1]

- **Treat the current model as a hypothesis.** See your current model for what it is, a model, rather than treating it as reality. View the decision you are about to make as an experiment and ask yourself: What are you hoping to learn from it? What hypothesis are you testing? Can you put mechanisms or review processes in place to monitor results and learn? The more you can think of your personal understanding as a hypothesis about reality rather than reality itself, the more you can free your thinking to engage in experimentation. If you look at your models as hypotheses, you will be better able to test them and to modify them. You need to be aware of your own biases in this process and try to adjust and compensate for them. Ian MacMillan and Rita Gunther McGrath present a systematic process of planning for new ventures in which companies actively identify their assumptions and test them along the way. This process of "Discovery-Driven Planning," using tools such as a "reverse income statement," make more explicit the vague hypotheses that are often embedded in business plans and allow business leaders to test them along the way to recognize when the results of the experiment no longer fit the initial hypothesis.[2]

- **Make a time and space for experimentation.** Often the process of experimentation is lost in the rush of business. On a personal level, set aside a part of your time to try new things and explore new ideas. On a professional level, find time for thinking creatively about how you see the world and exploring the meaning of your experiences. This could be a morning walk or even a car ride home from the office. You might even consider creating a space for this kind of thinking. For some, it might be a home office where you have the "equipment" you need to engage in experimentation (uninterrupted space, diverse resources for inspiration, etc.), a library or a local coffee shop where the stimulation of new ideas and activity can lead to original thinking. If you don't consciously create this time and space, the demands of day-to-day activity will tend to work against the process of experimentation.

■ *Make a conscious commitment.* In addition to setting aside a general time and place for experiments, it also can be helpful to make a specific commitment to experimenting, in the same way that companies allocate a certain percentage of their budgets to R&D. In coming up with a specific percentage of your time that should be ideally devoted to experiments, you need to consider the nature of your work and environment, as discussed above. Companies such as 3M allow employees to devote a percentage of their time to exploring their own original ideas. There may be times in your life or in the development of your organization when you will invest more or less in this R&D. Young children are engaged in constant experiments. As you finish school and reach maturity, an increasingly smaller portion of your time is generally devoted to cognitive R&D. At this point, you might consider making a conscious effort to increase your experimentation. If you think carefully about how much time and energy you should ideally allocate, it is more likely that you will actually take the time to engage in experimentation.

Whatever the percentage, you need to invest some portion of your time and resources in this cognitive R&D, or you will fail to see when your old models are not working or when new ones might be needed. When you don't do this ongoing work, you are much more likely to face catastrophic failures of your old models or leap into catastrophic failures by embracing new models that don't live up to their promise.

■ *Collaborate with others.* Experimentation doesn't occur in a vacuum. You can learn by studying the experiments of others and by sharing your challenges and results with others. Are others experiencing the same results with their experiments, or have they had a very different experience? The post-mortem, discussed above, is one process for this collaboration in focusing on specific mistakes or concerns. A broader approach is to develop communities of practice with others who are engaged in addressing similar concerns or areas of interest.

Ideally, these communities should represent diverse view-points, so you can constantly test your assumptions and results against very different perspectives. The communities should also have a mindset of experimentation rather than a rigid and static view of the world.

## LIFE AS A LABORATORY: CONTINUOUS ADAPTIVE EXPERIMENTATION

Cultivate the practice of experimentation in your life. When you read about companies in the media, ask yourself about the mental models that drove their decisions. What can you learn from these experiments? What mental models do commentators use to understand what happened? What would you do in their situation? Then watch the same companies over time and consider the outcomes. Were you able to make sense of things? If so, why? If not, why not?

This can be an important way to hone your mental-model skills and develop an attitude of experimentation. You might even keep a lab book or journal of insights from these experiments. Then do the same thing with a troublesome issue in your personal or business life. Systematically hypothesize new mental models or solicit them from others. What happens when you apply these models to the challenge? We'll explore the possibilities for this kind of work in more detail in Chapter 12.

With practice, the process of experimenting with new mental models and approaches will become second nature. It will become part of the way you address every new problem or situation you encounter. It will be the way you analyze the information that comes through. It will become a part of your intuition about addressing problems and making sense of the world.

At the same time, be careful not to become a prisoner of your approach to experimentation—like the scientist who tries to apply scientific method to the choice of a romantic partner. This is an experiment that probably has a high likelihood of failure, but a person who is dogmatically committed to applying the scientific process may not even be able to see the failure. Be aware of the process of experimentation, and experiment with your approaches. As part of your *adaptive experimentation,* experiment with experimentation itself. Be careful not to become too set in your ways of experimenting. Continue to challenge both your understanding and the approaches you use to gain it.

## IMPOSSIBLE THINKING

- What natural "experiments" are going on around you, and how can you create hypotheses that will allow you to learn from them?

- Think of a recent failure. How can you conduct a post-mortem to learn from this experience?

- How can you design new experiments to test the limits of your model or gain new insights that might suggest a new mental model?

- How do you capture the learning from these experiments and share it with others?

- When your hypotheses are confirmed or disproved by your experiments, how do you build on this knowledge to generate the next set of hypotheses and experiments?

# ENDNOTES

1. Brown, John Seely. "Peripheral Vision" Conference. The Wharton School, Philadelphia. 1–2 May 2003.
2. McGrath, Rita Gunther, and Ian C. MacMillan, "Discovery-Driven Planning." *Harvard Business Review.*73:4 (1995). pp. 44-52.

# TRANSFORM YOUR WORLD

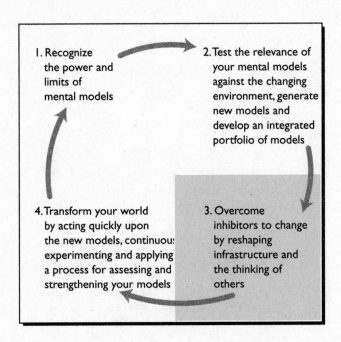

1. Recognize the power and limits of mental models

2. Test the relevance of your mental models against the changing environment, generate new models and develop an integrated portfolio of models

3. Overcome inhibitors to change by reshaping infrastructure and the thinking of others

4. Transform your world by acting quickly upon the new models, continuous experimenting and applying a process for assessing and strengthening your models

# 8

# DISMANTLE THE OLD ORDER

> If you have built castles in the air, your work need not be lost;
> that is where they should be. Now put the foundations under them.
>
> —Henry David Thoreau

## You want to give up smoking.

The only problem is that your whole life is built around it. You can get a patch to take care of the nicotine cravings, but what about your usual 10 a.m. cigarette break, talking with fellows smokers outside the building? You also have the cigarette in the car on the way to the office and one on the way home—the perfect end to your day. You walk into the store where you buy your cigarettes and always receive a warm greeting from the cashier. You have built an entire routine around cigarettes, and giving them up really means giving up a big part of your life.

Like the military systems and nuclear weapons built up during the Cold War, we build an infrastructure of processes and investments to support a given mental model, and these become very hard to dismantle. These skeletons of the old order tend to make it hard for us to change—even when we have a desire and capacity to change our mental models. We know we'd like to quit, but we still reach for another cigarette. How can we recognize and overcome these commitments to the past? Can we beat swords into plowshares? This chapter examines the challenges of dismantling the old order and strategies for addressing them.

Ozzie and Harriet may be fiction, but they represented a mental model about work and family life in the 1950s that was widely held, if less widely practiced. The father went to work, the mother took care of the home and child rearing. Supper was on the table in the evening when Ozzie walked in the door. This model saw the father committing to a career with a particular company, working to pay for a home and support a family, and saving for retirement. Even as this picture began to unravel, the model endured.

Women were stifled by this narrow definition of roles, and men began to find it unfulfilling, particularly as the idea of a job for life at a large corporation began to erode. As they began to change their models of the family, people found that it was not as simple as waking up in the morning with a new mental model. Everything about their marriages and work was built around this model. Relationships, routines, processes, investments and the legal system had all been shaped by it. A bridal and wedding industry was built around it. Company benefits were designed for it. The model for relationships could not be changed without altering the infrastructure and processes that supported them.

In some cases, couples were able to change their models of work and family without completely abandoning their past relationships. At other times, changing the model required going through the painful process of breaking up the old and trying to reestablish a new life based on a new model. Some people began to change the model of their work and family life without recognizing the shock waves that would result, and they were surprised when their lives unraveled as a result.

When we change our models, we need to pay attention to the world that we have already built around them. That world will hold us back from changing our models, making it more difficult, and the investments we made in that world need to be addressed explicitly in changing models. We cannot ignore the infrastructures of the old order, so we need a well-thought-out process for dismantling or repurposing them as we make our way from one world view to another. If we are aware of this process, we have a better opportunity to make the implementation of a new model much smoother—transforming our families or work life, for example, rather than watching them self-destruct.

This chapter is about how to change fundamental and tightly held mental models that have served us well in the past. We've looked at how we develop new ways of seeing things, but how do we actually begin to bring them into our lives? What changes do we need to make? What price will we need to pay? Are we willing? Do we abandon everything, or can we salvage something?

## PERSISTENCE OF MODELS

We are defined by our mental models, and giving them up means giving up part of ourselves. We don't like to give things up. Behavioral psychologists have long recognized that people have an aversion to loss that is not coldly rational. In simple experiments where subjects are given the choice of buying or selling mugs, the participants with the mugs (who are asked to give them up) typically demand a price that is two or three times higher than the price that those without the mugs are willing to pay to purchase them.[1] It is the same mug. These are not family heirlooms. Yet the desire to hold onto this "bird in the hand" makes them more valuable if we lose them than if they are ours to gain. We are predisposed to want to hold onto things, and this goes for our mental models.

Added to this internal problem of loss aversion is a network of external investments and relationships built around a given model. A person contemplating a change is very likely surrounded by a network of friends with perspectives and values that are similar to, or at least compatible with, his own. He is perhaps married to a spouse with similar views of the world and has supervisors, employees, coworkers, friends and family who come from similar backgrounds and reinforce the current model.

Our mental models are gated communities from which other models are locked out. If we try to change our models, we realize that these gates we have constructed not only protect us from the attack of foreign ideas, but also act as a cage that limits our ability to change. Our mental models represent considerable value. Letting go of these models will, in all likelihood, be traumatic. For organizations or businesses, considerable infrastructure or investment in such things as brands may be involved.

The pace of this change, and the infrastructure that supports the current model, varies by individuals or organizations. For institutions such as the Roman Catholic Church, the mental models change every 1,000 years, so to speak, and consequently immutable structures have emerged—massive and permanent physical structures such as cathedrals. It did not matter that it took hundreds of years for great cathedrals to be built (and rebuilt, as was Chartres). The Church had plenty of time. Similarly, its attitude toward many social issues remains constant, despite massive changes in society. The stability of the Church's mental models—its view of life and reality on Earth—has permitted long-term investments in plant and organization. If the Church changed basic theology every decade, this would be impossible. Its entire infrastructure—including organization, people, processes, and buildings—also makes it harder for the models to change.

While nations erect structures such as palaces that manifest a permanent view of things, in many instances these structures have been transformed for new purposes. The monarchy may persist in many European nations, but is much more related to decoration than to rule. The palaces of the kings are transformed into museums that support culture without supporting the old model of monarchy. Structures of the old order can be retained but converted to use in support of a different mental model. Similarly, in business, the power grid is being used to facilitate many producers of electricity, former retail outlets are being converted to new uses such as Starbucks' cafes, and the Williams Company converted miles of idle gas lines into conduits for fiber optics for broadband communication (an idea that was initially successful in the 1980s but ultimately fell victim to the problems of the Internet and telecommunications industry).

## CHANGING MODELS: REVOLUTION OR EVOLUTION

Sometimes these changes can be sudden and dramatic, such as Saul's conversion on the road to Damascus (or Bill Gates' about-face on the Internet). Saul changed his mental model and completely transformed his life, overnight. While this is dramatic, we hear little about how Saul's family and work associates took the news, but one might imagine that he shocked and alienated quite a few people in the process of changing his life. In this case, the acceptance of the new mental model is so dramatic, like a lightning strike, that the person's old life crumbles and disappears. This is a break with the old that obviously has a very high cost, and if a modern-day Saul made such a shift without addressing his existing relationships, he might find himself in divorce court, financial ruin and out of work because of unfulfilled obligations of his old life.

Other times, the shift in thinking is fundamental, but does not require quite as dramatic a break with the past. Albert Einstein was walking in Bern, Switzerland, when he suddenly had a shift in his thinking that led to the Special Theory of Relativity. He suddenly understood the problem and its solution. He was so excited that when he met his colleague Besso the next day, Einstein skipped his greetings and immediately announced to his astonished friend that the solution had come to him: time was not absolute, but was instead related to signal velocity.[2] This was a truly revolutionary development and caused massive problems for all the old mental models.

People may adopt new models by coming under the influence of a charismatic leader or organization, which supplies a new mental model as well as an infrastructure to support it. Cults often take followers completely out of their old world and into the jungle, where it is possible to create a whole world based upon the leader's particular view. There usually is a new infrastructure or way of life to support the new belief system, whether it is joining a cult or abandoning the world for a monastic life. Even the CEO of a corporation has a set of perks such as private jets and assistants, creating an infrastructure that may be hard to live without after retirement.

To accomplish conversions effectively, leaders recognize that they need not only to change thinking but also to put the structure in place to change actions as well. Even positive changes such as diet programs or an approach to life planning such as Stephen Covey's "7 Habits" program are reinforced by group meetings, software and day planners that allow people to reorganize their lives around this new way of thinking.

While we tend to think about conversion in a religious context, there are many similar examples. Enrolling in business school or going through a corporate training program are efforts to impart a new mindset to new converts and give them a different way of looking at the world. Weight-loss programs and 12-step programs such as Alcoholics Anonymous create structures of meetings, mentors and other support systems to change behavior. Since drinking is often a social behavior, such programs create new social settings and relationships to reinforce the changed behavior.

Sometimes the only way to make way for the new model is to clear away the infrastructure of the old, like a dilapidated building that needs to be leveled before new construction can begin. (This doesn't mean you never ever use the model again, but that it recedes into the background or is used in a different way, based on a different infrastructure.) The breakdown of the old order can be slow and gradual or it can be short and catastrophic, such as the fall of the Berlin Wall and the demise of the Soviet Union. With this collapse, the Cold War ended, and national leaders began shaping new sets of relationships and models to take its place. Part of this change was to shift the U.S. military focus from superpower conflicts to efforts such as humanitarian policing and fighting regional wars. With a network of military officers, all trained in the old style of war, not to mention nuclear subs and ACBMs, changing mental models is a very slow and painful process.

Whatever path we take to implement and embrace a new model in our lives, we almost always have to give something up, and this "something" is usually much more than a way of thinking.

## SMOOTHING THE WAY TO A NEW ORDER

This conversion can be less traumatic if we take a systems approach to carrying out change. The systems approach should address complex factors that support the old order, such as the individual needs of players and stakeholders, processes, structure and infrastructure, resources and information, technology, incentives and rewards, and culture. The process of dismantling must also draw a clear line from the old order to the new.

How can you dismantle the old order and build the infrastructure to support a new model? Among the approaches are:

- *Recognize how expectations of others tie you to a given model.* Starbucks set a very aggressive growth trajectory of expanding its stores from 6,000 to 10,000 worldwide in three years. Because growth was such a strong part of its appeal to investors, the company was locked into a pattern of growth by the stock market. Given this focus, it had to create the infrastructure to allow it to grow rapidly and move more aggressively into international markets. The company could not achieve this level of growth and penetration with its original model of wholly owned stores, but needed to move to a joint-venture model overseas. To fuel growth, it added more non-beverage revenue streams such as wireless Internet access and experiments with serving breakfast. It also allowed the use of its brand in supermarkets and service stations where it had much less control over quality, potentially eroding the brand as it expanded its market. Starbucks had little choice but to pursue such strategies to meet investor expectations, but is it a good strategy to change its organization to allow more partnerships? Will Starbucks be able to maintain the quality and integrity of this broader network? Could demographic shifts in Generation X already be undermining the Starbucks' model? If so, will the company be able to change quickly enough?

Companies and individuals both have aspirations. When they cannot meet their aspirations, they sometimes revise them downward. On the other hand, sometimes the existing infrastructure and commitments don't allow companies or individuals to adjust downward, as was the case of Starbucks. This is also the case with children held to the expectations of their parents, or managers held to expectations in a company or citizens held to the expectations of society. Companies and individuals can then become prisoners both to their models and to these commitments and expectations. This sometimes leads people to extreme measures to make the world fit the model instead of changing the model to fit the world.

You need to be aware of these constraints. It isn't always possible to change them—Starbucks can't step out of the stock market very easily—but by being aware of how commitments hold people into a certain model, you can better guard against situations where your investment in the model becomes dysfunctional and destructive. The investment of Sears in its department store model in the 1990s or of IBM in its commitment to mainframes in the 1980s are examples of what were ultimately dysfunctional commitments to old models, which were recognized only after substantial organizational and financial pain.

How do the expectations of others around you tie you into the current mental model? What can you do to change these expectations about your performance or actions to fit your new model?

■ *Understand how the infrastructure ties you to a given model.* Your "installed base" locks you into a certain model of the world. This is obvious with technology and plant investments. Enterprise software systems shape the way the organization approaches challenges, and the hiring and training of staff also limit your ability to change your mental model. When Xerox became the "document company," its sales force that was selling products on short cycles wasn't designed to sell high-concept network solutions to CIOs over very long purchasing cycles. All the elements of your personal life—your family and friends, the neighborhood you live in, the work you do and so on—affect your mental models. In what ways does the infrastructure around you tie you into the old model? How can this infrastructure be changed to support the new model?

■ **Be careful in making irreversible investments in a model.** When AOL merged with Time Warner, the belief was that the combined company represented a new model for joining premier content and diverse online and offline channels. This mental model was not successful in the wake of the dot-com collapse and the erosion of the advertising market after the 9/11 terrorist attacks. Much of the synergy was expected to result from a new media package for advertisers and the continued growth of online business. The company had invested a great deal in the infrastructure to create and support this new model. The result of the failure of the model was the largest operating loss in history and one of the largest balance-sheet write downs. The market was willing to write off huge losses when investors recognized that the model was wrong. Similarly, the Soviet Union scrapped rockets and submarines designed for the Cold War when that model disappeared. Sometimes you need to know when to walk away and accept your losses. Is there a way to reduce the investments you are making in your current model to preserve options for the future?

■ **Start with small changes that affect perceptions and actions in the broader system.** Sometimes a new mental model can be pushed forward through a series of apparently small initiatives that fundamentally transform the system. The transformation of the New York City Police Department by Mayor Rudolph Giuliani and Police Commissioner William Bratton began with "challenging every single assumption about urban policing."[3] Some small but significant changes such as the color of uniforms or a zero-tolerance policy on petty crimes had a big impact, because they began eroding a mindset of tolerating some crimes, and they moved from responding to crime after the fact to proactively preventing crime. The change also gave the police and public visible victories. In the past, for example, police didn't bother with panhandlers and squeegee people who washed windows of cars stopped at intersections, but when law enforcement began to crack down on these petty crimes, it changed the way residents looked at the law. They saw the benefits and took it more seriously. The department also began measuring crime patterns more effectively in real time and holding individual leaders accountable for the results. Felonies in the city fell 12.3 percent from 1993 to 1994, with New York's crime rate falling three to six times faster than the national average. Apparently small changes can become "tipping points" for fads or revolutions, which spread in epidemic fashion from a few initial carriers across the population.[4]

In December 2002, Coca-Cola took the simple step of announcing that it would stop issuing quarterly earnings forecasts. While it created a stir initially, Coke's move was quickly followed by other companies, such as McDonald's Corp., AT&T, Mattel and PepsiCo. These estimates tended to focus investor attention on the short-term rather than the long-term and to focus management on beating expectations. Coca-Cola and other companies took the practical step of changing their reporting processes to reshape their own models and attempt to change the perspective of investors. It changed the way investors and managers looked at their business. Sometimes a shift in infrastructure can be both a signal of a change in the old model and a support for a new model.[5] What small changes can you make to erode the old order and begin to build the new?

■ **Do the hard analysis and measurement.** In Giuliani's crusade against New York City crime, he realized that the old measures focused on arrest rates and reaction time to emergency calls, not on public safety and reducing crime. The national crime statistics that did exist were reported quarterly or annually—too slowly to have an impact. Part of the change in New York City policing was to develop measures that were more relevant and to report them *daily*. People were held responsible and accountable for improving results.

Sometimes the results of such analysis can offer stunning insights. Citibank had always considered its commercial real estate holdings as a strong balance-sheet asset and perhaps inadvertently became the largest owner of U.S. commercial real estate. But when its "work out" group took a hard look at its portfolio during its crisis in the early 1990s, it found that this and other hard "assets" turned out to be serious liabilities, given their overall problems. The result was a decision to get rid of large amounts of commercial real estate. Citibank also wrote down commercial loans and consumer debt through rigorous asset analysis.

With all the discussion of gender equality and the widely accepted concept of equal pay for equal work, one might think that there is wage parity between men and women. But rigorous analysis of salaries by gender shows that there is still a significant gap between the salaries of women and men. The U.S. Equal Pay Act of 1963 and the Civil Rights Act of 1964 prohibit unequal pay or wage discrimination based on race, color, sex, religion or national origin. Even so, 2000 U.S. Census data indicate that women's salaries are still only 73 percent of men's salaries (partly as a result of a higher percentage of women in lower-paid jobs and differences in education or experience). This is an increase from 57 percent in the early 1970s. Looking at the hard numbers offers a reality check in truly implementing a new model.[6]

What hard numbers can you look at to help erode the old models and build support for the new ones?

■ *Make the information visible.* To drive the change across the organization, these measures can be brought to everyone's attention or incorporated into "dashboards." If the right measures are selected and business leaders are alert to the emergence of a need to change them, these dashboards can keep the organization focused on business drivers. Offered by hundreds of vendors, they are increasingly being adopted by companies as a way to drive collaboration and focus behavior across the organization. The managers who are "driving" the business can use this real-time feedback to adjust their actions and develop a better intuitive feel for the business. On a more personal level, the simple installation of a bathroom scale is an infrastructure change that can aid in a realistic program of dieting and exercise to lose weight.

- *Align incentives.* Changing incentives can change behavior, as has been shown in many business reorganizations or mergers. The social "workfare" programs that are designed to get people who have long been on public assistance to rejoin the workforce is another example of how changing incentives can help to break apart the old infrastructure and mindsets. In London, the government has created a disincentive for driving cars into the city center by monitoring license plates and imposing a surcharge for drivers who come into the city in private vehicles rather than public transportation. The early signs are that traffic flow has improved, although there may be unintended consequences such as a drop in entertainment and dining in the city as well as a large backlog of unpaid fines. Incentives that might be viewed as positive from one mindset (city officials hoping to reduce traffic snarls) might be seen as negative from another (a restaurant owner or a city bureaucrat in charge of collecting fines).

  In what ways can you dismantle the incentives that support the old order and build different incentives to support the new?

- *When possible, beat "swords into plowshares" (or at least into better swords).* It is hard to write off your investments in the old infrastructure, and sometimes you don't have to. The U.S. military reoutfitted and redeployed warhorses such as its Trident missile submarines and B-52s to make them relevant to the new demands of war. Sometimes enabling technology can help in this transformation without making the change in models too expensive. Some local municipalities have transformed their trash dumps into public recreation areas, such as the "Mt. Trashmore" park in Virginia. Sometimes it is better to transform the old order rather than break it. How can you transform the current infrastructure to support the new model?

- *Be willing to tear down the walls when necessary.* Like the fall of the Berlin Wall, some transformations begin with a dramatic and symbolic destruction of the old model. Some organizations have actually gone as far as holding funeral services for their old processes and systems, to give a ceremonial finality to the end of the old order. Companies bring in a new CEO to launch a radical change in strategy and clean out the old order. In personal life, sometimes managers reach a point in their careers where they feel they need to quit their current jobs without having another position lined up. By getting rid of the old infrastructure, they create the room for the new one to develop. Sometimes you can't build a new building without bidding farewell to the old one. What do you have to let go of to build the new models?

■ **Build trust.** In making changes, recognize the importance of less "tangible" aspects of the infrastructure such as a culture that can facilitate the introduction of a new order. In particular, an environment of trust can greatly aid in the transition to a new mental model. Lack of trust in an organization can undermine this process. Organizations that are filled with distrustful people tend to become less flexible and less willing to try new things or listen to different perspectives. One of the fuels of the Cold War was an environment of suspicion and mistrust between the superpowers, and one of the keys to the end of the Cold War was a series of high-level talks between the United States and the Soviet Union that enhanced communications and built trust. Enhancing the level of trust in the organization can build a foundation for shifting mindsets and changing infrastructure.

# CASTLES IN THE AIR

As the Internet bubble rose in the late 1990s, Warren Buffett remained out of the high-tech market, even when investors began punishing his Berkshire-Hathaway stock. He held to his old models and investment strategies despite the critics, and his skepticism of the new order ultimately proved right. You need to know when to abandon the old order and when to defend it.

Abandoning the old order can lead to chaos. You need your current infrastructure to be able to carry on with life and act upon your models in the world. Otherwise, these models would be merely hypothetical and you would be unable to act at all. You cannot constantly question the validity of your fundamental mental models, because doing this would inevitably lead to dysfunctional people or institutions.

Knowing when to change and how to do it in an efficient, nondestructive way is of enormous value. Some cultures, corporate and personal, simply cannot tolerate discussions regarding change. When they let things get so far out of line with reality, they are on the path to breakdown and revolution. Others who can tolerate a process of adjustment have the capacity to adapt and transform not only their thinking but their worlds.

Personal resistance to change and new models can be a grave obstacle to the introduction of a new order of things. This is the focus of the next chapter, where we discuss the "adaptive disconnects" between people whose models are divergent or changing at different rates.

New mental models are like Henry David Thoreau's "castles in the air" that hover above the existing world and often have little visible impact. They are like the new idea that you read in a book or learn in an educational program that quickly is washed aside by the demands of your current life. These new models have little reality and little effect until you put the foundations under them. The ability to shift the infrastructure of the old order is what separates the person who wants to stop smoking from the person who actually quits. This ability also distinguishes the company that merely creates a compelling new "vision" for where it is headed from the company that implements a bold new strategy. Organizations and individuals that move forward in implementing new mental models have the ability to move with courage to change and dismantle the old infrastructures and build new ones.

IMPOSSIBLE THINKING

- What structures and processes in your life or organization support the current model?

- To change the model, what structures and processes need to be changed?

- How hard will it be to change them? Who are the stakeholders who are most likely to defend these skeletons of the past?

- What small changes can you set in motion that will face the least opposition and have the greatest effect in promoting your new model?

# ENDNOTES

1. Kahneman, Daniel, J. L. Knetsch, and R. Thaler. "Experimental Tests of the Endowment Effect and the Coase Theorem." *Journal of Political Economy*. 98 (1990). pp. 1325–1348.

2. Einstein, Albert. "How I Created the Theory of Relativity." Kyoto. 14 December 1922. Trans. Yoshimasa A. Ono. Reported in *Physics Today* 35 (1982). p. 46.

3. Giuliani, Rudolph. *Leadership*. New York: Hyperion, 2002. p. 71.

4. Gladwell, Malcolm. *The Tipping Point*. Boston: Little Brown and Company, 2000.

5. Byrnes, Nanette. "Commentary: With Earnings Guidance, Silence Is Golden." *Business Week*. 5 May 2003. p. 87.

6. National Committee on Pay Equity. "Questions and Answers on Pay Equity." *Feminist.Com* <http://www.feminist.com/fairpay/f_qape.htm>.

# 9

# FIND COMMON GROUND TO BRIDGE ADAPTIVE DISCONNECTS

The world hates change, yet it is the only thing that has brought progress.

—C. F. Kettering

## You are talking yourself blue in the face but nothing appears to be getting through.

It is hard enough to get your teenage daughter to take off her headphones long enough to even hear you, and when she does, you feel like you are living in parallel universes. You are talking about responsibility and learning. She is talking about hanging out with her friends at the mall. You are certain your lips are moving, but there is no hint that any of these messages are registering in the blank and bored eyes of your progeny. The longer you talk, the less interested she looks. Is there any hope of getting your message across this generation gap?

Whether it is a parent to a teen, U.S. President George W. Bush to Saddam Hussein, activists opposing producers of genetically modified foods or abortion protesters staring down medical personnel working in clinics, mindsets create divides between people. To change the mindsets of people around you, you have to recognize these disconnects and look for ways to bridge them.

Despite your worst fears, your daughter will, most likely, grow up and adopt a mindset that may be hauntingly similar to your own—for better or worse. Her mindset will change from the adolescent view of the world to a more adult view. This process can be faster or slower, depending on how you manage these adaptive disconnects. Very often this change comes about through the trials of adult responsibilities—holding down a job or raising a family. It is through these experiences that her mental models are shaped and reshaped. Through protests in the streets, activists raise awareness of their environmental views within corporations.

This chapter explores the divides that separate one mind from another and strategies for bridging these gaps and accelerating learning across mindsets.

---

In 1996, the journal *Social Text* published an article by Alan Sokal called "Transgressing the Boundaries: Towards a Transformative Hermeneutics of Quantum Gravity." The only boundaries Sokal actually transgressed were those of reason. The paper was gibberish and Sokal, a self-described "stodgy old scientist," submitted it primarily to see if a leading journal in the humanities would actually print an article that he saw as a parody of a scientific paper. The published article became known as the "Sokal hoax." It was one of the most famous broadsides in an ongoing guerilla war between science and the humanities, serving to highlight the disconnect between these two worlds.

This gap was the subject of C. P. Snow's famous book in the 1950s, *The Two Cultures,* which portrays science and the humanities as "two cultures."[1] He argued that these two worlds are so separated that they don't even have a common language and said that this gap represented a major obstacle in solving the world's problems. This disconnect between science and humanities is seen in the challenge facing policymakers in translating science into law and explaining these regulations to the public. It can be seen in attempts to address issues such as mad cow disease in Europe, genetically modified food, stem cell research and global warming. The problem becomes even more complex as scientists talk to policymakers who then have to communicate risk to a heterogeneous public—through the imperfect filter of the news media. While it may be an exaggeration to see humanities and science as separate worlds—and they grow closer every day—the separate evolution of these two cultures represents an "adaptive disconnect." It illustrates the difficulties such disconnects create for communication, cooperation and the sharing of mental models.

## ADAPTIVE DISCONNECTS

Adaptive disconnects occur when one individual or group of individuals changes mental models at a faster or slower rate than those around them. One person or group has taken steps toward embracing a new model while the other remains with the old one. The divide grows until, at the extreme, the two sides may not be able to communicate, because they interpret the world through such different lenses. We see these disconnects between individuals (couples who have drifted apart over the years), within organizations (battles between the old guard and the young Turks), and in societies (divides between the haves and have-nots, the developed and developing worlds). Hawks and doves. Liberals and conservatives. Scientists and evangelists. In new-product development, the technologists in R&D and the marketers taking products out to market are in separate worlds. Each side sees the world from a different model.

At a minimum, these disconnects impede the progress of the new mental model as it is implemented in the world. Like oceans, rivers and mountains in the natural world, sometimes these barriers between models can be crossed, bridged or tunneled through. When the disconnects are wide enough, they may be unbridgeable, leading to outright war and conflict. It is therefore important to know how to address our own disconnects and bridge those of others to carry new mental models out into the world.

Of course, it is assumed here that the proponent of change believes the new model is for the better and believes that others can be persuaded of this. In the process of bridging the adaptive disconnects of others, we need to pay attention to their arguments as well. We need to consider the possibility that they may be right, or that some new model can be sparked by the friction between the two positions. Perhaps through listening we will realize we need to challenge and transform our own models.

There is often hope for bridging these differences. The divide between humanities and science that Snow highlighted offers a case in point. These two worlds are increasingly finding common ground as they see the usefulness of their separate approaches. The ethical questions raised by advances in medicine such as human cloning are being addressed through perspectives from philosophy, ethics and other areas of the humanities. At the same time, philosophical questions in the humanities are now being tested by using advanced medical technology to look inside subjects' minds while they are making decisions. Woody Allen's quip about cheating on his metaphysics exam by looking into the soul of the student next to him is not as far-fetched as it once seemed. Humanities are also placing ancient works of literature on high-tech CD-ROMs that offer interactive access to background sources, commentary and multimedia adaptations of the work. As the humanities have recognized the utility of science, and science has recognized the utility of the humanities, these "two cultures" have found common ground. They may not always see eye-to-eye on the world, but they can increasingly see the world through one another's eyes.

During the Cold War between the United States and the Soviet Union, the disconnect between Communism and Capitalism was so great that conversation took place primarily on the actual or potential battlefield. We saw the standoff between the two sides during the Cuban Missile Crisis, wars in Korea and Vietnam, and other military actions between two superpowers that had little basis for dialogue. Finally, the silence became too painful and expensive. Gorbachev's policy of "glasnost" created an opportunity for strategic talks, a common language and cooperation that did not exist before. In part because of these changes, the Berlin Wall collapsed and we saw the emergence of market economies in the former Soviet Union.

As the world changes more rapidly, the disconnects between mental models become more common. Disparity across the world, in terms of changing our mental models, grows. For example, rapid advances in technology have left parts of the world behind that lacked these technologies or had a philosophical or cultural opposition to them. New technologies sometimes receive the same welcome as the balloons of early aviators, who landed in rural fields only to be met by angry farmers with pitchforks and torches. These gaps lead to stresses across groups who are adapting at different rates. These adaptive disconnects can become so severe that a shared view of the world or an issue becomes very difficult or even impossible.

When they are small enough, these islands can sometimes be bypassed. This is the case with Amish culture in the United States, which has maintained the farming traditions and more primitive technologies of the late 19th century. The Amish form an island in the midst of the surrounding culture of technological progress and modern world views. Similarly, smaller countries such as North Korea can adopt a very different view of reality, but ultimately this view may come into conflict with the surrounding world, as with the development of nuclear weapons capabilities.

## THE NEED FOR UNLEARNING

Neurophysiologist Walter Freeman concluded that each brain creates its own internally consistent world. He called this "a form of epistemological solipsism." This term probably separates the world of Freeman's mind from most of ours. What he means by "solipsism" is the theory that the self can know nothing but its own modifications and that the self is the only existent thing. The self is a separate world. The term "epistemological" refers to what we know and how we know it. So what can be done to jolt these separate worlds out of their own reinforcing orbits?

Freeman proposes that brains communicate primarily through a process of unlearning. Under the challenge or influence of others, the brain gives up current beliefs and learns new ones through socially cooperative action. This process of unlearning is quite difficult. First, we need to recognize the need to change our mental models, and then we have to be willing to dismantle our own world and begin to build a new one based on new information. When we unlearn, we start over the process of learning that we began as children, at least with regard to some part of our experience. When we learn an entirely new subject, we are flooded with a confusing array of information that makes little sense at first. As we work at it and continue to learn, slowly we build the models that allow us to make sense of it. Finally, it becomes quite easy and natural to see the world through this new model.

We all are aware of the need to keep learning, but many of us underestimate the importance of "unlearning." If we don't learn to deconstruct the models that shape our worlds, we may have a very difficult time in creating new ones. The old worlds will keep coming back to haunt us. Unlearning is critical to bridging adaptive disconnects.

## ADDRESSING ADAPTIVE DISCONNECTS

How can you recognize and bridge these disconnects? As discussed in more detail below, there are three basic ways to address these issues:

1. Recognizing your own adaptive disconnects,
2. Bridging the gaps of others, and
3. Developing processes to bridge the gap.

### Recognizing Your Own Adaptive Disconnects

Our mental models potentially isolate us from others, and this isolation and separation can lead to problems. No matter how homogeneous your organization or community, you will find yourself living in a world with other people who have very different mindsets. How do you avoid being disconnected? How are you able to remain open to other views without giving up your own?

- *Compartmentalize.* Sometimes people can deal with adaptive disconnects by limiting mindsets to particular situations. For example, a researcher who pursues a very scientific approach in her career might choose a completely different mindset to the choice of a spouse or participation in religious services. This may appear to be hypocritical, but actually it can be a very effective way of building bridges and applying the most useful mindset to the problem at hand. From a practical standpoint, the scientist who takes a coldly rational view of her personal life may not necessarily have a more fulfilling home life than the one who embraces a less rigorous approach to personal decisions. Recognize the limits of your models and be willing to adopt different models for different situations.

- *Have a portfolio of models in your own thinking.* The larger a portfolio of models you have to draw from, the more you will be able to understand or embrace the models of others. If you have learned to think about the world through the eyes of an artist—either through study of art history or through the practice of creating art—you may be better able to appreciate the perspective of the artist or the creative inventor on your staff who comes up with a harebrained idea that actually might transform your business. If you can appreciate these other models, you can at least engage in a dialogue with others about them. For example, the oil companies at first drew battle lines against the environmentalists. Later, however, the companies realized that this was counterproductive and began working with these same activists on issues such as global warming. Now some oil companies even employ environmentalists and use them in their advertising. By seeing the world through their eyes, the companies were able to work with them, even if they did not completely agree with them.

- *Pay attention to what other people are saying about you.* As hard as it may be to admit it, your mindset may be out of date or wrong for the situation you are in. You need to be aware of what the rest of the world is saying about you and give it credence. CEOs set up town meetings to solicit candid feedback from employees, open the CEO's e-mail box to all employees and survey their customers to find out how they are doing. Intel's infamous problems with its Pentium chip and Exxon's handling of the *Valdez* accident were examples of companies' taking a long time to listen to feedback from the world. Unless you listen closely and give credence to what you hear, you probably won't find out your mindset is out of sync with a good part of the world until much damage is done. Within organizations, this can mean creating transparency in sharing information.

- **Avoid fundamentalism.** Fundamentalism, by its nature, is a world view that embodies a reluctance to change. While there are many forms of fundamentalism, they share a common dogmatic belief in one model to the exclusion of others, and this creates battlefields. Strong commitment to a world view is necessary in advancing it against opposition and inertia, yet the inability to see other positions can sometimes be a detriment to advancing the view. It hardens the battle lines and also makes it impossible for the fundamentalist to see through the eyes of others. This puts an end to dialogue.

Consider the use of the word "evil" in remarks by President George Bush about Iraq and other countries suspected of supporting terrorism. This is a term with religious overtones that is seen by Europeans as a sign of the fundamentalist overtones of U.S. policy. Although the United States, as a nation, embraces the concept of separation of church and state, U.S. speech and practice often reflect a more fundamentalist view of the world.

Fundamentalism extends beyond religion to issues such as technology, where some companies create systems that depend on a certain software or hardware platform, in contrast to systems that are platform independent. These limits make it harder for them to communicate with others on different systems, creating disconnects.

## Bridging the Gaps

What do you do when you confront the challenge of introducing a new mindset into a hostile or incompatible culture? This is the challenge faced by new CEOs, management consultants, entrepreneurs and religious missionaries. How do you get people to see that you have discovered the next big thing? How do you change deeply entrenched views of the world that have been carried and reinforced for generations? How do you overcome the inertia in order to change the way others think?

Many of the approaches used in effective negotiations and dialogue can be applied in bridging these gaps. Approaches used in leading organizational change can also help generate hypotheses about what might work. Among the ways to carry forward a new mental model are to:

- **Create a dialogue.** If you are not talking, you are not doing anything to bridge your disconnects and you provide no opportunity for others to see your view or for you to better understand theirs. Get the different parties to the same table, or open lines of communication. A Camp David meeting won't necessarily lead to a peace accord, but there won't be a peace plan without a meeting. These dialogues cannot always be expected to yield shifts in mindsets, but a forum for communication does offer the first foundation for bridging disconnects and finding common ground. The dialogue need not be long or too specific. It may at least afford an opportunity to be around each other, perhaps afterward in a social context such as eating together, and this may facilitate offline discussions.

- **Emphasize utility.** The adoption of the automobile and computers in businesses and homes was accomplished by emphasizing their utility. If you can demonstrate the superior benefit of an approach, weighed against its cost and risk, you have a much better chance of encouraging others to adopt it. Once the car became technologically advanced enough to surpass horses on speed, performance and cost of ownership, it became widely adopted. Once the business benefits of computers began to be demonstrated—with both cost savings and improved customer service—companies set up IT departments and began automating their businesses. When Cyrus McCormick was trying to find customers for his newfangled mechanical reaper in the early 1830s, farmers at first laughed at this comical contraption. So McCormick organized demonstrations, where he showed that his mechanical reaper with two horses could do the work of six men with scythes. His machines swept the country and the world. Like Cyrus McCormick, if you can demonstrate the abundant harvest of a particular mental model, you will greatly facilitate the process of its acceptance, but you need to understand utility from the perspective of the person you are speaking to.

- *Change the culture.* If culture is not addressed in making a major change, it can lead to adaptive disconnects that are very destructive. Sony's acquisition of Columbia Pictures in 1989 seemed like a match made in heaven, but it was destroyed by a clash of cultures. Each culture is supported by its own mindset and infrastructure. Even if the mindsets can be joined in theory, can the infrastructures really be combined to create a new model?

- *If you can't come in through the front door, find a window.* W. Edwards Deming was a quality prophet without honor in his own country, but he brought his approaches to total quality management to a more receptive audience in Japan. Once he had converted the more receptive mindsets of Japan (who had less to lose in giving up old manufacturing approaches and more to gain than their U.S. rivals in improving their quality), Deming was then able to reimport his world view back into the United States. Tough competition from Japanese companies got the attention of U.S. manufacturers and made them see the utility of these new approaches to quality management.

It isn't always necessary to convert the whole world at once or even your target audience. You can sometimes start with the most receptive audiences, build a following and then come back en masse to the original group. If you can get leading users involved in helping to design a new product, they will be far more likely to adopt it—and then others will follow. Consulting companies and software firms often pursue this strategy in implementing new methodologies and technologies, working with a few lead customers on pilot projects, and then using that experience to carry the new mindset to a broader audience.

■ ***Precipitate a crisis.*** As managers know, sometimes the best way to change mindsets in an organization is to create or precipitate a crisis. By constraining budgets, you immediately encourage the entire organization to focus on cost cutting and creative use of resources. Similarly, a person with a substance-abuse problem may be forced to recognize it through an intervention by friends, who bring the issue to a crisis. A spouse in a troubled marriage might galvanize a partner's attention through a trial separation or threat of divorce. The creation of a crisis raises the stakes sufficiently to encourage a shift in mindset. External crises can have a similar effect. It was at the conclusion of World War I that the nations of the world began building the League of Nations and in the aftermath of World War II that the United Nations became a focal point of international discussions. The crisis of the wars led to a change in mindset from isolation to a more global view of geopolitical cooperation. If you are in the position to create a crisis, this process can be the flame that ignites the spread of changes in mindset.

■ ***Find boundary spanners.*** During a meeting with Chinese business executives, one of the authors (Colin Crook) was trying to explain some technical details of a project. It was a large room, and the expression on the faces of his audience showed that the ideas were not getting through. It was not only the language but also the immersion in technical detail. A colleague at Citibank, Nina Tsao, asked to take over. She launched into Cantonese, but it was not just the language that helped. She was able to translate the concepts into a form that was comprehensible to the audience. She was familiar enough with Colin's work and familiar enough with the specific audience that she was able to effectively translate between the two. Because she could see through both these perspectives, she could serve as a very effective interlocutor between the mental model of Colin and the models in the heads of the Chinese businessmen.

Even when there seem to be impassable gulfs between one world and another, there are usually bridges. These bridges are often in the form of "interlocutors" or "boundary spanners," people with one foot in one world and one in another. If you can find these people, they can serve as guides and translators, making these foreign worlds accessible to you. If you find yourself completely bewildered by exposure to a radical perspective, look around and see if you can find others who understand both your world and the new world and can bridge the gap.

These people can be a great aid in making the transition from one mindset to another. In science, for example, there have been a number of boundary spanners, such as Steven Pinker, Richard Dawkins or Stephen J. Gould, who make complex scientific subjects accessible to the masses. They are great communicators who bring a new view of the world to a great many people. The only danger with this approach is that your view of that particular discipline is through the eyes of a fairly narrow group of people. You lose some of the richness of the experience.

## A Process for Connecting

In general, there are three broad steps in carrying a new model out into the world and overcoming adaptive disconnects:

- **Can you communicate?** If you have no basis for dialogue, you will have a hard time carrying forward any new view of the world.
- **Can you share things of value?** If you can demonstrate the utility (the benefit versus the cost or risk) of the new view, you will increase the chances that it will be adopted.
- **Can you establish a shared or common view of things?** With a basis for dialogue and a demonstration of utility, you can now build a common view of the world.

You can create formal processes in your organization or life—such as establishing the role of devil's advocate—that help legitimize opposing perspectives and bridge these disconnects on a wide range of issues.

## ADAPTING THE WORLD

Progress sometimes comes from a radical model that is brought into the mainstream. The fringe movement of civil rights in the 1960s ended up shaping national debate and changing the mindset of the entire country. John F. Kennedy's view of putting a man on the moon by the end of the 1960s galvanized scientists and politicians around this compelling vision, helping to make it a reality. At the same time, the resistance of the old guard can also be valuable in the process of testing new ideas. It is this balance between the radical ideas and new mindsets, and the persistence of the old that allows us to select the model that offers the most utility for a specific situation.

Samuel Butler once said that "The reasonable man adapts himself to the world, but the unreasonable man tries to adapt the world to him—therefore all progress depends upon the unreasonable man." Butler's observation, while true, is not complete. If these "unreasonable" people cannot convince others of the reasonableness and usefulness of their views, little progress will result. The person with a "crazy" view will be isolated from the rest of society, if not in a padded cell. If Albert Einstein had not been able to convince others of the wisdom of his radical theories of relativity, or if abstract expressionist painter Jackson Pollock had not been able to convince the art world of the genius of his work, they would have remained footnotes in the history of their fields. All progress depends upon the process of the "unreasonable" people carrying their radical views across the adaptive disconnects of the world to make them "reasonable" views. They do this by bridging adaptive disconnects and joining separate worlds.

## IMPOSSIBLE THINKING

- What are the mental models around you that are different from your own? Who holds these models and why?

- How can you bridge these "adaptive disconnects"?

- What benefits do the proponents of alternative mental models gain from them?

- How can you demonstrate the utility of your new model?

- How can you create a dialogue with others who see the world through different models?

- Who are the boundary spanners who can help you bridge these gaps?

# ENDNOTE

1.   Snow, C. P. *The Two Cultures*. Cambridge and New York: Cambridge University Press, 1993.

# 4

# ACT QUICKLY
# AND EFFECTIVELY

1. Recognize the power and limits of mental models

2. Test the relevance of your mental models against the changing environment, generate new models and develop an integrated portfolio of models

3. Overcome inhibitors to change by reshaping infrastructure and the thinking of others

4. Transform your world by acting quickly upon the new models, continuously experimenting and applying a process for assessing and strengthening your models

# 10

# DEVELOP THE INTUITION TO ACT QUICKLY

*The supreme task is to arrive at those universal elementary laws from which the cosmos can be built up by pure deduction. There is no logical path to these laws; only intuition, resting on sympathetic understanding of experience, can lead to them.*

—Albert Einstein[1]

## Something just doesn't feel right.

You are in the last phases of completing a deal. As you look at the neat piles of papers on the table in front of you, all the details seem perfect. The lawyers and accountants have gone over all of it with a fine-tooth comb. All the i's are dotted. All the t's are crossed. This deal means a lot for your company, and you've pulled it off. But as you look across the table at your smiling partner, something about him strikes you the wrong way. Are you just getting cold feet, or is it something more?

You decide to trust your gut. You find an excuse to put off the completion of the deal. Your partner grumbles a little, but you gain time to do a more thorough background check. The first clue to possible trouble is your discovery that his internal auditor is engaged to become his wife. While all the books appear to be in order, you poke around a little more deeply and find some big holes under the plaster and patchwork. You back out of the deal, saving your company millions in losses and years of headaches.

But how do you explain the hunch that led you to question the deal? How do you know that your intuition, built upon hundreds of deals and thousands of interactions, is right?

Sometimes you have more knowledge than you are aware of. This is intuition. Your intuition allows you to access your mental models without thinking about them, and to act upon them. It is crucial to making real-world decisions. But it is very difficult to explain, and it can also be wrong, if it is based on a model that is out of sync with the current world.

What is intuition, and how does it help us make sense and act quickly? How can you improve your intuition? And how can you make sure your intuition continues to be relevant to your current environment?

---

In the late 1500s, tea master Sen Rikyu formalized the Japanese tea ceremony and, by virtue of long participation in its rituals, developed a high degree of intuition. Observing very subtle features of a sparse tea process, he was able to guess the intentions of Shogun Hideyoshi. The Shogun had not confided in anyone, yet the tea master, with his attention to detail and resulting sharp intuition, guessed that he was planning an invasion of Korea.

Sen Rikyu said, "I don't think you should invade Korea."

The Shogun was outraged, not only at the advice but at the fact that Sen Rikyu had guessed his hidden intentions. He instructed Sen Rikyu to commit seppuku (ritual suicide). A year later Hideyoshi sent 160,000 men in an invasion of Korea that proved disastrous.

Sen Rikyu had great intuition about the Shogun's thinking and the weaknesses of his military planning. But the tea master perhaps did not have such good intuition about what information to share with the Shogun.

As this story illustrates, intuition allows us to makes sense and act quickly, particularly in environments in which we face immediate danger. It can also lead us to take actions that we might reconsider upon careful reflection. Our intuition can be out of sync with our environment, and this can lead to serious errors.

In most of our decisions we don't have much time to make sense and take action. Intuition allows us to access our mental models and act on them quickly. Because the models have been refined and distilled into a "gut feel," we can apply them and make decisions much more quickly than we could using a more analytical approach. Intuition helps us shape, understand and access our mental models to make quick and effective decisions.

## WHAT IS INTUITION?

Some people with a deep knowledge of a given area are able to quickly make sense of the situation long before anyone else. The military leader on the battlefield, or the business leader in the midst of crisis, can cut through the extraneous detail, get a grasp of the situation and make a quick decision. They can often make sense of a situation with much less information than other people. Taking action requires decisions, and these are often made under conditions of stress, driven by time pressure, hampered by uncertainty and lack of information.

There are two basic approaches to the decision process: an analytical, formal process and an intuitive process. The analytical approach can be codified and explained to others. It is repeatable and follows a well-known process that is taught in business schools, medical schools and many other areas of society where important decisions have to be made. The analytical approach runs through a series of steps something like this: Problem formulation and information gathering, generation of options, evaluation of these options using a selected set of criteria, making a choice, and developing mechanisms for feedback, including measures of performance. Gather your information, conduct your analysis, generate options and select your decision.

Real decisions are not always made this way. In some cases, there is no time. In other cases, decision makers may just prefer not to follow a formal process. Instead, they trust their gut.

If we had infinite time to work out every move, we might be analytical, but if we need to make quick decisions, we need to rely more heavily on intuition. Consider a chess match in which both players have unlimited time in which to make their moves. If they had the mental capacity, they would then be able to analyze the implications of every possible move at each point along the way, all the way out to the end game. Even with time for careful analysis, it is still difficult for a strictly analytical machine to beat a human with excellent intuition, but it has now been done by IBM chess-playing computers. (These computers not only could analyze the moves but also had a database of grandmaster games to "get inside the head" of the opponent and analyze what a strong player might do.) If you take the same game, however, and give each player a five-second interval in which to play, or if, like the grand masters, one player goes against multiple opponents, the players will have to make moves that are much more intuitive. In this environment, they draw upon their experience through intuition rather than systematic analysis. Many of the decisions that face us are like a timed game of chess.

How important is intuition? In fast-paced, complex, high-stress environments such as the trading floor or the battlefield, the importance of intuition is particularly clear. A study that pitted Wall Street traders against seasoned Marines in war games on a mock battlefield found that the traders, surprisingly, came out on top on the battlefield. How could this be? It seemed that the traders had a much better sense of intuition—they were able to evaluate risks and act more quickly. The Marines were following more rigid rules. This experience led the Marines to set aside their formal analysis in the complex and fluid environment of the battlefield and urge their leaders to rely much more on intuition.[2] We see similar intuition developed in sports such as mountain climbing or whitewater kayaking, auto racing or surfing, where a deep knowledge and experience of the activity is translated into a set of reflexes and actions.

## Instinct, Insight and Intuition

Intuition is different from either insight or instinct in that it is generally based upon a deep experience in a certain area. Insight, in contrast, occurs suddenly and without warning, an "Aha!" moment. Intuition is rooted in deep, direct knowledge of a type different from that arrived at by reasoning or perception. Intuition puts one close to solving a problem before the solution is consciously apparent, and even before the problem is diagnosed and articulated.

Instincts operate in a way very similar to intuition. Both allow us to make very rapid assessments of situations and respond to them. But while intuition is generally based on very deep individual experience (an expertise that becomes a gut feel), instinct is based on some deep collective experience that we appear to be born with—or at least born with a predisposition to develop. Robin Hogarth discusses how some of our basic instincts, such as fear response, may be mechanisms that have evolved to protect us. When we hear a dog bark on a street, we might have an immediate impulse to jump or run away from the sound. This is automatic. We don't stop to think. After we stop and have time to look at the situation analytically, we may find the dog is tied up and so it is not a danger. This careful assessment is a different process for evaluating the risk of the situation, and much slower. But the immediate reaction is there to keep us from danger, and it is better to be wrong than to be torn to pieces by a wild dog.[3]

Studies have shown that some of this appears to be with us from the start. The location of the immediate fear response is the amygdala, a small organ in the back of the brain. The incoming sensory information is also processed by the neocortex, much more slowly and analytically. But this analysis is too late to help us if we face an immediate life-and-death situation. We are born with some hard wiring in our operating systems that predispose us to learn certain fears very easily, such as fear of heights and snakes.

## THE POWER OF CREATIVE LEAPS

Intuition also allows creative leaps. The intuitive decision process depends upon an individual; the decision may not be explainable. It is often emotional and sometimes even physical. Albert Einstein talked about a feeling in his fingertips, or "fingerspitzengefuehl." Starbucks founder Howard Schultz shook with excitement in an Italian café when he first had the idea for his U.S cafés.

Nobel Prize winning physicist Enrico Fermi, who demonstrated the first controlled atomic fission reaction, was carrying out some neutron experiments in Italy during the 1930s. During the course of debugging these experiments, he had a hunch to shoot the neutrons through paraffin wax instead of shaped lead. This led to the discovery of "neutron moderation," which ultimately permitted the development of the world's first nuclear reactor. Fermi had a deep knowledge of the physics, but he could not explain why he suddenly tried paraffin wax. The use of paraffin was accomplished "con intuition formidable." He felt it in his gut. Fermi became known as a great intuitive experimental physicist.

Studies of firefighters by cognitive psychologist Gary Klein found that they don't actually make formal decisions. They don't weigh alternatives. They grab the idea that looks best and then move on to the next. In his book, *Sources of Power,* Klein tells the story of a sudden decision of a firefighter to pull his crew from a burning building. He just sensed something was wrong. He couldn't explain why he made the decision. A short time later, the floor the firefighters had been standing on gave way. How could he possibly have known this? Somehow this experienced firefighter was able to draw together all his experience into a deep wisdom about the correct action without even taking the time to translate it into a conscious thought process.

## DANGERS OF INTUITION

Given the strengths of a well developed intuition, it is also important to recognize some of the weaknesses. First, when our intuition is wrong, our snap judgments will be off the mark. We might make decisions that are fast and efficient—but dead wrong.

Intuition can be wrong because it is out of sync with the environment. The initial instinct of a diver, drawn from a deep survival instinct, might be to surface rapidly after a deep-sea dive. But as the diver gains more experience in diving, he learns that he needs to fight this instinct and surface more slowly to avoid the bends. A driver's intuition for what to do when losing control of a car on a dry road would be to turn away from the direction of the skid, but on an icy road, the best strategy is to turn in the direction of the skid.

When the world changes, we are often left with an intuition that is highly developed but wrong for our current environment. For example, our intuition about human interactions from our home culture may lead us astray if we travel to a different culture where interactions are quite different. In this case, we need to train ourselves in a new intuition that fits with the situation, so that we know how to act in social situations in the foreign culture. Many Western business managers initially had trouble conducting business in Asia because of these differences. Their intuition was to move quickly into forging deals, for example, while their Asian partners stressed patience and relationship building. The hard-driving Western approach was all wrong, and managers needed to learn a new intuition.

The type of learning we do about our intuition depends on whether we are in what Robin Hogarth calls "kind" or "wicked" learning environments. In kind environments, we receive good feedback, so our intuition gets better. For example, if a weather forecaster is wrong, the rain or sun will clearly show the error of his mistake. In contrast, a waitress whose intuition says that during busy times she should focus on well-dressed patrons to earn better tips will fall victim to a self-fulfilling prophecy. The more attention she gives these well-dressed customers, and the more she ignores the others, the more her intuition will be confirmed. She'll get better tips from the well dressed. But she never tests whether she'd get better tips by paying attention to the poorly dressed patrons. Hogarth calls this a "wicked" environment, because it reinforces the existing intuition rather than testing and refining it.[4]

Another weakness of relying on intuition is the difficulty of communicating and coordinating with others. During World War II,

Adolph Hitler operated in a very intuitive way, and this made it difficult for his opponents to predict what he was going to do next. It also ultimately made it harder for his commanders and others to work with him, since they did not understand why he arrived at certain critical battle decisions. When his intuition failed him, the entire system failed, since he made all the critical decisions and no other system existed for overall coordination. In contrast, the Allies in World War II had a much more effective and rational system of joint working groups and committees that contributed to cooperation and coordination.

Smoke-jumping leader Wagner Dodge also had a brilliant intuition about how to escape a fire bearing down on his small team during the disastrous Mann Gulch fire in Montana in 1949. Smoke jumpers are firefighters who parachute into burning forests and use axes, shovels and other tools to contain, slow or stop forest fires. It is dangerous work, because the fires move quickly and unpredictably, and the firefighters always have to be concerned about being trapped by the blaze. This is what happened to Dodge and his team of 15 men at Mann Gulch. As the fire was racing toward him and his crew, Dodge stooped and lit a patch of grass to form a circle of burnt grass around him. This was not a backfire, which is designed to run up to meet the fire and stop it. Dodge's fire, instead, was one of the first recorded examples of the use of an "escape fire" designed to create a circle of burnt grass around the firefighter so the fire would rush by. While the escape fire eventually became part of the core knowledge of smoke jumpers, at this point it was an on-the-spot stroke of intuitive brilliance on the part of Dodge, a seasoned firefighter. It saved his life.

Unfortunately, because his crew did not share Dodge's intuition and didn't understand it (they knew there wasn't time to light an effective backfire), they couldn't make sense of what he was doing. They may have thought he had lost his mind. The men stormed passed him to their deaths as Dodge huddled safely in the ashes of his escape fire. Almost all of them perished in one of smoke-jumping's worst disasters. Dodge had brilliant intuition about what to do, but he could not communicate it to the men whom it could have saved. In this case, the roar of the fire made it difficult for

Dodge to communicate, but even when there is opportunity for dialogue, often the person with the intuition has trouble getting others to understand. Intuition is often hard to share.[5]

In our personal lives, we often trust intuition in making personal decisions such as a choice of a life partner. This intuition, expressed in experiences such as "love at first sight" or an instant connection or chemistry, can often show a deeper wisdom than we could ever have arrived at through analysis. On the other hand, the many relationships that are made and dissolved, formally or informally, offer ample evidence about how easy it is for this "intuition" to lead us astray or be clouded by other factors. These are often instances that "feel" right but turn out to be wrong. (It could also be that the intuition was right for the moment, but then the two people changed over time. This raises the question of the time frame of our intuition—are we focusing on the right decisions for the short term or for the long term?)

## DEVELOPING YOUR CAPACITY FOR INTUITION

How can you develop and act upon your intuition? Intuition is derived from having a superior repertoire of appropriate mental models and an instinctive way of accessing them to quickly make sense of things and solve problems. You also need a way to assess whether these models still fit the current reality and change them if necessary.

Intuitive skills are usually associated with specific individuals who consistently exhibit these capabilities. The rest of us marvel at their ability to just get things right—to make "gut feel" decisions that turn out to be good ones. We feel we are not part of this special intuitive community. Fortunately, we can develop intuitive skills by a deliberate effort to cultivate certain capabilities that will enable us to become more intuitive. The following process is suggested as a way of enhancing intuitive capabilities.

■ *Practice intuition only in your area of expertise.* Intuition is associated with deep knowledge in a given category. Therefore the first key decision is to practice intuition only in an area where you feel you have significant knowledge and experience. Attempting to become intuitive in areas outside your expertise is a fool's errand. Neophytes, except for the rare savant with a natural talent, do not generally have good intuition. Intuition comes from a deep immersion in the subject until it becomes a tactile feel rather than an analytical process. The musician who plays fluidly, the trader on the floor, the business deal maker who knows just the right move, the leader who always knows the right words to say—all have honed their intuitive reflexes through many years of experience and mistakes. People with deep experience in a certain area may have little or no solid intuition in another. A brilliant intuitive scientist may be totally inept in social situations, because his experience is completely in the laboratory.

- *Learn to trust your "gut."* The first requirement is to feel "good" or confident or comfortable with your area of expertise or knowledge. This is fundamental to having faith in your intuitive decisions. Create space to listen to your intuition. Cultivate the process of "letting go" and making your intuitive self manifest, stopping the world and listening to your intuition. Learn to exploit the full range of your human decision-making processes—including emotions, feelings or prejudices. From an analytical approach, many people dismiss these as irrelevant or dangerous. They are reluctant to say "I feel good about things" or "I feel bad about this." Emotional processes should be allowed to shape and determine the intuitive decision process, since they reflect a deeper sense of how one feels about things. This approach contrasts starkly with a cold, analytical decision process based upon hard data, rigorous analysis, decision option generation, and decision selection.

- *Bring others along.* Remember, you may have to say to others, "Trust me, I know this stuff." Analytical decision processes tend to drive us toward "optimal" decisions, based upon an extensive analysis of data. Intuitive decisions emphasize "getting it" (understanding) and seeking a quick solution that "works." This approach seeks to avoid an "optimum" criterion that systematically and painstakingly selects a solution out of many possible candidates. This inhibits flexibility. Therefore intuitive decisions, lacking data and depending on an incommunicable process will tend to give rise to contention. "Trust me" is not a very convincing argument. Successful thought leaders or gurus naturally command respect. To act successfully upon intuition in organizations or other groups, you need to find a way for your intuition to be respected.

■ *Practice, practice, practice.* Learning to quickly come to a decision under difficult conditions can be practiced and cultivated. Analytical training demands structured data and support tools to analyze problems. Deciding intuitively requires that you "get" the problem and "see" the solution. Such decision making can be practiced "off line" for a while. When some level of comfort is achieved, "on-line" decisions can follow.

Firefighters and other rescue workers spend a lot of time drilling in realistic conditions to refine their intuition. Their practice in making quick decisions in simulations can hone intuition and speed decision making in real-world environments, where these decisions have life-and-death implications. Airline pilots spend time in simulators learning how to deal quickly and effectively with sets of problems they might face in the cockpit. Similarly, managers engage in simulations, role playing and scenario planning to better tune their instincts for the rapid and fateful business decisions they need to make.

In particular, practice making intuitive decisions in situations of inadequate data, time pressure and high stress. By such practice you can get used to and enjoy your "gut feel" about the decision that arrives and avoid feeling desperate if a decision does not arrive. With more practice, it will become your mode of operation under decision conditions. A feeling of confidence will emerge.

■ *Build up your extended guru community.* Building deep expertise can be enhanced by gaining access to a broader community of knowledge. You may be smart and in touch, but so are many others, who may see things a bit differently. Encouraging dialog and feedback from this broader community shows a willingness to learn, and through this process you can improve your intuition.

- *Validate your intuition.* While you can't stop for validation at every point along the way without eroding the benefit of being able to act quickly, it is important to test your intuition periodically. Has it led you in the right direction, or has it led you astray? Is it out of step with your colleagues or out of step with your environment? Has your environment changed in a way that undermines the value of your past experience? Are you receiving negative feedback that you should be paying attention to?

- *Keep your intuition relevant.* In a complex and changing environment, maintain a healthy curiosity and an external focus to keep your intuition relevant. Since intuition is characterized by an unknowable process, you need to continue exploring a given area to maintain superior mental models. This includes openness to new ideas, experimentation and even outright speculation. Above all, learn to reflect on these novel things and consolidate the experiences. Keep an external focus. Become more aware and sensitive to external things— more observant of outside signals and patterns. Seek to see things others do not see, but use "gut discrimination" to avoid being overwhelmed by irrelevant data. Recall that people tend to jump from signals to conclusions, often "normalizing" variance to affirm their expectations and ignoring important signs.

- *Beware of confusion and uncertainty.* When you experience confusion and uncertainty, it may be a sign of the failure of your intuition. Deep expertise is associated with a superior repertoire of mental models. Intuition is the ability to subconsciously access these mental models in a repeatable and effective way in order to quickly make sense of things. This implies you are on top of things *always*, not just when you are within a decision process. If you feel confused about a decision and are not receiving a clear direction from your gut, it could mean your intuition has failed and you need a more analytical process, more experience, more knowledge or more information.

■ *Cultivate a practice of "letting go."* You need to cultivate the ability to frequently and consistently "let go" in order to listen to the still, small voice of intuition within you. On a regular basis, stop the world for a while, listen to your own heart, and examine the situation using your intuition. This process is cultivated in disciplines such as Zen meditation, which offer an opportunity to step back from active analytical processes by sitting quietly and observing body, mind and breath. To develop your intuition, break the habitual stream of normal activities and create space for contemplating new things. In normal life, you are bombarded by enormous amounts of information, requiring your mind to constantly operate within its mental-model repertoire. From time to time this process needs to be purposefully slowed down or halted. You can use techniques such as meditation or the less mystical approach of scheduling uninterrupted time for reflection. This will allow the mind to switch away from external stimuli, turn inward and seek a calm state.

Start "letting go" and giving a "light-touch" to things, rather than quickly jumping to a defined mental model in your thoughts. Becoming redirected to new things is a key ability and makes us more sensitive to the true nature of our world. Explore new ideas and expand your horizons, or indeed replace existing viewpoints with enhanced or more valid interpretations. You can go back over your recent past and look at events and experiences with a more sensitive eye. You can also contemplate and think about new ideas or thoughts. Having become self-focused and introspective, you calm down and become more contemplative, redirecting yourself to look for new things or for events in an early state of emergence. Eventually you can move toward a "phenomenological" viewpoint, establishing an ability to experience things without having to construct an elaborate explanatory theory.

■ *Combine intuition with analysis.* Cultivating good intuition doesn't mean you should give up rigorous analysis. When you have the time, information and resources to work out an analytical solution, it is often a good idea to do so. You can still test the results against your intuition, and they also might modify your intuition about the correct decision. You should work with the best analytical processes and intuitive processes, so that you can refine your mental models and apply them more effectively. Tools such as decision trees, value expectancy models, trade-off models such as conjoint analysis, optimization models, simulations, or the Analytic Hierarchy Process (AHP) can be used to help combine intuitive and subjective insights with rigorous analysis. Look for ways to combine the best of your head and your heart in making decisions.

## MODELS IN ACTION

You know more than you think you know. By accessing your intuition, you can tap into your implicit mental models, often more quickly than through a formal process. You need to be vigilant about the dangers of intuition—particularly that of having the wrong intuition for your current environment. With a healthy dose of caution and humility, you can learn to trust your intuition to make sense of the world.

This feeling in your fingers will often lead you in new directions that you might not have seen through an explicit process. In confusing environments, you might be tempted to fall back on extensive analysis to make decisions. While analysis can be extremely valuable, it is often best used to inform intuition rather than to take its place. Get the information that you need, but then learn to listen to your intuition.

Intuition allows you to focus the full capacity of your mental models and your experience, thought, and feeling into a decisive course of action. It can help you creatively rethink what you are seeing and reveal how certain aspects of the world are important in ways that might not be apparent to your mind. Intuition can help you see new patterns and arrive at new conclusions that can change the way you make sense of the world.

## IMPOSSIBLE THINKING

■ In what recent personal or professional decision have you trusted your intuition? What was the result?

■ Take a current critical challenge and, in a still moment, ask yourself: What does my intuition say to do in this case?

■ Can you set aside a few minutes every day to practice listening to your intuition (even if you don't act upon it)? What is your intuition telling you, and how does it differ from the solutions you develop through a more analytical process?

■ How have people around you or in news stories trusted or failed to trust their intuition, and what were the results?

■ In what ways has your intuition failed you, and how do you need to "refine" your intuition to fit the current realities of your environment?

# ENDNOTES

1. From address delivered at Max Planck's 60th birthday celebration (1918) before the Physical Society in Berlin.

2. Stewart, Thomas A. "Think with Your Gut." *Business 2.0.* November 2002. pp. 99–104.

3. Hogarth, Robin "Insurance and Safety after September 11: Has the World Become a 'Riskier' Place?" *Social Science Research Council.* <http://www.ssrc.org/sept11/essays/hogarth.htm>.

4. Hogarth, Robin. *Educating Intuition.* Chicago: University of Chicago Press, 2001.

5. Maclean, Norman. *Young Men and Fire.* Chicago: University of Chicago Press, 1992.

# 11

# THE POWER TO DO
# THE IMPOSSIBLE

What can people achieve with impossible thinking? We've seen how shifting mental models led to running the miracle mile, creating new businesses and transforming lives. This chapter presents three case studies of "impossible thinkers"—Howard Schultz, Oprah Winfrey and Andy Grove—to illustrate the power of new mental models. While these individuals differ in their spheres of action and impact, they all have challenged the thinking of people around them in ways that altered their own lives, their industries and the world.

## HOWARD SCHULTZ

It must have looked as if Howard Schultz had lost his mind.

He'd worked his way up from the housing projects of New York, earned a college degree, and risen to the rank of vice president and general manager of Hammarplast's housewares subsidiary, in charge of their U.S. operations. He had an apartment on Manhattan's Upper East Side, a good salary, a company car, and vacations in the Hamptons. He left it all behind—for the impossible.

In 1981, Schultz noticed that a small retailer in Seattle was ordering a very large number of drip coffee makers. He traveled across the country to visit Starbucks Coffee, Tea and Spices, a tiny company founded ten years earlier by a team of entrepreneurs and coffee aficionados. Starbucks now boasted four stores, selling high-quality dark-roasted coffee beans to a small but growing following of connoisseurs.

## Rethinking Coffee

Seattle in 1981 was in decline. Boeing; the city's largest employer, had made massive job cuts. The coffee industry was in its maturity, experiencing bitter price wars and declining quality. It was a commodity business with no proprietary intellectual property. Per capita coffee consumption was down from its 1961 peak of 3.1 cups a day in a slide that would continue until the late 1980s. To many outsiders, it looked like the worst possible time to enter the worst possible industry.

Yet Schultz saw something different—so different that in 1982 he gave up his job and moved 3,000 miles to join Starbucks as head of marketing. As he writes in *Pour Your Heart Into It*, life is "seeing what other people don't see, and pursuing that vision no matter who tells you not to."[1]

## A Journey of Discovery and Intuition

On a business trip to Italy for Starbucks in 1983, Schultz discovered the European espresso bar. His thinking shifted. He saw a model of coffee drinking and community interaction at cafés in Italy that he determined to bring back to the United States.

Starbucks at that time didn't sell brewed coffee; it only sold whole beans and equipment. As Schultz enthused about the prospect of American coffee bars, he found he could not shift the company's focus. The founders were not interested in changing the direction of their profitable and growing business. Schultz got permission to create a small experiment based on this new model, setting up an espresso bar in the corner of a Starbucks store. The experiment was successful, but the founders remained unwilling to change their model. They wanted to remain true to their roots as coffee roasters.

Facing this "adaptive disconnect," Schultz left Starbucks in 1985 to take his experiment onto a broader stage. He set up his own business of espresso bars, Il Giornale. Many people said it couldn't be done—it was impossible to change the way Americans viewed coffee. But, as Schultz writes, "No one ever accomplished anything by believing the naysayers." Two years later, his successful business bought Starbucks.

At the time of its initial public offer of stock in 1992, Starbucks had grown to 165 stores. By 2004, the company had nearly 7,500 stores and 75,000 partners (employees), with more than $4.4 billion in sales. The company had posted 142 consecutive months—nearly 12 years—of positive same-store growth. Since going public, this juggernaut has grown at a rate of 20 percent per year with an annual earnings-per-share growth of 20 to 25 percent.

## Bridging Adaptive Disconnects

Schultz not only transformed the thinking and actions of the company, he also revitalized a mature industry and changed the habits and perspectives of a generation of coffee drinkers. Most American coffee consumers were buying cans of coffee in the supermarket on the basis of price. Starbucks invested time and energy in educating people to appreciate fine coffee and a complex array of espresso drinks. The key to its success was to create an experience—the Starbucks experience—in its cafés. Gratified customers told others about the experience, and the phenomenon grew by word of mouth.

## Building a New Order

Beneath the transformation lay a lot of hard work. To change the American pattern of coffee drinking, Schultz had to rethink everything about the experience, from the design of furniture and stores to the training of baristas. He had to generate a supply of quality coffee large enough to support the enterprise along with a cadre of baristas who could create the coffee experience in city after city. He built a new infrastructure to support and deliver this mental model, giving this process the close attention to detail that was a big part of the company's success. Where other retail companies offered employees minimum wages and no benefits, Starbucks provided stock options and benefits even to part-time workers. While other coffee buyers took advantage of market downturns to cut the prices paid to growers, Starbucks sustained the prices it paid to growers, thus securing their loyalty and ensuring a long-term supply of fine coffees.

As Starbucks grew, Schultz had to continuously challenge his own thinking and conventional Wall Street wisdom, even as he remained true to the company's core values. To move from a small startup to a respected global brand, Schultz declared, the biggest personal challenge was "reinventing yourself." He reinvented himself from a dreamer who saw the possibilities of espresso bars and raised money to realize them, to an entrepreneur who built a successful business, to a professional manager who built a major corporation. He also had to challenge his own thinking about his personal success, leaving good-paying, secure jobs to pursue his passion.

## Zooming In and Out

During the 1995 Christmas season, Starbuck's hit a slow spot, and Wall Street complained that the company's leaders had taken their eye off the ball in their pursuit of rapid growth. The company made some short-term operational changes to address investors' concerns but continued to focus on long-term innovations, such as the introduction of ice cream and the forging of a strategic alliance with United Airlines that ultimately helped it emerge even stronger.

Over the years, Starbucks has introduced such innovations as prepaid cards (which grew to 70 million in 2002), sales of games and CDs in its stores, international partnerships and alliances with such firms as Pepsi-Cola, Capitol Records, Barnes & Noble, Nordstrom, and Kraft (for supermarket distribution) to expand its reach. Meanwhile, the company has kept an eye on vital short-term performance and operational issues. As Schultz observes, the CEO needs to be both nearsighted and farsighted. In other words, leaders need to be able to zoom out to see the big picture and zoom in to focus on the detail.

## Continuous Experimentation and Challenging the Model

As it continued to grow, the company transformed its product line, introducing drinks with both regular and nonfat milk as well as new beverages such as Frappuccinos. While managers have planned systematically and been resolute about protecting the culture and the brand, the pursuit of success and rapid growth has meant transforming their thinking along the way.

"We have been willing to change our minds about things, and as a consequence changed our company," said President and CEO Orin Smith, who joined the firm when the entire operation was supplied by a single coffee roaster in a drafty warehouse. He commented:

> The big barriers to growth are often self-imposed. When I came to this company, the big debate was that we are a coffee company. We buy the best coffee in the world and roast it in the best way. If people don't like it, too bad. What is this milk stuff we are putting in the coffee to create lattes? Then it was nonfat milk. Then we had Frappuccino (which now accounts for 20 percent of our business and is the most important innovation we have had). We were never going to franchise because we needed total control over the stores. Today, we are doing third-party licensing. We have been willing to change the things we'll never do, time and time again. We continue to redefine and expand what is the core business.

The company continues to experiment with innovations such as express preordering (tested in 60 stores in the Denver area), breakfast offerings (tested in 20 stores in Seattle), and wireless Internet connections throughout its network of stores in partnership with t-Mobile. Not all of these ventures succeed. A Starbucks furniture store—offering home versions of the furniture in its cafés—died a quiet death. But many experiments have led to new sources of revenue and profit, as well as keeping the brand and the stores fresh.

## Stretching Beyond the Possible

Throughout its history, Starbucks set out to do the impossible, and then achieved it. It set stretch objectives. As early as 1993, the company told Wall Street that by the year 2000 it would have 2,000 stores. It was a long shot, but seemed doable. By 2000, the company had already opened 3,000 units—and it just kept going.

As a small upstart, the company set the outrageous goal of building a brand that was as strong as Coca-Cola's. For the past few years Starbucks has been named one of the most respected brands in the world. "We set extraordinarily high expectations that border on the ridiculous," Smith said. "At every step, we set that bar really high and then tried to meet or exceed it."

In your travels around the world or into new domains of thought, what new ideas like Schultz's European espresso bar have you recognized? How can you bring them back home to change the way you approach your work and life? What can you learn from Starbucks about the difficulty and possibility of changing the mental models of people around you? Have you given up on your impossible ideas too soon?

---

# OPRAH WINFREY

Oprah Winfrey began her broadcasting career as an unlikely talk show host. She grew up in Kosciusko, Mississippi, in a house without electricity or indoor plumbing. Her unmarried parents separated soon after her birth, leaving her to be raised by a maternal grandmother. At age six, she moved to Milwaukee to live with her mother. As a child she was sexually abused by male relatives and friends. She ran away and was sent to a juvenile detention home at age 13. This difficult childhood later affected the way she approached her show and the topics she chose for her talk show and her books.

At the age of 14, she went to live with her father, whose guidance and discipline (for example, she went without dinner until she learned five new vocabulary words a day) helped put her on a path to success. She won a college scholarship for her oration and in 1971 was named Miss Black Tennessee. She graduated with a degree in communications and theater from Tennessee State University.

Oprah started broadcasting in college, becoming co-anchor of the evening news of the Nashville CBS affiliate. After graduating, she became reporter and co-anchor for Baltimore's ABC affiliate. She looked so little like what they envisioned as a successful anchor that the station sent her to New York for a beauty makeover. She was told that her hair was too thick, her nose too wide and her chin too big. But she was successful, not by fitting into the mold but by breaking it.

## Rethinking the Talk Show

In 1977, Oprah became co-host of the *Baltimore is Talking* show. Under her leadership it boasted better ratings than Donahue, who had been the reigning king of the format. After seven years in Baltimore, she was hired by ABC's Chicago affiliate, where she became anchor of the failing *A.M. Chicago* show in 1984. Because the show was doing poorly, she was given free reign to experiment. After she overhauled its contents, *A.M. Chicago* went from last place in the ratings to rank even with Donahue in just one month and then surged ahead. In September 1985, it was renamed *The Oprah Winfrey Show*. In less than a year it became the number one national talk show. She was on her way to a nearly two-decade reign as the Queen of Talk. The Oprah Winfrey Show is seen by about 23 million viewers in more than 100 countries.

Oprah had a very different model for the talk show. While Donahue worked his audience with microphone in hand like a reporter, interviewing for information, Winfrey met the audience as friends. She engaged in a dialog with them that was self-revealing. She told about her own challenges and experiences. Her style appealed to women viewers. She recognized the need for connection with viewers sitting in living rooms in the afternoon. She talked about personal issues, her childhood abuse, her relationship with her partner Stedman (who, like Oprah, is known to viewers by first name). She made a public medium into a private, intimate one—as intimate as several million viewers can become.

In the process, Oprah changed the nature of the talk show, democratizing it, and making it more personal. She adopted a goal to "transform people's lives." She changed the way people thought about talk shows and about their own lives—in effect, challenging their mental models. In her shows and choice of topics for her book club, Winfrey also dealt with difficult issues that were personally important to her. At the same time, she worked to transform the mindsets of viewers and readers, encouraging them to challenge themselves.

## Adaptive Experimentation: Books, Magazines and Other Media

Once Oprah had developed this new, personal view of the talk show and established a loyal group of followers, she could take her audience in new directions. She applied her new view to other areas, challenging the thinking in other industries in ways that sent shockwaves through them. In 1996, she created an on-air book club that encouraged millions of viewers to read serious fiction. These were not the kind of books that traditionally became popular successes, so she created a whole new segment of readers.

While book reviews had once been the domain of print publications such as *The New York Times,* her show represented a new format for discussing books with a very broad audience of viewers. This made Winfrey an arbiter of taste in the publishing industry, where her endorsement could mean an additional half-million or more copies in sales. Within two years she had helped two dozen books onto the best seller lists. *Time* writer Richard Lacayo remarked:

> It's not true that Oprah Winfrey's Book Club was the most important development in the history of literacy. For instance, there was the invention of the written word. Then there was movable type. So Oprah comes in third. But no lower, at least not in the opinion of publishers and booksellers, who binge every month on the demand for whatever title she features on her show.[2]

She then shook up magazine publishing in April 2000 with the creation of *O, The Oprah Magazine,* which became the most successful magazine startup in history, rapidly growing to more than two million readers monthly. As periodicals such as *Mademoiselle* folded in a tough advertising environment, hers continued to grow. While other magazines featured models on the cover, *O* featured Oprah Winfrey. She extended her personal connection and perspectives to this new channel. She broke the rules of some leading magazine publishers by placing her table of contents on page 2, instead of 22, so readers would not have to wade through countless ads. She also co-founded a cable and Internet company for women, Oxygen Media, in 1998 and created a movie production division that has turned out award-winning films such as *Tuesdays With Morrie.*

Her personal involvement doesn't end with her business activities. She has worked actively on behalf of many charities around the world. Her "Oprah's Angel Network" has raised millions of dollars from viewers to help build schools and aid children throughout the world. She also has been active in promoting legislation related to child abuse and other topics of importance to her.

## Bridging Adaptive Disconnects

In developing her book club, Oprah used the popularity of her talk show to bridge the "adaptive disconnects" between her audience and the intimidating world of modern literature. She showed the connections between the themes of these books and the themes that she addressed in her shows. She transformed this rarefied world into something personal, engaging and transformational for her audience. In the process, she was able to serve as a guide or interlocutor to lead millions of viewers into this new territory. This approach had tremendous power in creating a new segment of readers. It changed the way her viewers saw literature and changed the way many writers and publishers looked at their audiences. No longer were they publishing just for reviewers. They were publishing for Winfrey and the readers she represented. Once her audience began to follow her lead, she could take them in many directions because she was a trusted source of advice.

## Build a World Order: The Harpo Infrastructure to Support the Oprah Brand

Winfrey created an infrastructure to support her new model of a personal talk show. While others such as Martha Stewart went public or added their names to diverse products, Winfrey jealously guarded both her name and her growing empire, protecting the brand and her model for her entertainment company—a private company, Harpo, Inc. (Oprah spelled backward). This tight control not only helped to build her personal fortune, but also ensured control over the editorial content of her show, magazine and other projects. She made sure that these projects expressed her own thinking and personality.

The *Oprah Winfrey Show* won several Emmys for Best Talk Show, and Winfrey was honored as Best Talk Show Host. In 1993, she won the Horatio Alger Award, given to people who overcome adversity to become leaders in their fields. She was named by *Time* in 1996 as one of America's 25 most influential people. She has also appeared on the *Forbes* list of the highest-paid entertainers.

Along the way, she has consistently reinvented herself, her industry, and the thinking of her viewers. She brought her mental models to the talk show and transformed it. Her message to her viewers is to challenge themselves as well. She made her viewers aware of the limits of their own mental models and the possibilities in their own lives. As she said during one of her live "Live Your Best" road shows, "If you're open to the possibilities, your life gets grander, bigger, bolder!"[3]

What are the distinctive experiences of your own childhood and background, and how have they shaped the way you look at the world? What possibilities do your unique mental models allow you to see in the way that Oprah Winfrey saw the opportunity to re-envision the talk show? What new perspectives have you applied in one area that might be carried out to other areas, in the way that Winfrey transferred her personal approach to communication from broadcasting to the book club to magazines?

# ANDY GROVE

Andy Grove, who would become the fourth employee and the driving force of chipmaker Intel, began his life in turbulence. Born in 1936 of Jewish parents in Hungary, he lived through the harrowing times of World War II and the Holocaust. He then lived through the Communist takeover of Hungary and in 1956 fled to the United States at the time of the Hungarian uprising.[4] After studying chemical engineering and earning a Ph.D. from Berkeley in 1963, he joined the startup Fairchild Semiconductor at the outset of the semiconductor revolution. His very harsh childhood may have shaped his "resolute nature," determination and drive to succeed. The discipline of a deep engineering education provided him with formidable analytical skills, an understanding of the importance of detail, and a bias toward data and its meaning. He continued to build new perspectives on this base as he built Intel into a leading corporation and transformed his own thinking in the process.

## Continuous Reinvention and Experimentation

The founding of Intel by Bob Noyce and Gordon Moore forms the starting point for Grove's personal business journey. His initial responsibilities were engineering and production, and he brought a hard-driving focus to operations. Grove was known as the details guy. He was, observes Tim Jackson, the weekly technology columnist for the *Financial Times*, "brilliantly intelligent and articulate, driven, obsessive, neat, and disciplined." His personal and business experience led him to recognize the importance of impermanence, which led to what he later cultivated as an attitude of "paranoia" and a focus on the dynamics of changing his thinking and transforming the business.[5]

In the late 1970s, as the complexities of the microcomputer revolution took hold, multiple challenges faced Intel. To deal with them, the firm had a formidable set of management talent across many areas, including marketing and design. Its main strength lay in semiconductor manufacturing, a notoriously difficult technology to control. More innovative microprocessor designs began to appear in the market from Motorola and Zilog, and Intel felt the threat. The firm's reaction was the infamous "Operation Crush"—an uncompromising effort to destroy the burgeoning competition. It was quintessential Grove, total paranoia and a focused "no-holds-barred" effort to eliminate the threat. It worked, and Intel went on to dominate the world's microcomputer industry with a market share exceeding 90 percent.

Grove set a pace for continued leadership through experimentation and a planned obsolescence of chip designs, from the x86 series through multiple iterations of Pentium and beyond. This was a courageous path for a market leader, which suffers the most from disruption and cannibalization. But the relentless pace of change in the industry, Grove recognized, meant that either he would obsolete his own products or someone else would. He saw the opportunity to keep advancing chipmaking and creating new value. Intel was able to sustain profits and market leadership by continually moving forward. This model in itself differed radically from the classic one of protecting current technology and advantages. The pursuit of "smaller, faster and cheaper" led to experimentation in leading-edge fields such as nanotechnology. It also led to exploration of applications such as multimedia that would draw upon the added power of the chips.

## Changing Horses: The Strategic Inflection Point

The journey of both Intel and Grove, now at the epicenter of both the semiconductor and the microcomputer revolutions, was rife with change and stress. The industry undergoes periodic revolutions that require players to reinvent themselves along the way. The unrelenting progress predicted by "Moore's Law," enunciated by one of Intel's founders, Gordon Moore, required a continuous investment in all aspects of research and production on a staggering scale. Grove had to balance the need for discipline and predictability in the production of devices of ever-increasing complexity against the need to evolve and grow in areas where there was very little previous experience or knowledge.

During the 1980s, Intel made the courageous decision to abandon its core business, that of semiconductor dynamic memory (DRAM), and focus instead on the microcomputer. This decision and Intel's subsequent in microcomputer chips provide a dramatic example of a "strategic inflection point," one of Grove's evolving concepts. He has likened it to "a mental map of the New World," where the territory may be unknown but the need for a shift in thinking and action is recognized. He argues that these points can be found in businesses outside of high technology and even in one's career, where one sees the need to change horses.

In his writing, Grove describes the challenge of determining whether one has reached a true inflection point. Change is often a gradual process, and we normalize small changes until they become more serious. The problem is to detect whether the change we observe is a meaningful signal or just noise. The ideal is to make important changes while the business is still healthy. Often, warning signs are overlooked. Different people, too, can see the same picture and make very different interpretations, which Grove calls "strategic dissonance" and we have referred to as "adaptive disconnects."

## Using Paranoia and Cassandras to See Things Differently

Grove encourages the role of Cassandras, prophets of doom, within the business. These doomsayers can give early warning of impending change. They can also suggest new mental models that the business should consider. Grove encourages broad and extensive debate involving multiple levels of management and external perspectives, particularly those of customers. These diverse perspectives help to challenge the current mental model and change it when it needs to be changed. Given the uncertainty of the environment, Grove also argues for experimentation to resolve "strategic dissonance"—such as trying different techniques, products or sales channels.

## Intuition

Given Grove's reputation for valuing data and associated analytics, it is extremely interesting how he invokes the role of intuition. He has observed that data is usually about the past, whereas inflection points are about the future. While information and perspectives from customers and Cassandras can help, there is often no straightforward, logical path to the recognition of an inflection point. One must move beyond the rational extrapolation of data, and Grove has compared the leap from one business paradigm to another at these inflection points as going through "the valley of death."

## A Two-way Street: Adding Market Perspective to Engineering Through "Intel Inside"

While the technology continuously changes, the marketing of new chips demands continuity. Intel recognized this by developing the *Intel Inside* campaign to build the brand. Until then, chip making had been primarily a business-to-business (B2B) activity where chips were sold based on performance and price. With rising competition, a recognizable consumer brand had become more important. The branding strategy shifted the chip from a hidden piece of hardware inside the machine to something of value that consumers were willing to pay extra for. The brand advertising was iconic and emotional, without any mention of processor speed or other specs that were typical engineering concerns. This was a shift from a purely engineering view of the world to a marketcentric one.

The increasing brand recognition had its downside, posing a challenge to the thinking of an organization built upon engineering. The difficulty of balancing an engineering and marketing perspective showed up in the so-called floating-point problem in the 1990s. Intel microcomputer chips are hideously complex and carry out a wide range of complex actions, so testing all the possible permutations of use is immensely challenging. Intel had shipped a new product, and errors were detected in using the processors for certain complicated mathematical calculations. This was not surprising, and it affected only a small number of customers. It had been viewed as an engineering problem, but it became instead a major media event, of the sort engendered by defective consumer products, with CNN turning up at Grove's office for comment.

Because of its history and old mental models, Intel initially handled this problem the same old way—as an engineering problem. It did not recognize that its world was now radically different. Grove ultimately grasped the situation and initiated a consumer-style product recall, even though in most instances it was probably unnecessary. This cost Intel around $500 million, but preserved the company's reputation in the market. Grove later recounted the lesson this episode taught—that Intel needed to look at things in different ways than they had traditionally. The business could no longer be approached from an engineering perspective alone. Consumer perceptions were increasingly important, even though the "old order" of an engineering mindset continued to influence thinking in the company.

Grove and Intel have been phenomenally successful by consistently challenging their mental models and the models of their industry.

What are the "strategic inflection points" in your own business and life? How do you recognize them before it is too late? When you reach such a point, will you have the courage to give up your current mental model to embrace a new one, in the way that Grove shifted from DRAM chips to PC chips? Do you have the fortitude to cannibalize your current business to continue to shape the models of the future?

## CONCLUSIONS

Each of these profiles demonstrates the power of impossible thinking. Howard Schultz, Oprah Winfrey and Andy Grove were told at various points along the way that what they were trying to do was impossible. Yet they were able to embrace a different view of the world. For Schultz, it was the vision of an American espresso bar, for Winfrey it was an intimate talk-show format focused on the personal transformation of the audience, and for Grove it was a continuous evolution of the company and industry across discontinuous "inflection points." The stories of their successes reinforce some of the key messages of the book:

- *Recognizing the influence of childhood, education and early work in shaping their mental models.* These innovators drew upon their childhood and early career experiences to develop a distinctive world view. Schultz used his concern for workers developed while growing up in the housing projects as well as his experience in sales and his exposure to the coffee knowledge of the company's founders. Winfrey drew upon the themes of a difficult childhood and the transformation of her own life in re-creating the talk show. Groves drew perspectives from the chaos of war in Europe as well as his engineering education to combine hard-driving precision with a "paranoid" commitment to change. Each was able to leverage the distinctive perspectives arising from their early experiences, which some might have seen as a liability, as a platform for challenging the current view of their companies, their industries and the world. Part of their power was in tapping the perspectives of their personal lives and applying them to their business initiatives and to making changes in the broader society. *What unique perspectives have you have gained through your life and career experience that you can apply to current challenges in work, life and society? How can you use the parts of your experience that you might have thought of as failures or hardships to take a fresh view of these challenges?*

■ *Keeping their models relevant.* Even though they used their early experiences as a starting point to challenge current models of those around them, these innovators did not become fixed in their views. All three were committed to seeking out fresh perspectives and continuing to challenge the status quo. This allowed their organizations to continue to grow and helped them avoid the one-hit-wonder syndrome of a great idea that becomes calcified. They continued to experiment with fresh ideas. Starbucks experimented with global expansion, new channels such as supermarkets and new products in its stores. Winfrey stretched from her success in broadcasting to books, magazines and the Internet. Grove preserved the engineering genius of Intel with constant product innovations, even while embracing the foreign territory of marketing. Their models were not fixed and static. They were vibrant and alive, which allowed them to sustain growth and success long after their original model might have become mature or entered decline without this attention to renewal. *How are you challenging your current mental models? What are you doing to experiment to keep them fresh and relevant?*

■ *Making things happen by transforming the world around them.* Many people have radical ideas and perspectives on the world that amount to nothing. These three individuals have had a major impact on our world because they not only challenged existing models but were able to bring many other people along with them on this journey. They paid attention to the infrastructure needed to support the new order—from Starbucks' network of well-paid and trained baristas and coffee suppliers, to Winfrey's tightly controlled operating company, to Grove's initiatives in engineering, manufacturing and marketing. People who a decade ago had never heard of an espresso drink now find themselves ordering a "venti Caramel Macchiato" without a second thought. Television viewers who had never read a work of serious fiction are led by Oprah Winfrey into this new territory. Computer buyers who know nothing about hard drives and processing speed are looking for the "Intel Inside" symbol or thinking about how to speed up multimedia applications. These three leaders not only came up with a new way of seeing things, but they were able to change the way we look at the world and how we act. They reframed the dialog in a way that had broad repercussions across our society. To do this they addressed very hard operational and human issues, overcoming obstacles and converting the doubters. They built organizations to support their views of the world and created reinforcing infrastructures. They engaged in the difficult process of changing the minds of people around them, first in their own organizations and then in the broader world. All of this was what Edison referred to as the 99 percent perspiration that must support a dash of inspiration to comprise genius. This sweat and attention to operational details separates the radical thought from the transformational idea. *How can you get others to see and follow your new way of thinking? What combination of education and supporting infrastructure is needed to allow you to go from thinking the impossible to doing the impossible? How do you retain the humility to change your own thinking in the process?*

- **Acting quickly and effectively.** These three individuals were not afraid to act. While they continued to learn, challenge and change their models, they often acted on their own intuition against the advice of advisors. Schultz drove forward with his intuition about his espresso bar against the opposition of the Starbucks founders. Winfrey resisted attempts to make over her image and render her more mainstream, maintaining faith in the power of her distinctive view of the world. Grove was able to make the gutsy move out of DRAMs, abandoning the source of Intel's past success, to bet the company on the microcomputer chip business on the other side of this inflection point. *Do you tap into your intuition in making decisions? How do you ensure that you intuition is still valid in the current environment?*

These three profiles demonstrate the power of challenging the current model. Stories of this kind are easy to tell with hindsight, but very much harder to live with foresight. Thinking impossible thoughts and acting upon them takes great courage and perseverance. As these stories have shown, new mental models can have tremendous transformational power for the individuals who champion them, their companies and the world.

## IMPOSSIBLE THINKING

- Put yourself in the shoes of these three people early in their careers.

- Would you have had the guts and conviction to do what they did?

- If you look at your own world for areas where businesses are considered mature and products are commodities, do you have the power to break out of this model and reinvent them the way Schultz did with coffee drinking?

- Can you use insights from your personal experiences to transform the way you approach your work in the way that Oprah Winfrey brought her own personality into the redesign of the talk show?

- If you look to reinvent your products and services, do you have the courage—and paranoia—to cannibalize and destroy your existing business, as Grove did, even when you control the market?

# ENDNOTES

1. Schultz, Howard. *Pour Your Heart Into It,* New York: Hyperion, 1997, p. 44.

2. Lacayo, Richard. "Oprah Turns the Page," *Time,* 15 April 2002, p. 63.

3. Sellers, Patricia. "The Business of Being Oprah," *Fortune,* 1 April 2002.

   4. Jackson, Tim. *Inside Intel: The Story of Andrew Grove and the Rise of the World's Most Powerful Chip Company*, Dutton, 1997; Grove, Andrew S. *High Output Management*, Vintage Books, 1985.

   5. Grove, Andrew S. *Only the Paranoid Survive: How to Exploit the Crisis Points That Challenge Every Company*, New York: Doubleday, 1999.

# 12

# CHALLENGING YOUR OWN THINKING: PERSONAL, BUSINESS AND SOCIETY

Discovery consists of seeing what everybody has seen
and thinking what nobody has thought.

—Albert von Szent-Gyorgyi

## Friend or foe?

In the fog of war, you see a person standing in front of you with a weapon raised. In the midst of the battlefield noise and confusion, it has been a feat even to single out this one soldier. You have an instant to make a decision. Your ability to make sense of the situation could mean life or death for you or for a comrade. You choose. You fire.

The difficulty of making sense in these conditions is shown by the numerous deaths in wars from "friendly fire." The wrong mental model can be as dangerous as an enemy with an automatic weapon.

Every day you are faced with decisions in which you need to make sense of the world around you, quickly and with insufficient information. While the consequences of making sense are rarely so immediate and deadly as those on the battlefield, the models you adopt can have a tremendous impact on your world. They shape, often in dramatic ways, how you approach decisions about personal life (diet and exercise or work/life balance), your businesses (investing in e-business), and society (addressing terrorism or poverty). How do your mental models affect the way you understand and act in the world? In this chapter, we explore applications from personal life, business and society, and we invite you to challenge your own mental models.

Impossible thinking is not an academic curiosity. The goal of becoming better at impossible thinking is to be able to understand the world better, apply the most effective models for a particular situation and *act*. Models may appear ephemeral and abstract, but the costs and implications of our mental models are very real. The fact that most of what we see comes from inside our minds doesn't mean we should treat it as an illusion.

Our models shape our worlds and our actions. They affect our health, our relationships, our business performance and the quality of life in our society. The models used by business leaders can lead them to adulation or incarceration and can move their companies into boom times or bankruptcy. Mental models can keep groups of people in society in backward poverty and ignorance or propel them rapidly forward. We have seen how shifts in models by political leaders such as Konrad Adenauer in West Germany after World War II, Fidel Castro in Cuba, Pol Pot in Cambodia or Saddam Hussein in Iraq have retarded or advanced the quality of life for all the people of their nations. We also have seen how sudden shifts in long-held models, such as the end of the Cold War and its mindsets, can transform the lives of individual citizens and the dynamics of global politics. Our models shape our world in many ways.

In the three examples that follow, we explore ways of thinking about and challenging our mental models related to health (personal), the e-business (business), and addressing terrorism while protecting privacy (society). How can the insights in this book help address these issues? We then present a process for thinking through your own models and give you a diverse set of examples upon which to practice.

## HEALTHY THINKING: MAKING SENSE IN PERSONAL LIFE

The mental models we apply to our health and wellness can lead to very different actions and outcomes. There are Eastern models of treatment (such as acupuncture) and Western ones (such as pharmaceuticals and surgery). There are chiropractic professionals. There is a focus on nutrition and exercise. There is also a dividing line between a focus on *prevention* versus a focus on *treatment*. And there is a constant flow of information, some of it conflicting, about different strategies for diet and health.

Osteopathic medicine also initially offered a distinct alternative to traditional medicine. Its philosophy, developed by 19th-century physician Andrew Taylor Still, provided a holistic view of health in sharp contrast to the traditional medical approach. It was based on four principles—(1) body, mind and spirit are a unity; (2) the body is capable of self-regulation, (3) self-healing and health maintenance; (4) structure and function are reciprocally interrelated—and treatment is based on an understanding of these principles. While American osteopathic physicians are still trained in this philosophy, they also learn all aspects of medicine and surgery. As osteopaths have moved away from these core principles, the practice has become less distinctive. Their role has become more narrowly defined as the manipulation of bones for treating disease, and they have eroded their valuable mental model of using a systemic approach to treating disease.

Our mental models also have a direct impact on our health. Something that we believe will make us better may help to some extent because we believe in it. The well-known "placebo effect" demonstrates that some test subjects exhibit a positive benefit after taking a sugar pill that they believe is an actual medication. The pill itself has no effect, but they believe that it works, and this may make them better. There are obvious limits to the potential for positive thinking, but in some cases the best treatment could be the treatment you have the most confidence in.

How do you sort out the various mental models related to health and wellness and apply the most effective ones? Among the possible approaches are:

- **Seek out new models.** You first need to familiarize yourself with alternative approaches. What are other ways of treating illness and promoting wellness? Seek out new sources of information by reading widely or discussing with friends and alternative practitioners. What are the strengths and weaknesses of these various approaches? Look even at some alternatives that you consider absurd—there may be some hidden value in them or they might be combined with other approaches.

- *Create a portfolio of approaches.* A focus on preventive medicine doesn't exclude the use of medical interventions. Some proponents of alternative medicine may view the paradigm shift to a preventive approach as a one-way street away from more traditional approaches. But many people combine the two approaches. They choose to use a holistic approach when the risks are not too high compared to the potential side effects of medical treatments. For example, you might rely on chicken soup and other foods, teas and vitamins to treat a mild illness rather than going on antibiotics. As long as the disease is not serious, this may be a more effective approach. But if you contract Lyme disease, which can have serious consequences if not quickly treated with antibiotics, you use a pharmaceutical approach. Many individuals avoid becoming dogmatically attached to one approach or another, but select the best one for the specific situation. Often this selection is not explicit or conscious but intuitively happens as the mind uses what it considers to be a coherent set of models that work, addressing different aspects of experience—even though the models may appear to be logically incompatible on specific analysis. How can you build a portfolio of approaches to health and wellness?

- *Know when to shift from one approach to another.* It is important to find a physician or other health practitioner who can apply both approaches or to develop a set of diverse professionals that you can consult on treatment. If you rely entirely on a holistic practitioner, you might tend to overlook serious symptoms that should be treated with traditional medicine. On the other hand, if you rely entirely on a traditionally trained doctor, you might tend to overdo medical treatments when there could be an equally effective or more effective alternative approach.

- *Sift through complexity.* Medical information is constantly changing. Today's study may be disproved tomorrow. Alternative cures are riddled with fads and quack remedies that often are supported by compelling arguments but not by rigorous research. How do you sift through the complexities of this constant flow of information?

As discussed in Chapter 6, you can zoom in and zoom out, making a detailed examination of the studies upon which new medical approaches are based and then looking at the bigger picture. You might be focusing on perfecting your diet, for example, while still smoking a pack a day and living a sedentary life. It may turn out that giving up smoking and increasing exercise could have the greatest impact on the quality of your life and your health. Stepping back and looking at the broader picture is key in avoiding the pitfalls of cognitive fixation or being overwhelmed by data. This process of zooming in and out can keep you from being paralyzed by too broad a context and from jumping too quickly into new fads. Part of this process is to develop areas of interest that serve your needs, so that you don't have to examine everything. Any "advice" that excludes all others and wants your exclusive focus, promising incredible benefits, entails a loss of context and balance. You need to look more critically to sift for sense in this stream of shifting data.

■ *Understand your own models.* Assess the mental models that you use to filter health-related advice and information. What influences from your past cause you to view this information in this way? What is your interest level, and what is your attitude toward the topic overall? Is it: (1) fear of knowing (burying your head in the sand), (2) vague interest but a sense that this is not a priority in life, (3) interested but distracted by other competing concerns, (4) very interested and willing to spend time or (5) recognition of a major concern on which you are willing to spend extensive time and effort? Each of these attitudes and related mental models needs to be self-assessed. For example, the last one, recognition of a major concern, may well be shaped by either a health crisis or a medical examination highlighting a personal risk one may be under. Alternatively you may be a teenager, feel immortal, and have more pressing issues in your life, so your mental model is more along the lines of "vaguely interested." This attitude will shape the way you approach issues of health and well-being.

■ *Conduct your own experiments.* What works for one person in preserving health may not work for another. You can read all the medical research you want, but you also have to find out what works for you. Make changes in your diet and observe the result. Experiment with different forms of exercise. The fitness center or exercise video that works for one person might not work for you. Maybe a morning walk or weekend rollerblading might fit with your lifestyle and interests and so be more effective. Maybe one diet will work for a friend but be a disaster for you, either because it requires behavioral changes that are difficult to sustain or because you respond to it differently. Many people start a new exercise program or diet and then beat themselves up because they fail. If, instead, they see it as an experiment, they can note the results and move on to try another one. While it is important to exercise consistently to make progress, keep experimenting until you find something that works.

■ *Recognize the structures that reinforce the old models.* As we discussed in Chapter 8, our mental models are reinforced by the structures we have built around them. The smoking break at work reinforces this habit. To change our behavior, we have to address not only our mental models but also the structures that hold them in place. This can be the most difficult part of the process. Many diet programs address this challenge by creating social systems and mentors that reinforce the new behavior, by establishing systems of calorie counting that transform the way members see their diet or by setting up a complete set of meals that provide an alternative, and presumably healthier, universe with a more limited set of dietary options. Changing habits that affect your health and well-being requires a change in the structures that support these habits. You need to recognize that it is difficult to change behavior and begin to dismantle the infrastructure that locks you into the old order.

Your views of weight control, diet, exercise, cancer prevention, smoking, alcohol, stress and time management, and your attitudes toward medical advice, affect the quality of your life. What are your current models in these areas? How do they differ from those of the people around you? Try to find someone with a very different viewpoint whom you know personally or an author who has written on these subjects. If you adopted this viewpoint, how would the quality of your life change? Can you conduct a thought experiment, trying to see the world through this person's eyes?

How would your life be better or worse? Would this mental model be more useful to you? What are the risks?

If you have expressed the desire to change your behaviors related to health and wellness, consider that what holds you back may be not merely a "weak will" but rather the strength of your current models. You believe that what you see is, in fact, the world, while most of it is in your mind. If you can change your mind, you can think impossible thoughts and change the way you achieve your health and wellness goals.

## OTHER PERSONAL CHALLENGES AND THE MODELS BENEATH THEM

**Balancing work and personal life.** With the abandonment of the traditional career model of working one's way up through the ranks of a single company until retirement, we face a much more complex view of work and its balance with personal life. To balance professional achievements with personal fulfillment, employees are finding creative approaches such as job sharing, telecommuting and flexible work arrangements. What model of work and personal life shapes your thinking? Does it work well for you? What other models could you apply, and how would they change the quality of your career and life?

**Personal economics.** Economic downturns and corporate mismanagement have eroded faith in traditional company pensions as well as in the consistent returns from investments. As people live longer, planning carefully for retirement becomes more important. There are complex choices to make about financial planning for the future, and they are shaped by our mental models. The government cannot guarantee our retirement, so a tension arises between spending today and finding ways to effectively save and invest for a future that looks increasingly unpredictable. What are the mental models that shape your view of retirement? Are they still valid, given changes in the environment?

**Marriage and relationships.** With reality television shows in which would-be brides or grooms offer themselves for marriage to partners sight unseen, the models for our marriages and relationships have been stretched to the limits. Some have dismissed the need for formal institutions at all, and others have argued for a model of serial relationships. Same-sex couples are battling for the recognition of legal rights for their often long-standing unions against opponents who see this as a threat to the institution of marriage that might unravel the fabric of society. Even so, the enduring mental models of a "traditional family" still exert an influence, even if they never reflected the true reality of relationships and are even less relevant today. Attitudes toward divorce and particularly its impact on children have also changed over time. What is your current model for relationships, and how was it formed? What are the models held by your partners in your relationships? Does your current view still work? What are some alternative models you might adopt?

**Ad hoc work communities.** With even the U.S. Army, that most collective of all enterprises, touting a slogan of "an army of one," work has become a much more individual process. Employees are viewing work as an opportunity to develop marketable skills rather than as a step on a career path within a single firm. With outsourcing, organizations are much more like networks of individuals. Loyalty to an organization once was a key concern, but now with more ad hoc work communities, the loyalty is much more to a specific task. This has changed the model of what it means to be an organization. What work relationships do you have now? Upon what mental models are these relationships based? What other models could you adopt, and how would they change the way you act in the world?

## DOT-COM: MAKING SENSE IN BUSINESS

The Internet swept into our world like the tornado in *The Wizard of Oz*, lifting us up and transporting us out of our old world into a bizarre new one, with wonderful possibilities and unexpected dangers. Then, after a long and difficult journey along this yellow brick road, we clicked our heels together to find ourselves back where we started. Like Dorothy, of course, we are not completely back where we started, because our mental models have been shaken and stirred. We may be in Kansas again, but we will never look at it in the same way. And, unlike Dorothy's, our world has in fact been transformed in fundamental ways by this new technology. The perception of e-business moved from unstoppable fad to absolute failure and now is swinging back toward center. Our ability to take advantage of this technology depends upon our business models, which, in turn, depend upon our mental models. What can we learn about mental models from the dot-com bubble and its aftermath? Here are a few of the lessons:

- **_Understand your models._** During the bubble, much attention was given to compelling stories about potential ventures and very little to classical "business models" and their underlying mental models. Arguments were made to accept a new mental model that was not very clearly presented or understood. As events unfolded, instigators, observers, investors and customers were persuaded that they were all participants in truly revolutionary events. There was a widespread belief that they had entered a parallel universe where things were happening in "Web time." Managers were persuaded that the old mental models they employed to make sense of the world no longer worked here. Those who expressed skepticism "did not get it" and were viewed by many as regressive or out of touch. Previous experience was viewed as a liability. The growth rates were unique and the scale was phenomenal. Millions of users were joining the community every month at unprecedented rates.

  The unique nature of the experience was further reinforced by the financial and investment aspects of the various participating businesses. Simply put, the valuations and associated investments were outside everyone's experience. No one had seen such things before, so people had to create new models for their investments and understanding of businesses _on the fly._ The old models did not appear to explain what was going on, and the new models were so exciting that few looked carefully at their potential weaknesses. There was too little careful and rigorous examination of the strengths and weaknesses of either the old or new models.

What mental models shape your current view of the Internet and its value to your business? What alternative models could you use to assess its potential and apply it to your business?

- **Know when to switch horses.** As we saw with Lord Simpson, we need to be wary of being swept away by fads. With all the media hype about the Internet and all the investment dollars flowing in, it became hard to think rationally. There was also a problem of a lack of history, so that any story became credible. People gave up their old mental models without identifying a clearly articulated new model to replace them. Some did attempt to see these events through less rose-colored glasses by going back into history and comparing the meteoric rise of the dot-coms to events in the 17th century, such as the "South Sea Bubble" in England or the "Tulip Bubble" in Holland. Many companies also fell into the pattern of the midlife crisis, postponing change for long periods and then making dramatic and often destructive leaps. On the other hand, some investors knew when to jump in *and* jump out. They got in before the bubble, got out before it burst and profited greatly. Some were just lucky, but others apparently had a model that recognized the run-up as "irrational exuberance" and then found ways to exploit this understanding to profit from it.

What are the potential risks and rewards of sticking with your current mental models or changing them to embrace new technologies and other emerging opportunities?

- **Recognize that paradigm shifts are a two-way street.** The companies that saw the rise of the Internet as a revolution were like the people who sailed off on the *Titanic* without lifeboats. The ones who were able to see the world through multiple models and move back and forth between them often had the best chances of surviving. Webvan went bankrupt trying to sell groceries online, while retailer Tesco in the UK, with an established network of retail stores, found they could add on a very profitable online business, using their existing stores to facilitate local deliveries. Tesco realized it didn't have to throw away its current model in order to embrace the new model of the Internet. Even a strictly online retailer such as Amazon clearly understood the old models and used this understanding to transform its operations and economics, while other online businesses crashed and burned around it. It built partnerships with bricks-and-mortar retailers in toys and books and transformed its focus from building market share at any cost to producing returns.

The Internet revolutionaries claimed that everything needed to be changed: personnel policies, financial rewards and measurements, dress codes, software development methods, customer channels and so on. After the dot-com bubble burst, in established companies the pendulum swung entirely in the other direction, so the online businesses were abandoned with the same passion with which they were once embraced. As these firms returned with a vengeance to the old models, they may have overlooked some of the continued value and power of the new technology by becoming counterrevolutionaries.

What is the value of the old mental models in the new e-business world? How can the new models and the old be integrated? What does it cost to keep these different models open as options?

■ *See a new way of seeing.* Early in the development of the Internet, few companies had the experience to recognize its potential. The Internet was dismissed and marginalized for a long time before the development of Web browsers, and even then for a while its potential was recognized only by a few insiders. If companies had invited these wild-eyed Internet pioneers—the kids with the pierced ears and colored hair—into their organizations, they would have had a head start in gaining the kind of experience with the technology and the mental models of this subculture that could have helped in making later decisions. The Internet itself operated for many years as the exclusive domain of academics and programmers. Why weren't more companies already playing on this playground?

What are some emerging opportunities in the online world (such as blogs and wikis)? How can you tap into these developments and use them to rethink your business models and underlying mental models?

■ *Sift sense from streams of complexity.* In the 20/20 hindsight that was brought to bear on the Internet bubble, many people forgot how truly confusing and complex the emerging technologies of the 1990s had been. Just a few years before the Internet took off with the development of the Web browser, the transformational model was going to be "interactive television." Companies invested hundreds of millions of dollars into this technology. But how could companies recognize where the technology was headed and understand the implications? Some managers remained zoomed out and just looked at the big picture; some became so focused on a specific technology such as interactive television that they failed to see the potential of other technologies. The strategy of zooming in to understand and gain hands-on experience with the technologies (it was amazing how many CEOs in the early days of the Internet had never even been online) and then zooming out to look at the broader context could have helped in making sense of a very confusing picture.

What are the new areas of technology development and application on the horizon today? How can you discover them and recognize their potential to change mental models and business models?

■ *Engage in experiments.* Many experiments took place with the rise of the dot-coms, and at one stage it seemed as though the whole dot-com explosion was one gigantic personal and business experiment. Unfortunately many of these "experiments" were not designed in a way that maximized learning, and they were not done on a small enough scale to test some interesting hypotheses before larger investments were made. They were mostly large, parallel and often competing "bet the farm" activities with an unending flow of venture and corporate capital funding. The failures were big, and they swallowed a great deal of shareholder value. Some companies did make more careful experiments. In consumer goods, P&G's Reflect.com site for bath and beauty products offered a way for it to learn about the potential of e-business before making further investments or disrupting its existing retail partners. Most Internet experiments, however, were extremely costly and the payoffs very uncertain in terms of deep learning.

How can you learn from post-mortems of natural experiments of your company and other firms in using the Internet? What new experiments can you design?

- **Bridge adaptive disconnects.** One problem of the Internet was the dichotomy between insiders and outsiders. It was important to work to bridge the gap between these two worlds. Some companies recognized that their existing cultures would kill these new startups, so they wisely set them up as independent operations, often based in Silicon Valley. But often they didn't build bridges between these two worlds so that the startups could benefit from the experience of the old company and vice versa. These divides between the two worlds limited the usefulness of the different models and made it harder to recognize problems. A distinctive adaptive disconnect was the attitude of some in the dot-com arena who declared that the nonbelievers "did not get it" and that it was simply impossible to coexist. No attempt was made to bridge the gap, and this proved to be a major obstacle to mutual learning and the development of hybrid organizations.

How can you bridge the adaptive disconnects in your organization? How, for example, can you bring the technology leaders and business leaders together to understand the business implications of new technologies?

- **Consider the infrastructure.** Although the scaffolding that supports the old order is usually built up over a long period, in the case of the dot-coms the structures of our society supported the new models in ways that made their progress nearly irresistible. The amount of capital invested in the global telecommunications infrastructure proved to be vastly in excess of its real need. This investment became the basis for just having to believe the new model, since to not believe would have made this phenomenal investment, literally hundreds of billions of excess dollars, an irrational and inexplicable act. The growth of venture capital firms, the rise of the NASDAQ and the increase in individual investment created a supporting infrastructure that drove investments in these Internet startups to remarkable levels. The advance in equity values was so phenomenal for most dot-com companies that many ordinary people changed long-held investment habits and became day traders or simply less cautious investors, not wanting to lose out on these unprecedented gains. The rapid spread of personal computers in the office and home, together with falling computer and communication costs, also conspired to support these new businesses and their related mental models. At the same time, the strength of the "old world" infrastructure was eroded as traditional "hard goods" companies saw their market valuations collapse, even while they continued to post strong performance.

What investments, structures and processes of your current business make it hard for you to embrace new technologies and new mental models? What aspects of your infrastructure can be redesigned to support the new models you wish to embrace?

■ *Trust your intuition—but gain the experience to change it.*
During the dot-com revolution, very few people had the fortitude to hold out against the tide, trusting their own intuition against the relentless hype and the undeniable financial returns of the Internet. But the revolutionaries were right in noting that an intuition based on the past is often dangerous in a new environment. Like the old generals, you are fighting the last war. Intuition differs from insight in that it is grounded in experience. The challenge then is to gain enough experience in the new technology and models so that your intuition is drawn from deep experience. It was the rare senior executive who sought out this kind of experience. Many left the deep experience with the technology to the IT department—it makes sense to delegate this kind of technical detail—but what these leaders often failed to appreciate was the importance of having hands-on experience to refine their personal intuition. This was even more important because their customers, in the millions, were now embracing this technology. These were not

just technology decisions on the table but also strategic decisions with major implications for the organization. As a result of this lack of experience, business leaders either were convinced that they could not trust their current intuition or else embraced a new "intuition" about the potential of this technology that was not grounded in experience. In part, this also explains the rise of the Internet "gurus" who sought to be thought leaders. Some even achieved star-like status for a brief shining moment.

What does your intuition tell you about how you should use the Internet and other technologies? Can you trust your current intuition? How can you refine your intuition through new experiences?

## OTHER BUSINESS CHALLENGES AND THE MODELS BENEATH THEM

**Strategic planning.** How can organizations plan in a world of rapid change, complexity and uncertainty? It became clear to many large companies in the early 1980s that centralized planning was no longer fast, flexible or creative enough to address the challenges of the current environment. By the time the well-researched, five- or ten-year plans were released in big bound notebooks, they were already obsolete. These planning processes were based on the assumption that the future is predictable, so that viable long-term plans can be made accordingly, but the world has become increasingly unpredictable. In 1983, Jack Welch, CEO of General Electric, dismantled the company's heralded centralized planning initiatives. Over the decades that followed, there was a range of planning approaches. Some companies and consultants continued to develop new, more forward-looking approaches for creating a grand strategy. During the dot-com era, strategic planning sometimes consisted of little more than an optimistic business plan or story line. There was a series of revolutions in strategy making, some of them later viewed as fads. Some companies implemented broader and more flexible approaches such as scenario planning and options thinking to explicitly address the uncertainties of the environment. Other firms turned aside from strategy to focus more on achieving both operational efficiencies and short-term objectives. Some corporate leaders just abandoned strategic planning altogether, concluding that the environment was too uncertain to do anything else.

What is the current mental model that shapes your strategic planning? What are alternative models? Which of these models will work best for your organization?

**To grow or not to grow?** Many companies have built their strategies around a traditional model of consistent growth, but does this model become dysfunctional when growth is not possible or reaches its natural limits? The commitments of investors to value growth per se make it hard for companies to abandon this growth model, even when opportunities are becoming more constricted. There are increasing questions about this model. Another challenge for U.S.-based global firms is to grow in an environment of increasing anti-U.S. sentiment. Another recent phenomenon is deflation and slow growth of major economies, such as Japan or Germany, making growth across the global economy problematic.

Are there ways of creating value other than just growing the top line? How does a focus on growth constrain your opportunities and actions? What other models have companies used to build and sustain successful businesses? Could you apply them to your business?

**Mergers and acquisitions.** Mergers and acquisitions often look good on paper, but their high failure rate shows they are not easy to make successful in practice. There are incentives for investment bankers and management to take an overly optimistic view of the synergies, and this contributes to failures. Differences in culture and problems in implementation often make the difference. Before the fact, these combinations are usually assessed through financial models, but the returns from these arrangements often depend on softer issues such as integrating culture and leadership that are difficult to assess on a balance sheet.

What are the potential problems related to a pending merger or acquisition that you might not see because of your mental models? What are other models for achieving your goals besides mergers or acquisitions, and how might you use them?

**Startups.** Experienced corporate managers who have joined new startups find that they need to adopt very different mental models for business organizations that have little past history, no established brand or reputation and scarce resources. The arrival of these "professional managers" is often a line of demarcation between the creative and free-flowing startup phase and the more intense focus on operations of the larger established company. Making the transition between these two views of the company is one of the key transition points and a place where many initially successful startups fail to become enduring corporations.

If you are involved in a successful startup, what mental models shaped your initial growth? How do these mental models need to change, now that you are larger and more successful? What models are needed at each stage of a firm's progress? If you are in a mature firm, how could your thinking benefit from importing the mindset of a startup into parts of the business?

**Improving poor corporate performance.** The typical mental model for improving poor performance is to cut costs, change senior management, write off nonperforming assets and fire people. If people are an asset, though, this can be destructive in the long run, and cost cutting can take you only so far. Aggressive cuts can lead to loss of your best people, leaving only the "tree huggers." Are there alternatives to the usual litany of cost-cutting measures to improve corporate performance? The three great controls of P&L, balance sheet and cash flow have made all the traditional mental models very narrow in their utility. Other options, in addition to the usual cost measures, must be explored. Instead of being viewed as a negative, the crisis can be seen as an opportunity to change mental models.

What is your current view of how to define and improve corporate performance? What are alternative models for improving performance besides cost cutting? How could they be applied to your business?

**Corporate governance.** There are a variety of different models for corporate governance. Some CEOs saw the corporate board as a necessary evil, to be managed and kept in check, treated as a social club, dazzled with presentations and then sent on its way. Others saw the board as a resource and partner that could offer valuable insights on strategy and other matters. After Enron and other scandals, the board is seen much more in its traditional role as watchdog for the interests of investors, expected to rigorously challenge management and take an active role in identifying problems and resolving them.

What models are shaping your view of corporate governance? What are some other models that you could apply?

# TERRORISM AND INDIVIDUAL RIGHTS: MAKING SENSE IN SOCIETY

Democratic societies have a strong concern for individual rights and privacy, but these individual rights often make it harder for law enforcement to protect society. Legal restrictions on activities such as wiretapping phones or bugging offices protect the rights of individuals but place obstacles in the way of authorities collecting information about illicit activities. Past abuses by various governments and administrators such as J. Edgar Hoover (FBI) in the United States and MI5 in London have made citizens very wary of intrusions into their personal lives.

After the terrorist attacks of September 11, there was renewed debate about how to balance the war on terrorism with the protection of individual rights. If government agencies had possessed more extensive information about wire transfers and the purchase of one-way airline tickets, all in one place, could this have helped them prevent such attacks?

There was a proposal for a "TIPS" program through which postal workers and cable installers would contribute tips about suspicious activities to a central database. There were roundups of people of Arab descent for questioning or detention, raising charges of racial profiling. To avoid such charges, airline screeners moved to random processes that led to patdowns of congressional representatives and mild-mannered elderly women, who didn't have the physical strength to carry out a terrorist plot, even if, by some strange fluke, they had the inclination. This approach may be politically correct but it is foolish, because it assumes the searcher gains no valuable information whatsoever from direct observation.

As discussed in Chapter 6, the government's Total Information Awareness (TIA) initiative may lead to information overload, and it also raises other issues. The system is designed to draw together diverse financial and personal records to allow the government to identify potential terrorist threats. These intrusions can be seen as an attack on the core principles of the United States.

How can we sort through these conflicting models and manage the conflicts in ways that promote both privacy and security?

■ *Focus on the utility of different models.* While much of the debate over increased information collection has focused on privacy and civil rights, there are, as discussed earlier in the book, fundamental questions about the effectiveness of this approach. All the information in the world will not necessarily lead to better intelligence and deeper wisdom about potential threats. There may be more creative approaches for addressing this challenge that do not entail the same incursions upon the rights of citizens. Monitoring could be more focused, and existing systems, such as requiring court orders for wiretapping and warrants for searches, could be extended a bit without being abandoned in the collection and analysis of information. A careful assessment of the effectiveness of the approaches could lead to the development of other strategies for waging the war on terrorism without making such severe sacrifices of personal freedom. The recent terrorist experiences of the United States are extensions of global terrorist phenomena involving many countries and many terror groups with various agendas. The complexity of fighting terrorism has already revealed much experimental knowledge (UK and the IRA, Spain and the ETA, Italy and Red Brigades, Israel and Hezbollah, etc.). This can be combined to build a rich mental-model repertoire for balancing the needs of individuals and the needs of the state fighting a ruthless terrorist adversary. The strength of a culture and its shared mental models, such as individuality in the United States, can be turned into a potent force for fighting terrorism instead of requiring the culture be changed in fundamental ways as part of the fight. What is the utility of different approaches to fighting terrorism and protecting privacy?

- **Encourage debate.** The presentation of these different views is critical in making sure the issues and implications of different strategies are carefully considered. By allowing the views both of the proponents of individual freedom and of those focusing on the challenge of finding terrorists, both goals can be more effectively addressed. The danger in such a situation is that the imperative of one side or the other becomes so great that opposing views are denied or dismissed. At the extreme, we move toward the kind of "Big Brother" mind control described by George Orwell in *1984*, where competing views are eliminated. The other extreme is the rise of local militias and an "every man for himself" paradigm with the loss of cohesion, shared values and mental models. By maintaining the ability to look at the issue from both individual and state viewpoints, we can better protect individual freedoms while identifying potential threats. How can we encourage debate about these issues to highlight the strengths and weaknesses of the different models?

- **Recognize different perspectives.** An individual may be willing to give up certain liberties in the short term, provided that they are restored when the problem disappears. The government, on the other hand, may have a different perspective. In the UK at the start of World War I, hours for consuming alcohol in pubs were restricted to aid the war effort. Not till 80 years later was this restriction substantially abated. Individuals and their governments, especially the bureaucracy, despite elections, may look at things completely differently. Because of these different perspectives, many individuals are reluctant to give up fundamental rights or to see them eroded. What are the different perspectives and players who are involved in addressing these issues? How do their mindsets differ?

## OTHER SOCIETAL CHALLENGES AND THE MODELS BENEATH THEM

**Market economy and democracy.** During the Cold War, the U.S. view of market economies and democracy presented a stark contrast to the Soviet view of centrally controlled economies and communism. Since the end of the Cold War, there has been more refinement of the views of market economies and democratic societies. What should these look like? What different models are available for creating democratic societies with free markets? The emergence of the United States as the sole global superpower has tended to make people more wary of the market economy. It is blamed, via globalization, for promoting U.S. interests and rendering companies no longer answerable to individual countries.

The concepts of globalization and the market economy are now being turned into negative aspects of the United States and are being used to shape mental models around the world. Also the unconstrained market economy has sometimes led to customer abuse and undesirable outcomes, making people think that a free market has to be subject to some type of control.

What are the various models for free markets, and what are their strengths and weaknesses in particular situations?

What model of economics and politics do you currently support? What other models might you adopt and what would be the implications of adopting them?

**Disparities between the "haves" and "have-nots."** There is a sharp contrast between the developed nations of the world and the emerging economies. These different "worlds" look at issues from very different perspectives. The dividing lines can be seen in debates over globalization, technological progress and the environment. Even within nations, there are sharp contrasts between the richer and poorer sectors of society, and these divides have been more sharply polarized with the shrinking of the middle class. The tax breaks that primarily benefit wealthier citizens are seen as stimulants for the economy from the perspective of the "haves." In the view of the "have-nots," on the other hand, these moves are seen as placing a larger tax burden on the poor, who can least afford to bear it, to put money in the pockets of the rich. The adaptive disconnects between these two groups worldwide is a critical challenge for government and society.

How do mental models contribute to the gaps between haves and have-nots? How could changes in mental models help to bridge the gaps and benefit both sides?

**Mental illness.** The way society has addressed mental illness has changed radically over time. In the Middle Ages, mental illness was usually seen as a form of possession that required exorcism or other religious interventions to remove the demons. Medicine took over by the end of the 18th century, but a prevailing view was that people with mental illness had regressed to the state of beasts and had to be shocked back to humanity. Doctors prescribed brutal regimens of confinement, blistering and cold immersion to the point of drowning. The mid 1800s, led by Quaker reformers, saw the rise of "moral treatments," in which patients were treated with respect and kindness and given activities, good food and clothing.

From the early 1900s up to the middle of the century, a genetic view of the world led to the rising popularity of eugenics, the view that the human race could be bred for success by weeding out "defective" individuals and races. This led to increased confinement of the mentally ill, the rise of large institutions and the promotion of lobotomies and other surgeries and forced sterilizations. This view, which had a wide following around the world, was taken to its ultimate and destructive extreme in the gas chambers of Nazi Germany. Subsequent decades saw the rise of pharmaceutical treatments, then the deinstitutionalizing of treatment, as large institutions were closed amid scandals and allegations of shocking mistreatment. There is still intense debate about the causes and treatment of mental illness—and even the existence of mental illness. In 1961, a U.S. commission on mental illness noted that it is a field "where fads and fancies flourish." The mental models held by society and individuals have led to significantly different treatments, laws and actions.[1]

What are the models that currently shape our treatment of mental illness in society? What other models from other eras or other parts of the world might be applied?

**Organizing global protests.** One aspect of society that has been changed by the emergence of the World Wide Web is that of social organization and interaction with government. Groups can organize much more quickly and interact much more directly with government officials around the globe as a result of e-mail and Web sites. Small grassroots movements can rapidly become national and international by organizing through the Internet, as exemplified by the protests against globalization at WTO meetings and the antiwar protests before and during the war in Iraq in 2003. We could say: *New York Times* columnist Patrick Tyler and other commentators have referred to this rise of global public opinion as a second "superpower" to challenge the United States.[2]

But is this an accurate model? Do the new online channels for political organization change the mental models of global geopolitics?

**U.S. and UN models for running the world.** The debate in the United Nations in early 2003 over military action against Iraq highlighted very different views of world governance. The United States presented a view of its right to take preemptive action against prospective threats from nations developing weapons of mass destruction. It moved forward with a "coalition of the willing." The UN stressed the need for multilateral action and the preservation of international institutions. From the U.S. viewpoint, the United Nations was weak-willed and ineffective in addressing this threat and Americans had a right to protect their own interests. From the UN perspective, the United States acted outside the international community, eroding its systems and structures.

What are the differences between these two models? What are the implications for the world of adopting either one? Are there other models that should be considered? How can both models exist side-by-side? If you are a proponent of one view, how could you bring people holding the other view around to your model?

## Keep Your Eye on the Model

Every issue you come across in your life can provide opportunities for exploring the impact of mental models and for developing or adopting new models. As you read stories in the morning paper, as you face challenges in your personal life, as you make decisions at work, ask yourself: What mental models are shaping the way I look at this decision? How do these models limit or expand my opportunities in this situation? What models do others hold, and what other models are possible? How can I avoid being overwhelmed by complexity? How can I design experiments? What is my intuition saying about this issue?

The issues posed in the sidebars in this chapter provide some grist for the mill in three areas: personal life, business, and society. Pick a few of these issues that attract your attention and consider how your own models affect your view, and the potential alternatives for looking at these concerns. Then look for other issues that are important to you. Mental models affect every aspect of life, so these examples are everywhere. In this way, you can increase your awareness of mental models and your practice in impossible thinking. When you are confronted by new information or situations, this continuous practice will help you improve your ability for impossible thinking and to act quickly and effectively.

## IMPOSSIBLE THINKING

- Pick one example from each of the three areas (personal, business and society). What model do you currently use to assess the situation? What other models could be used? How does the choice of models shape your position on the issue and your decisions about it?

- When you read news stories, cultivate a practice of asking: What mental models underlie the decisions and actions reported upon? What are some different models for looking at the same situation, and how do they change the options available? Pay particular attention to national and international political debates or court cases, where different models often define the battle lines.

- As you encounter situations throughout the day, identify and explicitly articulate the mental models at work. How can you get better at recognizing the underlying models?

# ENDNOTES

1. Whitaker, Robert. *Mad in America: Bad Science, Bad Medicine and the Enduring Mistreatment of the Mentally Ill.* Cambridge: Perseus Publishing, 2002.

2. Tyler, Patrick E. "A New Power in the Streets," *The New York Times*, February 17, 2003.

# WHAT YOU THINK IS WHAT YOU DO

The future enters into us, in order to transform us, long before it happens.

—Rainer Maria Rilke

When you face a new decision or new challenge, step back a moment and consider whether you have the right model for it:

- **Recognize how models limit or expand your scope of actions.** What is your current model? What parts of the world are you not seeing because of it? What opportunities are you missing? What parts of the world or new potential paths could you see with a new model?

- **Know when to shift horses.** Does your model fit the current environment? Does a proposed new model really work better? What are the risks of implementing it? Can you use gradual experiments to reduce these risks? How can you avoid the twin perils of either failing to recognize an important new model or leaping to it too soon and too enthusiastically?

- **Recognize that paradigm shifts are a two-way street.** Old models are not always toppled like statues of the old order when new models emerge. What old models might be applied to your current challenge? If everyone else is using automobiles, can you use a horse? What are the implications of the new model for the way the old model is used? How can you build and access this diverse portfolio of models? In what situations are specific models valuable?

235

- **See a new way of seeing.** Where can you find new models? Who are the people around you and what are the situations you can enter into that will expand your set of models? Are you talking to people older and younger than you? In different professions? Do you have a dialogue with the radicals who might just be creating the new order?

- **Zoom in and out to make sense from complexity.** Are you overwhelmed by data and information? If so, practice zooming out so you can see the forest for the trees. Are you too far back from a problem? If so, zoom in to examine the details before coming back to the big picture. How can you cultivate the habit of zooming in and out in your life?

- **Engage in experiments.** What hypotheses are suggested by the new mental models you are considering, and how can you design experiments to test them? What are opportunities for experiments in your personal and business life? Eleanor Roosevelt once advised, "Do one thing every day that scares you." What small actions can you take today that represent a daring break from the past without entailing too much risk?

To carry your new view out into the world, pay attention to the factors that keep you locked in the old model or enable you to bring others into your world.

- **Dismantle the old order.** What infrastructure have you erected around your old model, and how do you need to change it to support the new model? Is your desire to change evanescent like a New Year's resolution, or are there ways to ensure that you follow through? What forces keep you trapped in the old model (a smoker's addition to nicotine, or the integration of smoking breaks into your life)? What are the forces (like a nicotine patch) that can help you adopt a new model? What structural aspects of your organization need to be rethought to support the new model?

- **Find common ground to bridge adaptive disconnects.** Which people around you do not share your model? Why are they not changing? What is the value of their current model to them? What models are they working from? Are there boundary spanners who can help you bridge these adaptive disconnects, or levers that can drive the change? Where can you find common ground between the old model and the new?

Develop and practice broader capabilities to access your models and act quickly and effectively:

- **Develop and refine your intuition.** Do you use intuition? If not, are there ways you can flex your intuitive "muscle" to gain more practice? Practice using intuition instead of analysis in making small decisions, and note the results. Are there times when intuition is most useful? How can you put yourself in the frame of mind to use your intuition? Is your intuition still valid? How do you need to refine it?

- **Transform your actions.** The goal of changing the way you think is to change the way you act. How do you carry your new insights into the world and use the transformation of your thinking as a basis for the transformation of your life, your organization and society?

## Beyond Possibility

The world is more malleable than you think. This means that the limiting factor in seizing new opportunities—whether in personal health or economic value creation or world peace—is often your own mental models. Your own mind creates the fences that you live in. Your thinking is bounded by the limits of the possible.

Some of these limitations are very real. But because of the nature of mental models, there are often holes in these fences that you are unable to see. Once someone finds these holes, they are usually obvious in retrospect, but you need to be able to think creatively to see them first. Stop and think. If you can cultivate the ability to think in new directions, you have the possibility to transform the business of your life and the life of your business. There are so many opportunities for transformation if you could only see them. To see these opportunities and seize them, you need the courage and understanding to think impossible thoughts—and then act upon them.

# THE NEUROSCIENCE BEHIND MENTAL MODELS

The subject of neuroscience is vast, complex and changing rapidly as new discoveries are made. Indeed, it is said that we have learned more about how the central nervous system works in the past ten years than in all previous history. This has been made possible in large part by developments in science and technology that have permitted direct access to the brain and nervous system. We no longer have to just "think about thinking." Neuroscience and even philosophy can now start to have a deep empirical basis. While the science is changing rapidly and the details of our understanding of the brain are continuing to evolve, our discussions in this book have focused on core concepts that have been robust, and in many cases have been strengthened, as a result of recent scientific advances.

Any discussion of this topic is humbling. The more we know about the brain, the more we realize that most fundamental aspects of the mind remain a complete mystery. Yet we need to act today in our businesses, personal lives and society, so we do not have the luxury of waiting for all these mysteries to be unraveled (assuming that this can be done at all). Despite the limitations of our knowledge, our emerging understanding of neuroscience does offer some insights into how we make sense of the world and provides the basis for changing our thinking and actions.

The general topic of mental models has been examined through the unique lenses of many different disciplines, and we have tried to draw upon these diverse sources in formulating our broader view of the subject. Writers on topics ranging from competitive strategy to cultural anthropology have invoked ideas of mental models to understand their subjects. Like the parable of the blind men and the elephant (in which they touch the trunk, leg or tail and came away with a different view of the animal), each of these disciplines offers a distinctive view, and quite often a corresponding set of limitations. The language that members of each discipline use to discuss mental models is usually shaped by the given model they use to make sense of the world.

While we have not tried to explicitly make all these diverse connections within this book or even this appendix, it is important for us to recognize the underlying concepts and for individual readers to relate these ideas to their own language and frameworks. In essence, while we recognize that there are diverse "languages" that these ideas can be translated into, we have not attempted the complex and confusing task of explicitly making all these translations.

The following annotations present richer discussion of the sources for some of the key insights of the book:

- We live together in separate worlds
- We use only a small part of what we see
- Reality is a story the brain and the world work out together
- Mental models
- The Cartesian Theater
- The reality of reality

We also offer a few explications of some specific statements:

- Walking on a dark street at midnight
- Shaking hands with Bugs Bunny (the nature of memory)
- Overlooking gorillas (inattention blindness)
- Hardwiring (nature vs. nurture)

- Seeing things differently
- Zooming in and out to sift sense from streams of complexity
- A self-reflexive world (epistemological solipsism)
- Intuition
- Cultivating a practice of "letting go"

While this set of insights is not exhaustive, it does suggest some of the underpinnings of the book, and we close with a set of resources for readers who wish to explore these ideas in more detail.

# CORE CONCEPTS

## We Live Together in Separate Worlds

We all make sense of things in the same fundamental way, but each of us brings to this common capability an additional individual interpretation. Nobel laureate biochemist Gerald Edelman has observed that while individual brains are extraordinarily diverse, they share "common experiences, characteristics and neural patterns" particularly in sensory experience.[1] Without this common ground, it would be impossible to make sense except in individual, self-contained worlds.

Yet while we may live in the same world, Edelman points out that even our interactions with physical objects in this world are shaped by our distinctive sets of experiences and current concerns. For example, when a fire engine goes by with lights flashing, one person worries about victims and property, another about travel delays, and a third has "Proustian reminiscences" of evenings spent with his grandfather, who was a fire chief.[2] The personal experience of making sense means we all do it in slightly different ways.

Humberto Maturana and Francisco Varela observed that we see our experiences as certain, objective and absolute, yet our experiences are much more malleable than we typically recognize.

Maturana and Varela claim that cognition is not merely a passive process of seeing the world, but rather an active process of creating our world of experience.[3]

So, making sense uses a common human neurological basis but individual and unique implementations. Given the power of mental models in shaping reality and communications, their great danger and great possibilities are readily apparent.

## We Use Only a Part of What We See

The other side of this story, which has emerged from studies of neuroscience, is that we apparently ignore much of what we take in through our senses. From their work on the brain's nervous systems, Maturana and Varela have observed that we use only a small part of the available information and create the remainder from our minds. Indeed it has been observed that the brain knows no difference between perception and hallucinations, with both having similar patterns of neural activation.

Neurologist Walter Freeman discovered that the neural activity due to sensory stimuli disappears in the cortex.[4] This stimulation flows into the brain, and it appears to evoke in its place an internal pattern, which the brain uses to represent the external situation. External reality is sensed and processed by a phenomenal number of processes and activities, of which we are mostly unaware. The brain, based upon its knowledge of the world, fills in the broad detail, thus creating a complete picture or context.[5]

We may not even be consciously aware of what we are looking at. Scientists have observed an incredible but rare phenomenon called "blindsight," in which a person who is blind can reach out and pick up an object when asked to do so.[6] Apparently the "evolutionary old" optical system permits a person to do practical things, such as guiding a hand movement, without being conscious of it. An evolutionary new system, involving a conscious awareness of seeing things, was damaged in this person. These two different optical systems, having evolved at different times, provide an explanation for this strange ability; to be blind yet be able to reach out and touch something.

As an extreme example of this ability to "see" without any visual input, Australian psychologist Zoltan Torey, who was blinded in an accident at the age of 21, worked hard to build and sustain an imagined visual world that he used as a basis for action. This imagined world was so complete that Torey was able to climb a ladder and replace the roof guttering of his home singlehandedly—a feat made more terrifying to his neighbors by the fact that he accomplished it in the pitch darkness of the middle of the night.[7]

The brain apparently makes no distinction between the image seen by the eye and the various details it has filled in. We are all unaware of the significant blind spot in our eye at the point where the optical nerve enters. The brain makes a guess at what should be there, fills in the missing gap and it all looks quite consistent.

## Reality Is a Story the Brain and World Work Out Together

Susan Blackmore has argued that the brain and the world work together to construct a story or "great confabulation."[8] Reality is a story that the brain and the world come up with together.

The brain does not build up detailed representational internal models of a scene.[9] For example, the brain has some 30 different areas that have evolved over time to handle visual information. The external visual information is broken down and sent across these 30 areas, and the brain then somehow reassembles the responses of these 30 areas to give the self some sense of what is out there.[10]

Some even argue that the mind may use the external world as an external memory, since all the details are there anyway. It does not need to have detailed internal information; it can locate this from the external scene.[11] In this view, instead of memory being inside our minds and reality outside, these are reversed. The mind has an overall model or context for the external scene and then can actively explore it for details, using its established understanding of categories, and so on.

## Mental Models

In this book we employ the phrase "mental model" as a short form for all the complex neuronal activities that we use in making sense of something and then deciding what action to take. There is some confusion about the term, because various groups have used the phrase "mental model" in different ways and in a narrower sense.[12] Some see it as a synonym for "mental representation." Others define it in a narrower sense in the context of the theory of thinking and reasoning. Others use it as part of a methodology of how to develop information technology systems.

As psychological representations of real, hypothetical, or imaginary situations, mental models were first postulated by the Scottish psychologist Kenneth Craik, who wrote in 1943 that the mind constructs "small-scale models" of reality to anticipate events, to reason and to underlie explanation.[13] More recent work at MIT defines "mental models" as deeply ingrained assumptions, generalizations, or even pictures or images that influence how we understand the world and how we take action.

Vilayanur S. Ramachandran, Director of the Centre for Brain and Cognition at the University of California (San Diego), commenting in a BBC broadcast, described our brains as "model-making machines."[14] He compares this process to virtual reality simulations and points out that we not only create models of our own minds but also of other people's thinking so that we can try to predict their behaviors.

## The Cartesian Theater

Research shows that the brain, just like the rest of our body, is a product of the evolutionary process.[15] Its general structure and various features exhibit all the complexity of the evolutionary process, and this throws into question some of our deeply held beliefs—in the dualism of mind and body and the existence of objective reality.

Rene Descartes advanced the concept of dualism, or the fundamental philosophical distinction between mind and body. His dualism leads to the concept of objective, external reality and a model for how we perceive and think, called the "Cartesian theater."[16] This is the idea that an external scene is faithfully projected inside the brain, much as a movie is projected, and something intelligent inside the brain, a homunculus (Latin for "little man"), views it in an objective way. (See Figure A.1.) This, of course, begs the question of how this intelligent agent inside us actually works; so that we have an infinite regression of homunculi.

The Cartesian theater has been itself a powerful mental model for how we think about our own thinking. The influence of dualism has been profound, including the sense of an objective reality out there and an ability to make sense of it by an objective observer. This is a contentious issue invoking considerable debate.[17]

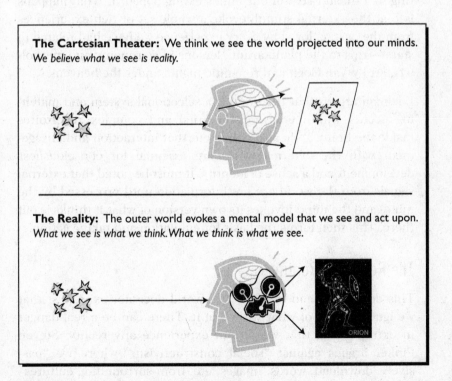

**The Cartesian Theater:** We think we see the world projected into our minds. *We believe what we see is reality.*

**The Reality:** The outer world evokes a mental model that we see and act upon. *What we see is what we think. What we think is what we see.*

ORION

**FIGURE A.1** The illusion of the Cartesian theater

Research evidence is accumulating that this process is not as straightforward as the Cartesian model suggests. Instead of resembling a direct projection, the images and information that come in through our eyes and other senses appear to evoke neural patterns. Imagine that a person outside the theater sees a few stars and rushes in with a rough-drawn sketch to the projectionist, who hunts through the reels on hand and finds something related. This reel is then projected in our minds. We think we are seeing the reality of the external world, when we are primarily seeing a world of our own making (as illustrated in the lower part of Figure A.1).

Yet even this analogy of a motion picture projector is not a completely accurate representation of what happens in our minds. There is no projector, of course, because this again assumes a "little man" inside to watch the movie. There is no homunculus sitting in a theater seat of our minds eating popcorn. What happens is that the external stimuli evoke a whole set of rich experiences from the past, colored by every experience we have had related to stars—trips to the planetarium, lessons in astronomy and mythology, art by Van Gogh and romantic nights under the heavens.

Edelman argues that the brain is a selectional system and matching occurs within enormously varied and complex repertoires inside the brain.[18] He also points out that interaction and engagement with the external world are essential for consciousness development and a sense of identity. It must be noted that external signals from the world are not information until processed by the mind, and the mind invokes its own version of what it thinks is out there. This then forms the basis for emulation and taking action.

## The Reality of Reality

This does not mean that the real world does not exist, just that we ignore much of what we see in it. There can be a real danger in extrapolating that we do not experience any reality. Steven Pinker argues against "social constructivism" where we "passively 'download' words, images, etc. from surrounding cultures" and where "scientists are unequipped to grasp an objective reality."[19] He argues that "people do have access to facts about the real world."

Edelman argues that an animal can generate a "mental image" of real events in its immediate environment. However, humans are not bound to the immediate present and can invoke semantic capabilities—thus enabling the construction of both past and future scenes which enrich the sense of the present reality.

Reality just requires a lot of interpretation. Francis Crick makes the point:

> What you see is not really there; it is what your brain believes is there…Seeing is an active construction process. Your brain makes the best interpretation it can according to its previous experience and the limited and ambiguous information provided by your eye.[20]

The debate continues whether we experience "reality" or suffer from some "illusion." To some degree, this is a false debate. It is clear that our internal and external experiences are transformed into a complex neural pattern inside our brains and that these patterns are not a strict representation of things. How could they be? We cannot literally take the world into our minds, so it is some vague reflection of it that we are able to grasp in our minds, and we work from sketchy details in building our internal reality. It would appear that the brain registers its various sensory signals, which are then transformed and trigger a rich set of stored patterns based upon past experiences. This complex neural activity in our brains constitutes our reality. In most cases, this is an accurate and efficient process. Problems arise when our experience and stored patterns do not effectively relate to our current environment.

The discussion on mental models therefore does not imply that we are out of touch with reality. On the contrary, we are superbly equipped to inhabit a real world of living things, inanimate objects and people. The sheer overwhelming complexity of our environment has shaped the evolution of our brain so that it can handle this complexity with both efficiency and effectiveness. To this end, we look at a scene and are remarkably successful at making sense of it. We just need to recognize our limitations.

# EXPLICATIONS

## Walking on a Dark City Street at Midnight (Book Opening)

The opening story of a person who hears footsteps behind him on a dark city street illustrates the interaction between the models in our heads and the ambiguous information in our environment. Walking alone down a dark city street at midnight is not the ideal condition for exercising cool decision theory, yet it is another example of the way we create an emotive set of interpretations, in addition to trying to make sense of the obvious sensory inputs from the eyes and ears.

Hearing the footsteps behind us evokes many thoughts and memories. Antonio Damasio discusses what he calls "the somatic marker hypothesis," noting that the mind is not a "blank slate." Instead it has a set of images, such as past stories of crime on dark streets. This set of images is then generated in harmony with the situation you are in and the consciousness is "entertained" and "excited" by this rich show.[21]

The person on the street then has to make a rapid decision about what is going on and how to respond to it (speed up, run, call for help, etc.) Decision making under the conditions described in the story is not simple to explain. As Damasio comments, the mind facing a decision evokes and considers images related to many different options for action and possible outcomes of these actions. In additions to images, the mind is generating related words and sentences, resulting in "a richly diverse juxtaposition of images."[22] This mix of actual stimuli and internal thoughts and experiences leads to an overall emotional and visceral reaction.

## Shaking Hands with Bugs Bunny: The Nature of Memory (Book Opening)

Since our current experiences elicit models based on past experience, memory is critical to making sense of things. Yet memory is much more malleable than most of us believe, as demonstrated by the theme park visitors who were convinced they had shaken hands with Bugs Bunny in Disneyland. Researcher Elizabeth Loftus, who conducted the "Bugs Bunny" study, notes that: "Memory is more prone to error than many people realize."[23]

Our memory has an egocentric bias, which means we remember things in a self-enhancing way. The individual encodes memories and recalls them more effectively if they are self-relevant. This places great emphasis on personal experiences or self-centric events, such as shaking hands with a theme park character. As people develop and mature, their own self-stability will be changed and their own view of their life's journey as well as of self will evolve and change. A study of political attitudes showed that people misremembered their past attitudes in line with their present attitudes.[24]

Although memory is subject to many distortions,[25] most people believe memory is generally reliable. Criminal trial juries tend to believe those witnesses who give an assured performance of their recall of events. Yet over 90 percent of wrong convictions are attributed to errors by eyewitnesses.[26] When a memory is distorted, it can result in overreacting to certain triggers from past experience. Importantly, we tend to introduce a significant bias into what we memorize or recall.

We also have trouble distinguishing real memories from illusions. Psychological studies show that it is almost impossible for us to distinguish between a real memory and the product of imagination.[27] As Edelman points out, since memory is nonrepresentational, this allows perception to alter recall and vice versa. Our memory has no fixed capacity limit and generates information by using a construction process which is robust, dynamic, associative and adaptive. Essentially, memory is a system property of the brain and is creative and not strictly replicative.

This should not cause us to lose faith in the integrity of our memories, but it should help us to understand the characteristics of memory and to exercise some care when our recall of events is used in serious situations. It also cautions us to make contemporaneous notes of events for future reference rather than relying on memory, especially after long periods of time.

## Overlooking Gorillas: Inattention Blindness (Book Opening)

The gorilla experiment, in which subjects failed to see a gorilla walking through videotaped scenes of players passing a basketball, is part of a series of tests on phenomena described as "change blindness" and "inattention blindness." There have been various attempts to explain what is going on.[28] There is no generally accepted explanation, though one thing is clear, contrary to some conventional theories; the mind is not assembling a series of exquisitely detailed images of everything out there.

Overlooking gorillas may well be the result of assembling a series of fairly poor images and filling in the details from the mind. It has been noted that the brain apparently makes no distinction between the image and the various details it has filled in. In the process, huge chunks of reality such as the gorilla, can be essentially painted over.

Attention distorts our perception, so when subjects in the study were asked to count how many times players in white shirts passed the basketball, they were predisposed to ignore dark objects such as the gorilla. The things that interest you shape your perception. Things that change, even in your direct field of view, may not be seen. Also perception is gist dependent; things that change the gist of things are more likely to be noticed.

## Hard Wiring: Nature vs. Nurture (Chapter 1)

The brain is *not* "hard wired" per se, though it does have a genetically determined structure. Gerald Edelman points out that genetics appears to shape the overall architecture of the brain and the sequence of its development. For this reason humans have very similar brain structures.[29] How we make sense of the world, however, is based on a combination of genetics, experience, and other factors. Edelman notes that the brain continues to evolve so every individual's brain development takes a unique path—even those of identical twins.

Pinker makes the point that education helps develop intuition in areas of human knowledge that are too new for a species-wide instinct to have developed.[30] Neuroscientist Jean Pierre Changeux notes that education is not simply data collection but a complex process of generating representations, assumptions and models that are tested against experience.[31]

## Seeing Things Differently (Chapter 5)

The basis for seeing things differently is driven by the brain's willingness to consider something "interesting." What we find interesting is, in turn, affected by our past experiences. A connoisseur of art pays attention to "how a work that he contemplated compares with others that he has committed to memory."[32] Some people by nature or their roles in organizations have a broader scope of what they find interesting. For example, the IBM researchers were looking for new ideas, which made them more open to exploring developments in open-source software.

There is an overwhelming tendency to see things according your past experience and knowledge. Finding a way to avoid being "channeled" into the usual ways of seeing things is difficult. A key technique is to avoid a rush to judgment and to look for "interesting or novel" things, even if their usefulness may not be immediately apparent.

## Zooming In and Out to Sift for Sense from Streams of Complexity (Chapter 6)

The basis for some of the methodology and reasoning behind this approach is the way the eye/brain (really all part of the brain) has evolved to make sense of our incredibly complex environment. We are normally presented with a visual field of enormous complexity. The eye/brain tends to focus on a small part of it to examine in detail. The remainder of the visual field provides an "out of focus" context. Details are registered best in the center of the eye, the fovea centralis, where there is a higher density of cones. The eye switches its gaze to interesting things, not dwelling on anything for long, and has a process for changing called "saccades," in which attention shifts and then the eye is directed.

Interestingly, if the eye/brain dwells on something for too long, the brain no longer makes sense of it. Too narrow a focus can lead to fixation of vision that results in the eyes glazing over, like the hypnosis of a driver focused on the passing lines of a monotonous highway. On the other hand, too broad a focus can lead to confusion. To keep making sense, the eye is in constant motion, moving across the scene, and over time building up a sense of context. The establishment of context then enables the brain to create a consistent understanding of the whole scene by filling in missing detail.[33]

## A Self-reflexive World: Epistemological Solipsism (Chapter 9)

Freeman argues that the brain experiences various sensory inputs which are translated into an internal, self-consistent world, which he refers to as "epistemological solipsism." Both Freeman and Pinker argue that human brains have evolved primarily as organs of social organization, which permit broader cooperation and sharing beyond the self.[34]

Varela offers an interesting observation on this sense of self, influenced by his interest in Buddhist thought. These teachings propose the concept of a "virtual self," or "selfless self" that is a lived experience inside us.[35]

## Intuition (Chapter 10)

Intuition is distinct from our basic instincts, which are not learned, but these instincts do contribute to our intuition and shape our actions. Our nature is complex and reveals the fundamental influence of our animal evolution. For example, we can infer intent by watching the eyes of others—an ancient animal capability that we can use in reacting to situations. We have brainstem coordination for what is referred to as the 4 F's: fleeing, fighting, feeding and…reproducing. These provide us with a capacity and often a bias to quickly make sense and to take drastic action, if needed.[36]

Our intuitive abilities have evolved from interaction with our natural world.[37] When examining the process for making decisions, Damasio and Poincare have pointed out that when we solve problems, we pre-select options to consider rather than trying to examine every possible option. This process of pre-selection, which can be conscious or more covert, is typically based upon intuition even if the final choice may be based on analysis.[38]

While emotion has tended to be rejected as part of the basis for a "logical decision process" (we complain, for example, that "you are being emotional"), research is increasingly recognizing emotion as an important, some would even argue integral, part of our decision process. Feeling and emotions are a fundamental part of how we make sense and make decisions. Emotions elicit cognitive evaluations which result in feelings; and like all other aspects of cognition, feelings contribute to the total network of images that constitute an object's or an event's meaning.[39]

## Cultivating a Practice of "Letting Go" (Chapter 10)

Francisco Varela has described a process for accessing first-person or personal experience. He describes this method as deriving from the intersection of introspection, phenomenology and contemplative traditions. His research took these traditions and tried to extract commonalities. He argues that to become more aware and access our experience requires three gestures: suspension, redirection and *letting go*.[40]

In an interview, Brian Arthur has also discussed reaching a "deeper region of consciousness,"[41] noting that to access this deeper knowing requires three steps: total immersion (observe, observe, observe), retreating and reflecting (allowing the inner knowledge to emerge), and acting in an instant (bringing forth the new as it desires). This process is consistent with the practice of "letting go."

# ENDNOTES

1. Edelman, Gerald. *Universe of Consciousness: How Matter Becomes Imagination*. New York: Basic Books, 2000.

2. *Ibid*.

3. Maturana, Humberto, and Francisco Varela. *The Tree of Knowledge: The Biological Roots of Human Understanding*. Boston: Shambhala, 1987.

4. Freeman, Walter J. *Societies of Brains: A Study in the Neuroscience of Love and Hate*. Hillsdale, NJ: Lawrence Erlbaum Associates, 1995.

5. *Ibid*.

6. "Synapses and the Self." *Reith Lecture Series 2003: The Emerging Mind*. By Vilayanur S. Ramachandran. BBC Radio 4. 9 April 2003.

7. Sacks, Oliver. "The Mind's Eye: What the Blind See." *The New Yorker*. 28 July 2003. p. 51.

8. Blackmore, Susan. *New Scientist Magazine*, 18 November 2000.

9. Clark, Andy. "Is Seeing All It Seems? Action, Reason and the Grand Illusion." *Journal of Consciousness Studies* 9:5–6 (2002). pp. 181–202.

10. "Synapses and the Self." *Reith Lecture Series 2003: The Emerging Mind*. By Vilayanur S. Ramachandran. BBC Radio 4. 9 April 2003.

11. Clark, Andy. "Is Seeing All It Seems? Action, Reason and the Grand Illusion." *Journal of Consciousness Studies*. 9:5–6 (2002). pp. 181–202.

12. See for example, Johnson-Laird, Phil, and Ruth Byrne. *Mental Models*. May 2000. </Psychology/Ruth_Byrne/mental_models/>; Senge, P. *The Fifth Discipline* & various articles; Psychology.org definitions. *Encyclopedia of Psychology*. 17 September 2003.

13. Craik, K. *The Nature of Explanation*. Cambridge: Cambridge University Press, 1943.

14. "Neuroscience: The New Philosophy." *Reith Lecture Series 2003: The Emerging Mind*. By Vilayanur S. Ramachandran. BBC Radio 4. 30 April 2003.

15. Churchland, Patricia. *The Self: From Soul to Brain: A New York Academy of Sciences Conference*. New York City. 26–28 September 2002.

16. Dennett, Daniel. *Consciousness Explained*. Boston: Little, Brown and Co., 1991. Explains & rejects the Cartesian theater model of phenomenal consciousness.

17. Weinberg, Steven. "Sokal's Hoax." *The New York Review of Books*. 43:13 (1996). pp. 11–15.

18. Edelman, Gerald. *Universe of Consciousness: How Matter Becomes Imagination*. New York: Basic Books, 2000.

19. Pinker, Steven. *The Blank Slate: The Modern Denial of Human Nature*. New York: Viking, 2002.

20. Crick, Francis. *The Astonishing Hypothesis: The Scientific Search for the Soul*. New York: Simon & Schuster, 1995. Reprinted with permission of Scribner, an imprint of Simon & Schuster Adult Publishing Group from *The Astonishing Hypothesis* by Francis Crick. Copyright © 1994 by The Francis H. C. Crick and Odile Crick Revocable Trust.

21. Damasio, Antonio R. *Descartes' Error: Emotion, Reason and the Human Brain*. New York: G.P Putnam, 1994.

22. *Ibid*

23. Loftus, Elizabeth. "Our Changeable Memories: Legal and Practical Implications." *Neuroscience* 4 (2003). pp. 231–234.

24. Schacter, Daniel L. *The Self: From Soul to Brain: A New York Academy of Sciences Conference*. New York City. 26–28 September 2002.

25. *Ibid*.

26. Loftus, Elizabeth. "Our Changeable Memories: Legal and Practical Implications." *Neuroscience* 4 (2003). pp. 231–234.

27. Loftus, Elizabeth. "Memory Faults and Fixes." *Issues in Science & Technology*. Summer 2002. pp. 41–50.

28. Clark, Andy. "Is Seeing All It Seems? Action, Reason and the Grand Illusion." *Journal of Consciousness Studies* 9:5–6 (2002). pp. 181-202.

29. Edelman, Gerald. *Universe of Consciousness: How Matter Becomes Imagination*. New York: Basic Books, 2000.

30. Pinker, Steven. *The Blank Slate: The Modern Denial of Human Nature*. New York: Viking, 2002.

31. Changeux, Jean Pierre. *L'Homme de Verite*. Paris: Odile Jacob, 2002.

32. Gardner, Howard. "Mind and Brain: Only the Right Connections." *Project Zero*. July 2000. <harvard.edu/PIs/HG_Changeux.htm>.

33. Crick, Francis. *The Astonishing Hypothesis: The Scientific Search for the Soul.* New York: Simon & Schuster, 1995.

34. Freeman, Walter J. *Societies of Brains: A Study in the Neuroscience of Love and Hate.* Hillsdale, NJ: Lawrence Erlbaum Associates, 1995.

35. Varela, F., and J. Shear, eds. *The View from Within: First Person Approaches to the Study of Consciousness.* Exeter: Imprint Academic, 1999.

36. Churchland, Patricia. *The Self: From Soul to Brain: A New York Academy of Sciences Conference.* New York City. 26–28 September 2002.

37. Pinker, Steven. *The Blank Slate: The Modern Denial of Human Nature.* New York: Viking, 2002.

38. Damasio, Antonio R. *Descartes' Error: Emotion, Reason and the Human Brain.* New York: G.P Putnam, 1994.

39. *Ibid.* p. 149.

40. Excerpted from Brockman, John. *The Third Culture: Beyond the Scientific Revolution.* New York: Simon & Schuster, 1995. Francisco, Varela. Interview. "Three Gestures of Becoming Aware." *Dialogues on Leadership.* 12 January 2000. <http://www.dialogonleadership.org/Varela-2000.pdf.> This interview provides a fascinating dialog on Varela's process for becoming aware.

41. Arthur, W. Brian. Interview. "Three Gestures of Becoming Aware." *Dialogues on Leadership.* 16 April 1999. <http://www.dialogonleadership.org/Varela-2000.pdf.> The conversation with Brian Arthur took place as part of a global interview project with 25 eminent thinkers on knowledge and leadership. The project was sponsored by McKinsey & Company and the Society for Organizational Learning (formerly the MIT Center for Organizational Learning).

# SELECTED BIBLIOGRAPHY

A large and increasing number of books are accessible to the lay audience on neuroscience, consciousness, mind and brain and neurophilosophy. The following books represent an illustrative cross section of publications on related topics.

1. Carter, Rita. *Mapping the Brain.* Berkeley: University of California Press, 1998; *Exploring Consciousness.* Berkeley: University of California Press, 2003.

   Carter provides an illustrated survey of discoveries related to brain structure and function and examines diverse ideas and people in the field of consciousness research.

2. Crick, Francis. *The Astonishing Hypothesis: The Scientific Search for the Soul.* New York: Simon & Schuster, 1995.

   Using the neurobiology of vision, Crick explores fundamental questions of consciousness, free will, and other topics.

3. Damasio, Antonio R. *Descartes' Error: Emotion, Reason and the Human Brain.* New York: G.P. Putnam, 1994; *The Feeling of What Happens: Body and Emotion in the Making of Consciousness.* New York: Harcourt Brace, 1999; *Looking for Spinoza: Joy, Sorrow and the Feeling Brain.* Orlando: Harcourt, 2003.

In these books, Damasio discusses emotion, reason and the human brain, challenges traditional views on the nature of rationality, and discusses the role of the body and our emotions in explaining consciousness.

4. Dennett, Daniel. *Consciousness Explained*. Boston: Little, Brown and Co., 1991; *Darwin's Dangerous Idea: Evolution and the Meanings of Life*. New York: Simon & Schuster, 1995; *Freedom Evolves*. New York: Viking, 2003.

5. Edelman, Gerald. *Universe of Consciousness: How Matter Becomes Imagination*. New York: Basic Books, 2000.

Edelman builds on the radical ideas he introduced in his monumental trilogy, *Neural Darwinism, Topobiology,* and *The Remembered Present*, to present for the first time an empirically supported full-scale theory of consciousness. He and the neurobiologist Giulio Tononi show how they use ingenious technology to detect the most minute brain currents and to identify the specific brain waves that correlate with particular conscious experiences. The results of this pioneering work challenge the conventional wisdom about consciousness.

6. Goleman, Daniel. *Emotional Intelligence: Why It Can Matter More Than IQ*. New York: Bantam, 1995.

Goleman argues that human competencies such as self-awareness, self-discipline, persistence and empathy are of greater consequence than IQ in much of life, and that we ignore the decline in these competencies at our peril.

7. Horgan, John. *The Undiscovered Mind: How the Human Brain Defies Replication, Medication, and Explanation*. New York: Free Press, 1999.

Horgan, author of the controversial and bestselling *The End of Science*, turns a quizzical eye to the claims of contemporary scientists, psychologists, philosophers and medical researchers who, through mind and brain science, hope to explain rationally human consciousness and behavior.

8. LeDoux, Joseph. *The Emotional Brain: The Mysterious Understanding of Emotional Life*. New York: Simon & Schuster, 1996.

LeDoux argues that we should not study emotion or cognition separately but should explore both as aspect of the "mind in its brain."

9. Maturana, Humberto, and Francisco Varela. *The Tree of Knowledge: The Biological Roots of Human Understanding*. Boston: Shambhala, 1987.

Humberto and Varela apply science, especially what is known of neural systems, to philosophical questions about human perception and understanding. The arguments are built up methodically, beginning with the origin of life and continuing through the development of language in humans.

10. Pinker, Steven. *The Blank Slate: The Modern Denial of Human Nature.* New York: Viking, 2002.

    Pinker discusses human nature, the role of genetics and questions the "blank slate" view that we are all born as blank slates upon which the environment writes.

11. Searle, John R. *The Rediscovery of the Mind.* Cambridge: MIT Press, 1992.

    Searle attacks conventional wisdom about the philosophy of mind and argues that the lack of consideration of consciousness weakens work in psychology, the philosophy of mind, and cognitive science.

# ACKNOWLEDGMENTS

Like many projects that have been percolating over a number of years, we owe a debt of gratitude to countless people who have shaped our thinking and speaking on this topic. We are particularly grateful for the many members of the Wharton Fellows community who listened to and reacted to early versions of these ideas and offered insights and encouragement to continue this work. We appreciate their willingness to engage in dialog about the process of making sense, and their intellectual curiosity and courage in exploring their own challenges of personal and organizational transformation. We also benefited from the support of Al West and the SEI Center for Advanced Studies in Management, and the creative insights of Center board members.

As we developed the manuscript, we benefited greatly from the insightful comments of many reviewers, including Paul Kleindorfer, J. Allen Kosowsky, Vijay Mahajan, Nick Pudar, Kathleen Levinson, Bob Wallace, Lee Wind, Catherine McDermott and Justine Lewis. The errors, of course, are our own, but the content was strengthened and the flow greatly improved as a result of their many suggestions for improvements.

We were aided by the skillful comments and editing of Russ Hall in helping us "make sense" throughout the process, the buoyant enthusiasm of Tim Moore in driving this book forward from a rough outline to a publishable manuscript and to Patti Guerrieri for turning that manuscript into a book. We also would like to thank Tricia Adelman for providing the administrative support that is so crucial to a project of this scale and Deeksha Hebbar for her assistance with research.

Finally, we would like to acknowledge the support of our wives, Dina and Dorothy, and families, who not only accepted the intrusion of this book into many nights and weekends but also encouraged its progress.

Jerry Wind
Colin Crook

# INDEX

# M

# Nightly Business Report Presents Lasting Leadership
## What You Can Learn from the Top 25 Business People of our Times

### BY MUKUL PANDYA, ROBBIE SHELL, SUSAN WARNER, SANDEEP JUNNARKAR, AND JEFFREY BROWN

Two of the world's leaders in business knowledge and insight come together to select and profile the 25 most influential businesspeople of the past quarter century. The team: *Nightly Business Report,* the United States' #1 daily TV business news program, and *Knowledge@Wharton,* the Wharton School's online journal of research and business analysis. The book's incisive profiles show exactly how each business leader became so influential. They teach lessons you can use to discover, refine, and nurture your own leadership style—and gain powerful influence in your own career. You'll gain new insights into familiar faces (Jack Welch, Lou Gerstner, Bill Gates). But you'll also gain greater appreciation for less heralded individuals—from Mary Kay's Mary Kay Ash to Mohammed Yunus, whose 'microlending' revolution is helping millions of poor people around the world transform themselves into entrepreneurs. No other book offers this much actionable insight into this many extraordinary business leaders.

ISBN 0131877305, © 2006, 304 pp., $16.99

# The Fortune at the Bottom of the Pyramid
## Eradicating Poverty Through Profits

### BY C. K. PRAHALAD

**The world's most exciting, fastest-growing new market?** It's where you least expect it: *at the bottom of the pyramid.* Collectively, the world's billions of poor people have immense entrepreneurial capabilities and buying power. You can learn how to serve them and help millions of the world's poorest people escape poverty.

It is being done—*profitably.* Whether you're a business leader or an anti-poverty activist, business guru Prahalad shows why you can't afford to ignore "Bottom of the Pyramid" (BOP) markets.

ISBN 0131877291, © 2006, 304 pp., $16.99

> "Great schools have…endeavored to do more than keep up to the respectable standard of a recent past; they have labored to supply the needs of an advancing and exacting world…"
>
> — **Joseph Wharton,** *Entrepreneur and Founder of the Wharton School*

**The Wharton School is recognized around the world** for its innovative leadership and broad academic strengths across every major discipline and at every level of business education. It is one of four undergraduate and 12 graduate and professional schools of the University of Pennsylvania. Founded in 1881 as the nation's first collegiate business school, Wharton is dedicated to creating the highest value and impact on the practice of business and management worldwide through intellectual leadership and innovation in teaching, research, publishing and service.

Wharton's tradition of innovation includes many firsts—the first business textbooks, the first research center, the MBA in health care management—and continues to innovate with new programs, new learning approaches, and new initiatives. Today Wharton is an interconnected community of students, faculty, and alumni who are shaping global business education, practice, and policy.

Wharton is located in the center of the University of Pennsylvania (Penn) in Philadelphia, the fifth-largest city in the United States. Students and faculty enjoy some of the world's most technologically advanced academic facilities. In the midst of Penn's tree-lined, 269-acre urban campus, Wharton students have access to the full resources of an Ivy League university, including libraries, museums, galleries, athletic facilities, and performance halls. In recent years, Wharton has expanded access to its management education with the addition of Wharton West, a San Francisco academic center, and The Alliance with INSEAD in France, creating a global network.

Wharton
UNIVERSITY *of* PENNSYLVANIA

# University of Pennsylvania

www.wharton.upenn.edu

## Academic Programs:

Wharton continues to pioneer innovations in education across its leading undergraduate, MBA, executive MBA, doctoral, and executive education programs.

*More information about Wharton's academic programs can be found at:*
http://www.wharton.upenn.edu/academics

## Executive Education:

Wharton Executive Education is committed to offering programs that equip executives with the tools and skills to compete, and meet the challenges inherent in today's corporate environment. With a mix of more than 200 programs, including both open enrollment and custom offerings, a world-class faculty, and educational facilities second to none, Wharton offers leading-edge solutions to close to 10,000 executives annually, worldwide.

*For more information and a complete program listing:*
execed@wharton.upenn.edu (sub 4033)
215.898.1776 or 800.255.3932 ext. 4033
http://execed.wharton.upenn.edu

## Research and Analysis:

*Knowledge@Wharton* is a unique, free resource that offers the best of business—the latest trends; the latest research on a vast range of business issues; original insights of Wharton faculty; studies, paper and analyses of hundreds of topics and industries. *Knowledge@Wharton* has over 400,000 users from more than 189 countries.

*For free subscription:*
http://knowledge.wharton.upenn.edu

*For licensing and content information, please contact:*
Jamie Hammond,
Associate Marketing Director,
hammondj@wharton.upenn.edu • 215.898.2388

## Wharton School Publishing:

Wharton School Publishing is an innovative new player in global publishing, dedicated to providing thoughtful business readers access to practical knowledge and actionable ideas that add impact and value to their professional lives. All titles are approved by a Wharton senior faculty review board to ensure they are relevant, timely, important, empirically based and/or conceptually sound, and implementable.

*For author inquiries or information about corporate education and affinity programs or, please contact:*
Barbara Gydé, Managing Director,
gydeb@wharton.upenn.edu • 215.898.4764

---

**The Wharton School:** http://www.wharton.upenn.edu
**Executive Education:** http://execed.wharton.upenn.edu
**Wharton School Publishing:** http://whartonsp.com
**Knowledge@Wharton:** http://knowledge.wharton.upenn.edu

## *An Invitation from the Editors:*
# Join the
# Wharton School Publishing Membership Program

**Dear Reader,**

We hope that you've discovered valuable ideas in this book, which will help you affect real change in your professional life. Each of our titles is evaluated by the Wharton School Publishing editorial board and earns the Wharton Seal of Approval — ensuring that books are timely, important, conceptually sound and/or empirically based and — key for you — implementable.

We encourage you to join the Wharton School Publishing Membership Program. Registration is simple and free, and you will receive these and other valuable benefits:

- **Access to valuable content** — receive access to additional content, including audio summaries, articles, case studies, chapters of forthcoming books, updates, and appendices.
- **Online savings** — save up to 30% on books purchased everyday at Whartonsp.com by joining the site.
- **Exclusive discounts** — receive a special discount on the Financial Times and FT.com when you join today.
- **Up to the minute information** — subscribe to select Wharton School Publishing newsletters to be the first to learn about new releases, special promotions, author appearances, and events.

Becoming a member is easy; please visit Whartonsp.com and click "Join WSP" today.

Wharton School Publishing welcomes your comments and feedback. Please let us know what interests you, so that we can refer you to an appropriate resource or develop future learning in that area. Your suggestions will help us serve you better.

Sincerely,

Jerry Wind                          Tim Moore
windj@wharton.upenn.edu             tim_moore@prenhall.com

**Become a member today at Whartonsp.com**

Wharton School Publishing
www.whartonsp.com

PEARSON
Education

Wharton
UNIVERSITY *of* PENNSYLVANIA